POLITICS

AN INTRODUCTION TO

POLITICS

AN INTRODUCTION TO

ALAN ISAAK
Western Michigan University

■ HarperCollins*Publishers*

Credit lines for the photos and copyrighted materials appear on page 338. This constitutes an extension of the copyright page.

Library of Congress Cataloging-in-Publication Data

Isaak, Alan C., 1940-
  An introduction to politics.

  Includes bibliographies and index.
  1. Political science. I. Title.
JA66.I77 1987   320   86-28008
ISBN 0-673-15312-6

4   5   6-KPF   94

PREFACE

People enjoy politics for different reasons. Some view it primarily as a spectator sport—watching the votes come in on election night can be exciting. Others enjoy participating in the political process—working in a campaign or demonstrating for an important issue. *An Introduction to Politics* has been written for both spectators and participants, as well as the politically unaware.

The text's basic assumption is that politics affects all of our lives. A functioning political system is essential to a functioning society. So, to the political spectators, I hope this book makes politics even more fascinating; to active political participants, I hope this book opens up new avenues for your interest and activism; and to the politically unaware, I hope this book demonstrates how valuable involvement in politics is both for the individual and for society.

This text covers as many political topics as possible, but its major strategy is to emphasize the *functions* of politics. In particular, politics is examined as a function of how societies distribute benefits and costs. This approach gives the book a framework, yet it is not a constricting one.

While a book written primarily to introduce students to politics will draw on the American system for examples, it should not be an American government text. *An Introduction to Politics* draws on many cross-national comparisons and examples to illustrate the concepts and relationships discussed.

The text is organized in five parts. Part I analyzes several definitions and conceptions of politics. A chapter on "Models of Politics" attempts to explain politics by comparing it to familiar games such as football and chess. This Part concludes with the notion that politics develops as a means of deciding who gets what in a society.

Part II examines politics within the environments of power, political culture, economic and ideological systems.

Part III discusses the roles of institutions—legislatures, executives, bureaucracies, and courts—in political systems.

Part IV looks at politics from the standpoint of the individual or group who wants to have an impact on the political process. It is here that we discuss various forms of political participation, including voting, and the activities of political interest groups. We also consider why some people feel it is necessary to resort to more direct, even violent, forms of participation.

Part V looks at the international political system, focusing on the question, "Is politics among nations different from politics within nations?"

The introduction to any field draws upon the research and analyses of many scholars; I thank those whose work helped in the writing of this text. Of course, any errors in fact or interpretation are entirely my own. A number of people have had a more direct hand in the development of this book. I appreciate the critical reviews provided by Loch Johnson, University of Georgia; William McCraw, San Jose University; Donald G. Tannenbaum, Gettysburg College; and Alan Wyner, University of California, Santa Barbara. The professional advice, encouragement, and understanding of the people at Scott, Foresman and Company, especially Scott Hardy and Paula Fitzpatrick, have also helped immeasurably.

I would also like to thank my colleagues at Western Michigan University for creating an atmosphere which makes one want to write books, and my students over the years for helping me write this one.

Finally, I owe a special debt to my wife, Betty, and my children, Eric, Greta, and Josh, for their encouragement and understanding during this long project.

Alan Isaak

CONTENTS

PART THREE

POLITICS FROM THE TOP DOWN: INSTITUTIONAL CONTEXTS   161

CHAPTER 8

GOVERNMENT: FUNCTIONS AND LEVELS   163

CHAPTER 9

LEGISLATIVE-EXECUTIVE INSTITUTIONS   176

CHAPTER 16

NATURE OF POLITICS

1

CONCEPTIONS OF POLITICS

Politics is everywhere. The President of the United States makes public his priorities for the next year by presenting a new budget to Congress while interest groups work to preserve or increase their shares of the one trillion dollar pie. In nations all over the world, debates take place over the proper role of government; some people say it does too much, others too little. But in some nations, such as Lebanon, the issue is even more fundamental; there, an almost invisible government finds it impossible to maintain basic order in a society wracked by ten years of civil war. In the Soviet Union, a new leader of the ruling party maneuvers to make his power more secure. In Central America, the ideologically opposite leaders of Nicaragua and El Salvador continue to repel rebel fighters who wish to topple their governments. Meanwhile, back in the United States, as the President tries to cope with budget deficits and terrorism, would-be Presidents begin to map out their strategies for the next election, still several years away. Across the Pacific in the Philippines, a presidential election has ended, bringing about a change in leadership but, more significantly, affirming the integrity of the democratic process itself.

What do all of these situations have in common? What do drawing up a budget, maintaining order, and seeking power have to do with each other? Most of us would answer, "They all involve politics." But what is it that makes them political? Producing an answer is not easy. The fact that most of us would identify these situations as political does not mean that each of us has a precise definition of politics in mind. As a matter of fact, because it is such a widely used word, *politics* probably has taken on a variety of meanings. This does not create great problems in everyday conversation, but in a book intended to be an introduction to politics, an ambiguously defined central concept is unacceptable. Thus, in order to study politics systematically, a more precise definition of politics must be fashioned. This is the main purpose of the first chapter. Some preliminary work must be done before our definition of politics makes complete sense, but a brief statement of the definition at this point will lay the foundation for what follows. **Politics** is that process in any society, usually working through the institutions of government and involving the use of power, which decides who receives the benefits and who pays the costs of society.

Fifty years ago, political scientist Harold Lasswell wrote *Politics: Who Gets What, When and How*, a book about the basics of politics.[1] The subtitle of his book opens the door to our understanding of politics. It tells us that politics is a process; that is, an activity, a type of human behavior that performs certain functions for the society. Saying that politics is the process of deciding who gets what assumes several things about people and the societies they live in. First, to be human is to have needs, wants, and desires. Second, the resources that satisfy human needs are usually scarce: not everyone can be as wealthy, powerful, or prestigious as they would like to be. Third, most of the things we want (let's call them *benefits*) are costly; they must be paid for with economic resources, time, sometimes even human lives. The most important implication of these assumptions is that every society must find a way to decide how benefits and costs are to be distributed. This process of distribution is politics, and it seems to follow that politics is an essential part of every society; without a political process a society cannot function.

A point of clarification should be made. It is incorrect to assume that, when resources are plentiful, decisions about who gets what no longer have to be made. Even when supply is greater than demand, the problem of distribution remains. Consider the political implications of an oversupply of oil or wheat. Political decisions still have to be made about what to do with the surplus. Thus, even when there is an economic surplus, the political question of **"who gets what"** remains.

It must be recognized that not everyone shares this positive, functional view of politics. To many, the terms *politics* and *corruption* are synonomous and the Watergate scandal of the 1970s was a significant but not surprising event. Politics, to some, is simply the way that politicians use power and position for their own special interests.

These days, one would have to be very naive to believe that politics is immune from corruption.[2] However, it is misleading to assume that politics is inherently corrupt. This book suggests that while dishonesty and corruption do exist in every political system, their incidence is probably no greater than in other segments of human society, such as business, labor, education, and athletics. Consider, for instance, the revelations appearing in the press from time to time concerning the unlawful behavior of many of the best-known corporations, banks, labor unions, and university athletic programs.

Even though it is counterproductive to view politics as inherently corrupt, it is not unreasonable to treat political corruption, when it appears, with special concern. After all, the political process stands at the center of every society. Corrupt political decisions affect all of society— they are rarely isolated. Corruption in a single corporation or labor union is a serious matter and might affect thousands of people. But a corrupt government affects an entire people.

An even more negative attitude suggests that politics is not to be taken seriously. This kind of assumption provides the basis for those who are called **anarchists**.[3] They see the political process as, at best, an unnecessary appendage to society and, at worst, the cause of most of society's ills. Some anarchists advocate peaceful withdrawal from, others violent opposition to, society. What they all have in common is the belief that politics is unnecessary and is not essential to the functioning of society. Clearly, the anarchist position runs counter to the core assumptions of this book.

We now know that a number of people view politics as either unnecessary, unimportant, oppressive, or corrupt—some would probably feel comfortable with all of these adjectives. In fact, each contains a grain of truth. Some politicians think mainly of their own interests and some are even corrupt; some governments are oppressive; some political activities are no doubt unnecessary. But emphasizing the negative can lead to a failure to appreciate the essential functions that political systems perform. An analysis of these functions is, in a sense, the primary purpose of this book.

POLITICS: GOVERNMENT AND POWER

So what is this "elusive something" called politics? We have started the process of definition, but we must now proceed more systematically. In thinking about politics, two concepts come readily to mind—government and power. Each is central to an understanding of politics, but as we shall see, neither by itself can serve as the defining characteristic of politics. For many people, politics is equivalent to the institutions of government. Politics is what goes on in the White House, Parliament, and the Kremlin. After all, the institutions of government are all around us. We hear about them, read about them, and actually feel them affect our lives. That the institutions of government are important, even essential, to politics, seems obvious. But to make government the defining characteristic of politics (as many do) limits our understanding. In most societies the institutions of government are at the heart of the political process; but it does not follow that politics is found only in formal institutions. There is more to it than that.

These conclusions have led most political scientists to look for a broader and more inclusive definition which, while including government, goes beyond it to encompass those political activities which are not part of the formal institutions of government. The realization that politics is all around us implies that politics is something that takes place not only in governmental institutions but throughout society. And something that "takes place" is an activity, a process, not a static physical object. Politics exists when a certain type of human behavior takes place. The question is, what type of behavior are we talking about?

The attempts of individuals to control other individuals—and of nations to control other nations—has gone on for ages and has not been ignored by those who study politics. Thus, many political thinkers have identified power as the defining characteristic of politics. According to this view, whenever one exercises power over another—that is, controls their behavior—a political situation exists. Power can be exercised in families, in labor unions and, of course, in governments. In fact, power is likely to be found whenever people get together. If politics equals power, it seems to follow that politics exists in all the nooks and crannies of society.

Almost five hundred years ago, the Italian political philosopher Niccolo Machiavelli drew these conclusions and used them as a basis for his very influential analysis of politics.[4] His name is still identified with power politics, and has in fact been used in an adjective, *Machiavellian,* which characterizes a ruthless, even amoral, political outlook.

Like other political thinkers, Machiavelli began his theories of politics with an assumption about human nature. He assumed that people are naturally self-centered and competitive. Thus, power becomes the most natural of human relationships. And, since it is an ever-shifting relationship, Machiavelli suggested that a politician should never be complacent or overconfident. Power is something that must be constantly cultivated and nurtured, according to Machiavelli, not simply locked in a vault and possessed. (The concept of power will be discussed in greater detail in Chapter 4.)

Such a notion is indeed appealing; the political scientist's canvas is broad if power is as pervasive as it seems. However, its apparently limitless range is what makes many political scientists uneasy. If all power situations are political, then it seems that politics includes too much. What concerns us is not power, but *political* power. The question is, what makes power political?

FUNCTIONAL DEFINITIONS OF POLITICS

We now know that politics often takes place in government and involves the use of power. But why does government exist and how is power used politically? Answers to these questions take us one step closer to the heart of politics, and the best way to take the next step is to consider the functions of politics, that is, what politics does for society.

Maintaining Order

More than three hundred years ago, the great English political thinker Thomas Hobbes argued that political systems exist to maintain order among highly competitive and selfish human beings.[5] Because people cannot regulate themselves they must establish a process that will do it for them, a process called politics. Here then is the most extreme and pessimistic of functional definitions. According to Hobbes, maintaining order is the only thing we should expect politics to do. Today, most of us would no doubt want to go beyond this limited view. We would probably also disagree with Hobbes' belief that only an absolute authoritarian government can carry out this basic task. However, the significance of his argument lies in its assertion that politics can be understood only if we realize that it is a human invention designed to provide a particular service. Modern governments do much more than maintain order, a point that will become increasingly evident as we progress through this text. But it is not unrealistic to argue that maintaining order or resolving conflict is "where it all begins." Observations made by anthropologists in primitive societies seem to support this conclusion; they usually find that in their earliest stages, most tribal societies are mainly concerned with finding ways to resolve disputes among their members. Whether this is done by a chief or by reliance on a set of traditional values, the result is the beginnings of politics.[6]

It is important at this point to reiterate that every definition of politics begins with a conception of human nature. Nowhere is this clearer than in the case of Hobbes. His functional definition depends upon the assumption that humans are selfish and competitive. Thus it follows that without the order maintained by an effective political system, the "life of man is solitary, poor, nasty, brutish, and short."[7]

Achieving the Good Life

Far removed from the pessimistic theory of Hobbes is the view that rather than being a necessary evil, politics is the means to the good life. That is, politics allows humans to reach their highest levels of development. The Greek philosopher Aristotle went so far as to argue that politics itself is the ultimate activity.[8] His theory states that because people are naturally social and cooperative, they can organize themselves and accomplish things that no individual could.

It is highly unlikely that many people in today's world would accept Aristotle's theory in its pure form. While Hobbes' theory may seem too pessimistic, the ideas of Aristotle appear too optimistic. The point seems to be that while politics is usually viewed as a process that exists to perform functions for the society and not as something good in itself, it is equally reasonable to assume that its functions are richer and more extensive than Hobbes envisioned.

Deciding Who Gets What

A richer and more functional definition of politics is possible if we make several initial assumptions about human nature and human society. First of all, we assume that people have appetites (needs, wants, and desires). This suggests a fairly large dose of self-interest. At the same time, humans seem able to cooperate with each other—to work together to accomplish certain goals. In this sense, we are social animals. It thus seems reasonable to assume that humans have a dualistic nature; a theologian might say that humans are part good and part evil. Modern psychologists would probably put it another way: humans have no inherent nature but are instead the product of their environment. They are, in short, born as blank slates, with personalities and attitudes yet to be shaped. The **blank-slate theory** suggests that in societies that emphasize competition, people will learn to compete; in societies that emphasize cooperation, people will learn to cooperate.

Whether the result of inherent characteristics or social conditioning, the dualistic conception of human nature seems a reasonable basis for a working definition of politics. By itself it does not explain politics. But when combined with the additional assumption that there is a scarcity of most of the things that people want (whether wealth, status, power, knowledge or freedom) we have something to work with. For if there is usually not enough to go around, the logical result is the need for a way to decide, in the words of Lassell, "who gets what." As we have already seen, this short phrase gets to the heart of politics and so will serve as the core of our definition. This is what governments and politicians spend most of their time doing, whether in primitive tribal societies or incredibly complex industrialized states. The methods and techniques will vary from system to system, but the function of politics remains constant. Formulating budgets, competing for public office, passing regulations, and trying to dominate other political systems all boil down to the question of "who gets what."

In each case there is a need to reconcile conflicting interests, to resolve questions about how limited resources are to be distributed, whether they be money, government position, or control over others' lives or territory. So it is not a question of whether politics exists in a given society, but what form the political process takes—deciding who gets what will go on in one way or another.

There is another way of stating the who gets what definition of politics. First formulated by the political scientist David Easton, it adds an important dimension to our definition.[9] According to Easton, politics is the process that *authoritatively allocates values for the society.* "Allocating values" is another way of saying "deciding who gets what."

When we allocate we decide how to hand out or distribute something. *Values* refers to what is handed out.

So far, the definitions are similar. But now we add the notion that the allocations must be authoritative, that is, they must be potentially enforceable by someone or something, a tribal chief, a king, a dictator, or a constitutional political institution. Anyone can decide who should get what; but only some can back up their decision. I might go to Washington, D.C., stand in front of the White House, and announce that, beginning next Monday, all those receiving Social Security benefits will have their payments increased by 50 percent. Although my proposal might appeal to some, it would not become a reality because I have neither the authority nor power to enforce it—the proposal is not authoritative. Thus politics involves allocations of values, decisions about who gets what, which are either made by those who have been given the right to make such decisions for the society or are enforceable through an act of power. This leads to the hypothesis, one we will be testing throughout the book, that those with the most authority and power, tend to control the political process. This should not imply that every political system is controlled by a small elite who take everything for themselves; it is possible to have benevolent elitist systems and even systems in which almost everyone can participate in the basic process of allocation. The major implication of this discussion is that in most societies, it is the institutions of government that have the power and authority to make such binding decisions.

In emphasizing the need to make these kinds of hard decisions we must not lose sight of something else that seems to take place in political systems. The "who gets what" definition should not imply that politics is simply a battle over limited goods and resources. Somewhere along the line, a society realizes that there are significant things that can be done more effectively through collective rather than individual action. This is perhaps one of the great social discoveries and is of course not limited to human society (consider for instance the elaborate colonies of ants and bees).

Philosophers and politicians might disagree over what should be done through collective action, but most would accept the basic principle involved: Can individuals maintain a national defense or a welfare system? The point is that we have moved several steps in the direction of Aristotle's notion that politics can achieve the good life. We need not go as far as he did to recognize that together, people can often accomplish what they cannot accomplish as individuals and that some of these activities might increase the quality of human life.

A political system allocates benefits. But there is another side to the political coin. Few of the good things come free. Thus, we must recognize that a necessary consequence of the political process is the

Collective action often proves to be an effective way to achieve certain goals. Here, a group of Gray Panthers meet with Senator Don Riegle of Michigan about national health insurance.

distribution of costs. Armies, police forces, and welfare programs, to name only a few, are costly; decisions must be made about who will foot the bill. This decision is as political as the allocation of benefits, for just as it is reasonable to assume that most people seek what they believe is a fair share of the benefits, it seems clear that most would prefer to reduce their share of the costs. The most obvious costs levied by the political system are taxes and service in the armed forces, but there are many other less tangible ones that will come up later in our discussion.

THE ORIGINS OF POLITICS

There is another way to get an initial feel for politics. If we can identify some of the ways that politics begins, our understanding of what functions politics performs might increase. Actually, no one really knows how politics begins. But anthropologists have observed the development of primitive societies and these studies provide us with clues about how politics might have begun in the more developed nations of the world.[10] It does seem clear that as a society becomes more complex, its political system becomes more complex and extensive. That is, it takes on more functions. We can also study the writings of political historians who trace the development of different kinds of political systems—tribes, city-states, empires, and nation-states.

So, realizing that there are no final answers, let us speculate about the origins of politics to see if we can shed some light on the nature of politics. We are going to discuss three such theories, each with a long tradition behind it and each explaining the origins of politics in a different way. They are the **conquest theory,** the **contract theory,** and the **natural development theory.** The first two theories flow from the assumption that humans are selfish and competitive; the latter adopts the more positive view that humans are naturally social and cooperative.

Conquest Theory

Let us begin with what is probably the least complex theory. It states that politics begins with an act of *conquest*. In the primitive state of nature, people compete with each other on fairly equal terms. There is no ordered process for deciding who gets what. Instead it is a matter of taking what you can when you can take it. After a while, one individual becomes more proficient at this game than others, beginning to develop more skill and accumulate more wealth, weapons, and followers until he or she is able to dominate the others. What has happened is that control has been concentrated in the hands of one, or perhaps a few, individuals. It seems clear, according to the conquest theory, that politics and government begin at this point only because the most powerful individual is able to impose himself or herself on everyone else. From that point on, people no longer live in a state of nature or natural freedom. Now, the dominant ruler establishes a set of rules that define what is right and wrong, and then backs them up with superior force. The point is clear: Politics begins with an act of power and is maintained through the continued use of power. People don't choose to establish a political system; they are forced to accept one.

Clearly, modern political systems are so complex that it is impossible to trace their origins back to an act of conquest. In addition, many governments seem to be based on the consent of the people. Thus, those who accept the conquest theory must assemble bits of circumstantial evidence and speculate back in time to show that their theory makes sense. They point out, as Machiavelli did, the seemingly unending struggle for power between politicians and groups and the regular outbreak of wars as nations attempt to control each other's people and territory. To those tuned into the conquest theory, this is all proof that somewhere in the distant past, every political system began with an act of conquest; thus, even today politics is primarily the process of gaining and using power.

Contract Theory

One can assume that humans are self-interested and competitive without concluding that politics is simply the result of conquest and superior power. Remember the arguments of Hobbes: because people do compete, their lives are insecure and so they finally agree to establish a government which has as its main function the maintenance of order. A contract is offered and accepted by the people and the new ruler. The form of government may appear very similar to that resulting from an act of conquest, but there is a fundamental difference. According to the **contract theory**, politics begins with and lasts only if it is based on consent; people agree to be governed. This is the significance of a contract—all parties agree to be bound by it because they all stand to benefit.

As we have already pointed out, Hobbes took a very limited view of the functions of politics; others like John Locke, the political philosopher who so influenced the writers of the American Constitution, greatly expand the duties of the political system to include the protection of a number of natural rights, such as property.[11] But once again, the idea of contract is there. People agree to be governed only because they expect the resulting political system to make their lives better.

Natural Development Theory

The third theory of how politics begins takes us back to Aristotle and his notion that people are naturally social, cooperative, and political. By this he meant that to be fully human means to be part of the political system. What this leads to is the notion that one doesn't really have to explain the origins of politics because politics develops naturally. Politics is neither the result of an act of conquest by a power-hungry individual nor the creation of an insecure people. Rather, it is something that should be expected given the basic social instincts of humans.

We need not resolve the debate among these three theories to appreciate their significance. In trying to identify the origins of politics each suggests a particular view of what politics is all about. The working definition we have arrived at takes elements from each; from the conquest theory, the centrality of power; from the contract theory, the functional nature of politics; and from the natural development theory, the recognition that humans do have some social instincts and can cooperate to achieve what is perhaps a better life.

SUMMARY

This book begins with, indeed is based on, the assumption that politics is an essential feature of every functioning society. This positive and functional conception of politics does not ignore the negative attitudes that some people have toward politics. It simply puts them in the proper perspective; they are based on real concerns that should nevertheless not blind us to the essential nature of politics.

In attempting to define politics, the concepts of power and government must be included, but neither by itself can define politics. A more fruitful approach to a definition is to consider the functions that politics performs for a society. Among its primary functions are maintaining order and helping people achieve "the good life." It is clear that identifying central functions depends to a large extent on one's conception of human nature.

Thus, combining the crucial elements discussed in this chapter leads to the following definition of politics: politics is that process, usually working through the institutions of government and involving the use of power, that decides who receives the benefits—and who pays the costs—of society. Today, most political scientists label the results of the political process *public policy* and thus politics itself becomes the policymaking process.

A good way to get a feel for politics and the functions it performs is to consider the ways that politics might have begun: from an act of conquest, a contract, or through natural development. Our working definition of politics takes elements from each of the theories of the origins of politics: from the contract theory, the realization that politics is functional and performs important functions for the society; from the conquest theory, the recognition that power is often the most important factor in the making of political decisions; and from the natural development theory, the recognition that humans can cooperate to make their lives better.

NOTES

1. Harold Lasswell, *Politics: Who Gets What, When, How* (New York: McGraw-Hill, 1936).
2. See, for instance George Benson, Steven Maaranen and Alan Heslop, *Political Corruption in America* (Lexington, Mass.: Lexington Books, 1978).
3. For a discussion of anarchism, see George Woodcock, *Anarchism* (New York: Meridian Books, 1962).
4. Machiavelli's most famous book is *The Prince*, published in 1532.
5. Hobbes' most famous book is *The Leviathan*, published in 1651.
6. See Lucy Mair, *Primitive Government* (London: Penguin Books, 1961).
7. Hobbes, *The Leviathan*, p. 100.
8. Aristotle's most famous political work is *The Politics*.

9. David Easton, *The Political System* (New York: Alfred A. Knopf, 1953).

10. Mair, *Primitive Government.*

11. Locke's most famous book on politics is *Two Treatises of Government,* published in 1690.

2

MODELS OF POLITICS

Politics can be compared to games such as football, basketball, or chess, and to systems such as the solar system, the human body, or the automobile. In making these comparisons, the objective is not to prove that politics *is* a game or a system, but rather to use some of the basic elements and relationships that are common to popular games and well-known systems as a way to get a handle on the complexity of politics. A simplified means of thinking about something complex, often by analogy between the familiar thing and the less familiar one, is called a **model**. Using a model in studying politics can create greater understanding in two ways: first, the model will help us organize or bring order to the confusing world of politics, and second, it will hopefully produce what political scientists call **hypotheses**, or educated guesses about the way the political process works.

POLITICS AS A GAME

People have probably always played games. How long they have made comparisons between games and other aspects of their lives is less certain.[1] All we can say is that writers throughout history have made such comparisons to illustrate their ideas. Consider these lines from an English writer of almost two hundred years ago: "But war's a game which, were their subjects wise, kings would not play at."[2] The notion that the kings "play" at war opens our minds to a number of interesting hypotheses, including one suggesting that political leaders get away with a great deal because of the ignorance of their subjects.

Moving from the past to the present, it is common knowledge that a number of presidents have used the language of games in their speeches and other public comments. Popular contemporary novelist Philip Roth even went so far as to suggest, in one of his satirical works, that a recent President made his important decisions in a simulated football locker room in the White House basement.[3] While this seems far-fetched, it is not unusual to hear politicians talk about "game plans," "strategies," and "payoffs"; all are taken from the language of games and suggest that it is probably very natural to think of politics as a game.

The news media also find the game analogy appealing. During the 1984 presidential campaign, when Walter Mondale won the endorsements of two major labor unions and the support of the Democratic party leaders of the state of Maine within a single 24-hour period, one news magazine called it a "political triple play."

Why is it so easy for politicians and political reporters to think of politics as a game? In answering this question, one point must be made clear. Politics is not being compared to football and chess because games are fun to play. Though many people are attracted to politics because it promises to be an entertaining participant sport, this is not what makes politics a game. Rather, it has something to do with the way games are played—with the fact that football and chess are filled with competition and conflict, with contestants using their brains, muscles, and capacities to cooperate to gain their objectives, all apparently within a set of rules. Doesn't this also sound like the typical political situation? After all, we have already established politics as the process of deciding who gets what.

Isn't this definition of politics also a fairly accurate description of the typical game? At the end of any game, gains and losses are added up—sometimes there are primarily winners, sometimes there are primarily losers. But in one way or another, football, chess, and politics deal with the process of deciding who gets what. Now, the task before us is to go beyond this general discussion of games to see just how much the game model can tell us about politics.

Chance, Skill, and Strategy

The games that we watch and play fall into three categories. First are **games of chance** such as roulette, the card game War (also called Battle), and the lottery. In each case, the outcome of the game is beyond the control of the players and almost everything depends upon chance or luck: that is, the way the cards happen to be shuffled or the number of times the wheel spins. Such games are basically a competition between the player and chance: if you're lucky, you win; if not, you lose. Knowing the probability of any particular card or number being selected might help one in deciding which number to bet on, or even which game to play. But a player cannot affect the odds since he or she has no control over the game.

In contrast to games of chance, the outcomes of **games of skill** are affected mainly by the skill or expertise of the players. Some obvious examples are golf, bowling, and archery. In the real world, such games involve some luck. Golf balls sometimes hit unseen rocks and unexpected gusts of wind can blow an arrow off course, but the outcome is usually within the control of the players. In golf tournaments, for example, the most skillful players tend to win.

Politics is neither a game of mere chance nor total skill—it involves a mixture of both. The same thing can be said of all team sports and most of the more complex parlor games. But these games have something else in common, which serves as the defining characteristic of the third category, **games of strategy**. Such games are more complex than games of skill or chance because they always involve several interacting players. The outcome of the game is a result of how the various players deal with each other. Not only must players plan their own moves wisely, but they must also keep in mind the goals and possible moves of their opponents.

Consider, for example, the game of basketball. Good coaches analyze not only their own team's strengths and weaknesses but those of the opponent. The winning game plan accentuates one team's strengths and capitalizes on the opposing team's weaknesses. In addition, good coaches try to anticipate their opponents' moves, while their opponent does the same. Only when one team has overwhelming physical superiority can strategy be downplayed; but even in that case, the superior team will win by a smaller margin than it might have with a good strategy.

Anticipating the opponent's move is of major importance, too, in the game of chess. No chess player can succeed without constant attention to the possible moves of the opponent.

What is true of basketball and chess is also true of politics. Politics—whether taking place among individuals, groups, governments, or nations—is strategic because each player must continually think about what others in the game are up to. Politicians who forget or fail to realize this rarely achieve their goals. In short, they must devise strategies, or plans of action, that indicate how to react to the possible strategies of the other players. This means not only reacting to the moves that are made, but trying to figure out what moves will be made. Thus the best strategic thinkers, whether coaches, chess champions, or secretaries of state, are those who anticipate what others will do.

The Elements of Strategic Games

As a game of strategy, much can be learned about politics if we compare it to some more familiar games. In order to do this, we must identify the elements that all strategic games have in common. This then will provide us with a framework for a closer look at the game of politics.

All strategic games have the following elements: *players* using their *resources* and developing *strategies* within a set of *rules* in order to achieve their *goals*. Let us take each element and see to what extent it helps us understand politics.

First, it is obvious that a game requires players; in politics they include individuals, groups, and nations. Players bring two basic things to the game: goals and resources. It is reasonable to assume that in a football game, each team's goal is to score more points than the other; in short, to win. In politics, as we will see time and time again, the goals are more varied and complex. Some political players seek personal gain (wealth, power, status, recognition); others compete for the good of their group (ethnic, economic, racial, religious); still others work for a societal goal (justice, freedom, equality, order). Often, more than one kind of goal is pursued at the same time—there is no contradiction, for instance, in wanting more security for yourself and advocating a more ordered society for others.

Sometimes, an entire society pulls together and works for a common goal—winning a war, for instance. But just as often the policies pursued by political systems result from a series of smaller decisions in which factors such as power are of crucial importance. Also important is the extent to which the goals of a player are compatible with the goals of other players and with the rules of the game (more about these points a bit later). What this all suggests is that the game of politics determines who achieves their goals and who doesn't.

The success of the players depends on more than the goals that they bring to the game. Resources are also required; they will of course vary from game to game, and from player to player. In basketball, height and quickness are important; in chess, intelligence and the ability to concentrate definitely help. The resources of politics are too numerous to list at this point, but among the more obvious are wealth, numbers, prestige, position, and persuasive skill.

We now return to the heart of the strategic game, the use of strategies. Each player devises a strategy or game plan designed to maximize his or her chances of winning and minimize chances of losing. The strategy is based not only on the player's own goals and resources, but on what he or she thinks others might do. Sometimes in football, a coach will decide to emphasize passing rather than running because he assumes that the opponent expects just the opposite. An analogous situation in politics might be the reelection strategy of an incumbent President to stay in the White House and "act presidential" rather than getting out on the campaign trail and debating his challenger. This strategy is based on the assumption that voters expect their President to act in a dignified manner, (and is often used when the challenger is a superior debater who would benefit from direct confrontation with the President). Thus, in any game, the results are as much a result of the appropriateness of the strategy as the resources that the players have to draw upon.

The Rules of the Game

While intrinsically competitive, games are supposed to take place within a framework, or a set of rules. The rules specify how the outcome of the game is determined: what it takes to win (whether measured in runs, points, or votes); what roles or positions the players fill (quarterback or end, voter or president) and the powers, responsibilities, and limitations assigned to each role; and who can play the game (anyone or only those with appropriate skills, wealth, or color).

Outcome. It is easy to describe the way that the outcome of a football game is determined. The rules say that after a specified period of time the team that has scored the most points by performing certain tasks is declared the winner. In some political situations, the rules in this regard are also fairly clear. In democratic elections, for instance, the date of the election is specified, the election is held, and then a rule indicates how a winner is declared—whoever has the most votes; whoever has a majority of the votes; or whoever has at least 60 percent of the votes.

In many other political situations, the rules are not so clear. This can result from several factors. Some political games differ from a football game or an election in that they do not have clear-cut beginnings or endings. In many political situations, the players are playing for different goals. And, the rules that describe the outcome may be fuzzy, ambiguous, or unwritten. We will return to this point a little later.

Roles. The roles of a game may be one, a few, or many. Most political games fall into the third category, with roles ranging from citizen to president, prime minister, or monarch. The various roles are distinguished from each other according to what those filling them can do (power), should do (responsibilities), and should not do (limitations). The President of the United States has more power than the average voter, but he also has more responsibilities. One of the major questions that arises in the analysis of any political system is, How are political powers and responsibilities distributed and what limitations are placed on the various political participants?

Who Can Play. In most games, the question of who can play is not a major issue. A neighborhood poker or bridge game involves friends who don't worry about such things. But in politics, since the game will ultimately decide who gets what in the real—perhaps even life or death—sense, the question of who can get into the game is crucial. Many of the great political conflicts in history have revolved around the question of who is allowed to participate in the political system. After all, until you become a player, your chances of benefiting from the game are slight. Consider the century-and-a-half struggle of various groups in the United States to gain the right to vote. First nonproperty holders, then blacks, and finally women were added to the electorate. In each case, change occurred only after a long period of struggle, during which a number of political strategies were used. Even now, a struggle con-

Various groups, especially blacks, have struggled long and hard to gain the right to vote.

tinues over opening up the South African political system to more players. This exemplifies the movement toward greater democracy.

Penalties. The rules we have discussed so far provide the basic
outline of a game. But most games also have at least one rule specifying
what happens to those who violate the other rules. Football, basketball,
and hockey provide for immediate enforcement. Every political game
has enforcement rules, but they usually are not as clear-cut nor easily
administered as is a foul shot in basketball or a trip to the penalty box
in hockey. In fact, some political actors discover that certain rules exist
only after they have violated them. We will soon see why.

Changing Rules. Because games must be updated from time to time, some provisions for change ought to be built into the original set of rules. In the popular team sports, changes are made periodically to make them safer or more exciting. Political rules also change, either formally or informally. Amending a written constitution is an example of a formal change. For instance, the amending process described in the Constitution of the United States has been used a number of times to make changes in the basic rules of American politics. What amazes some observers, however, is the fact that the formal amending process has been employed successfully fewer than 30 times in 200 years. This does not suggest that the rules of American politics change only occasionally. As a matter of fact, the rules of politics change so often that it is sometimes difficult for the players to know which rules apply. The solution to these apparently contradictory statements comes from the realization that the rules of politics are found in places other than a nation's written constitution, and thus can be changed informally as well as through the formal amending process.

SOURCES OF POLITICAL RULES

We have discussed the kinds of rules that every game must have. What we now want to know is where to go to find the rules of a particular political system. Most games have a rule book containing a neat (and usually consistent) set of rules. Such is not the case with the game of politics. Let us see why.

Constitutions

If you were given the task of putting together a list of rules to describe the political game that takes place in your nation, state, or city, where would you start? Most people would probably look first to the **constitution**. This makes sense, because a constitution is supposed to provide a political system with a basic framework. Citizens of the United States tend to believe that a constitution must be a written document. After all, we can go to Washington and look at our nation's Constitution preserved in a glass case. But the situation is different in Great Britain. The British have no document labeled the "British Constitution." Instead, they have a number of written items which, together with unwritten traditions, make up their constitution.[4] The point is that it is best to think of the constitution of any particular political system as that set of fundamental rules, written or unwritten, which gives the system its basic shape or character.

Because the typical constitution is supposed to serve as a framework, it is by its very nature broad and general. This implies that many questions will arise which are not directly covered by the constitution or are covered only by general constitutional principles. The U.S. Constitution does not provide all the answers; it does not itself give us all the rules. Someone or something has to tell each generation what it means. In short, the Constitution must be interpreted if it is to be truly useful as an authoritative guide for political action. In the game of American politics, the Supreme Court has responsibility for **judicial review.** Only a few countries around the world have given their courts this significant power.

Judicial review is based on the assumption that whenever a government enforces a rule, a citizen or group could be adversely affected. If such a citizen or group concludes that it has been harmed by the application of a government rule, it might appeal to the courts, in some cases all the way to the Supreme Court. The function of the Court is clear: to decide if the Constitution was truly violated by the governments' action. In most cases, something more significant is happening. The Supreme Court must first decide what the Constitution says on this particular issue; it must interpret the basic rule of the game before it decides if it was violated.

Consider how the Supreme Court has handled the issue of segregation in American society. In 1896, the Court heard *Plessy* v. *Ferguson,* a case involving the segregation of the races on Louisiana trains.[5] The fundamental question was, Does a clause in the Fourteenth Amendment of the Constitution (which says, "No state shall make or enforce any laws which shall—deny to any person within its jurisdiction the equal protection of the laws") prohibit the separation of the races in public facilities? The Supreme Court decided that as long as the facilities were equal, they could be separate. That is, an individual is not denied equal protection of the law just because he or she is not allowed to sit in a particular part of a train. Thus was born the famous "separate but equal" doctrine, which became the law of the land, one of the basic "rules of the game," until 1954.

By 1954, however, society had changed, values had changed, and most importantly, the Supreme Court had changed. Thus, when the Court heard **Brown v. Board of Education,** a case involving segregation in the Topeka, Kansas, school system, it totally reversed the Court's 1896 decision, overturning the "separate but equal" doctrine and proclaiming that any separation of the races automatically implies that one is inferior.[6] The separation of the races, the decision stated, is inherently unconstitutional because separate facilities cannot be equal. Here, then, is a perfect example of how the basic framework of a political system is subject to interpretation and reinterpretation.

Legislative and Executive Decisions

Unfortunately for those who would like an easy route to the rules of politics, there are places to look other than constitutions and court decisions. One must also review the major decisions of the legislative and executive branches of government. In the United States this means acts of Congress, Executive Orders of the President, and decisions of various bureaucratic agencies; in the Soviet Union, decisions of the Council of Ministers, Politburo, and Secretariat; and in Great Britain, those of the Parliament and Cabinet. As we will see in more detail in a later chapter, institutional arrangements vary from nation to nation, but all have institutions which make decisions that become basic rules of the political game. Continuing our example of the rules affecting race and politics in the United States, consider the Voting Rights Act, passed by Congress in 1965. As one of a series of decisions that extended the antisegregation rule laid down in *Brown* v. *Board of Education,* the Voting Rights Act made it more difficult for states to prevent blacks from voting. The result was an increase in black registration and voting. The rules had been revised once again to allow more players to enter the game.

Custom and Tradition

So far, most of the rules discussed in this chapter can be found in written documents and statute books. However, one source of political rules—custom and tradition—is much more difficult to pin down and identify, yet in some political systems, it is the most important. Earlier it was mentioned that the rules of English politics are not written down anywhere. Rather, they are unwritten customs and traditions, some of them several centuries old. This is true to a greater or lesser extent for all nations. Custom and tradition refer to processes and patterns of behavior that are widely accepted and practiced by a society or a portion of a society, but which are not part of its formal set of political rules. Custom is closely related to culture, something we will delve into in a later chapter.

Every society has such informal rules that shape its political system. It is probably true that the more primitive the political system, the more important are custom and tradition. Thus, in a primitive tribal society, we might expect to find that all political rules are customary; in a more modern society, only some. We have already mentioned Great Britain's reliance on unwritten custom, but many people don't realize that the Constitution of the United States says nothing about political parties, surely one of the most important features of the American political system.[7] While some laws have been passed to regulate their activities, parties have grown largely outside the formal set of rules. Another example of political tradition is the unwritten agreement in multiculture systems like Canada (with its French- and English-speaking populations) and Switzerland (with its German, French, and Italian groups) that each important ethnic group be represented in its government.

PROBLEMS OF POLITICAL RULES

We have established the fact that like other games, politics has rules. But now we encounter some special problems which seem to apply only to the game of politics. Several have been touched on already. The rules of politics are found in many places; sometimes, those playing the game are not even aware that some of the rules exist and many of the well-known rules are ambiguous because of their generality. Finally, the rules of politics are probably more changeable than those of any other game.

The last point deserves more attention for it definitely complicates the game of politics. As we have already seen, the rules of most team sports change from time to time, always after the season is over. In the game of politics, the rules often change in the middle of the game. One of the reasons is, of course, that politics, in the broad sense, is a continual process—it has no seasons. Thus, any rule change would have to take place in the middle of the game. But even if we classify politics into a series of separate games—presidential elections, acts of Congress, coup d'états—we find that rules are often changed while the game is still in progress.

The complications do not stop here, for the rules are often changed in the middle of the game by those who are playing the game; in short, by those who stand to win or lose the most. It is as if a football coach who discovers during the first half of the first game of the season that he has an incredibly accurate field goal kicker, comes out for the second half and proposes that field goals now count as six instead of three points. Football fans would be shocked. Comparable events happen all the time in politics, however, for every astute political actor knows that if one can get the rules rewritten in one's favor, there is a better chance of achieving one's goals.

Examples of this phenomenon are not hard to find. Consider what happened at the beginning of the 1980 National Democratic Convention. Incumbent President Jimmy Carter came to the convention with more than enough delegates pledged to him to be renominated as the Democratic candidate; if all of them voted as pledged, the President could not lose. However, just to ensure the outcome, Carter forces worked for a convention rule that would *require* delegates to vote for the candidate they were pledged to support. Opposing the issue was Senator Edward Kennedy, Carter's main challenger for the Democratic nomination. Coming into the convention, Kennedy did not have enough delegates to win the nomination, so he worked against the effort to bind the delegates. He favored a rule that would allow delegates to "vote their conscience." The Kennedy forces defended their position as being more "democratic"; the Carter people rejected it as destructive of the moral commitment of delegates to those who voted for them in state primaries. While many players on either side of the game were no doubt sincere in these claims, the real stake was the presidential nomination. If Carter could get his rule accepted by the Convention Rules Committee, the game would be over for Kennedy. If Kennedy could prevail, he had a fighting chance of picking up defecting Carter delegates during the next several days. As a matter of fact, the game ended when Carter's rule was adopted.

Or, consider how four years later, agents of President Ronald Reagan and Democratic challenger Walter Mondale negotiated rules for the 1984 presidential debates. Not surprisingly, each side worked for rules that favored its candidate. The rules specified the number and format of the debates. Since televised debates tend to give needed exposure to the challenger, the Mondale people wanted six or seven debates; the incumbent's people preferred as few as possible. The decision (probably favoring President Reagan) was to have only two debates. Possible debate formats ranged from free-wheeling, one-on-one discussions (probably more in line with Mondale's style) to more tightly controlled, question-and-answer sessions, with a panel of reporters providing the questions (probably more in line with Reagan's style). The decision was to adopt the second format. And, since both candidates feared "unfair" questions, each insisted that they be given the right to veto any unacceptable reporters.

TYPES OF POLITICAL GAMES

Up to this point, it might seem as if all games, including politics, are based on conflict. This is not surprising, since nearly all the games discussed so far in this chapter are competitions among two or more players, each of whom is presumably playing to win. Games involve conflict—of this there can be no doubt. But the richness of politics is not captured by the total-conflict situation alone. Many political situations involve conflict *and* cooperation. Thus, to totally describe the world of politics, we must consider several types of games, ranging from those of total conflict over a single goal to those in which players com-

	TABLE 2.1			
TYPES OF POLITICAL GAMES				
Type of Game	Typical Conditions	Typical Strategies	Consequences (payoff)	Examples
Zero-Sum	Total conflict	Each side seeking total victory	A winner and a loser (winnings and losses cancel each other out)	Total war; two-person election
Positive Nonzero-Sum	Some disagreement but some interests in common	Bargaining	More winners than losers; everyone can win	Vote-trading in legislatures
Negative Nonzero-Sum	Total conflict or no perceived interests in common	Each side seeking total victory	More losers than winners; everyone can lose	Total nuclear war

pete for several goals and must cooperate to achieve them. (See Table 2.1.)

Zero-Sum Games

The first, simplest and most familiar game situation is the **zero-sum game.** This is the game of total conflict in which neither player is satisfied with anything short of total victory. Thus, the game ends when one player wins and other loses. The term *zero-sum* comes from the fact that winnings of one player equal the losses of the other. In a poker game, for instance, if one player wins $50, the other must lose $50; and in a two-candidate election, one candidate wins and the other loses. Or, consider a war between two nations, each one seeking total victory. Neither will accept anything short of the complete subjugation of the other. Again, if either is successful the result will be a zero-sum game.

Nonzero-Sum Games

Some real-world situations have the characteristics of the zero-sum game, but most are more complicated. Another category, the **nonzero-sum game,** describes those political games that are not simple, total-conflict situations. Games in this category usually involve more than two players and never result in winnings and losses adding up to zero. That is, there are either more winners than losers, or more losers than winners; we call the first situation a *positive* game, the second a *negative* game. The significance of the nonzero-sum game is its recognition that there are many real-world situations which do not fit the neat either-or conditions of the zero-sum game.

Let us consider several political examples of the nonzero-sum game. The ultimate negative game would be a massive nuclear exchange between the United States and Soviet Union. Each side would probably suffer such devastation that it would be difficult to identify a winner. Thus, it would be reasonable to conclude that everyone, including other sections of the world, would end up losers. Fortunately, this is probably an extreme case. There are few political situations where no one wins.

Much more typical is the political game in which more than two players compete for a single prize. Consider, for instance, a campaign for political office among three candidates. Only one can win and so the other two must lose—the sum must be a negative number. This result is a common one in politics since so many political situations involve the distribution of limited goods and resources. At these times, the losers outnumber the winners.

But the reverse, the positive game, is also possible—in fact, it might be more typical, under certain circumstances, than the negative game. While politics does involve conflict, it also requires a significant degree of cooperation. Many political goals cannot be achieved unless individuals, groups, and sometimes even nations work together. At times, this is possible because the parties involved see eye to eye, have the same values, perhaps agree on all the important issues. Thus, cooperation comes naturally just as it does between two completely understanding friends or spouses. But a more common situation is one of mixed interests; that is, the parties agree on some things but disagree on others. As the game proceeds, it becomes evident that the only way to achieve a portion of their goals is for each to cooperate with the others. The words we use to describe this situation are *compromise* and *bargaining*, words that are essential to an understanding of real-world politics.

Bargaining takes place among political actors who realize that in order to gain some of their objectives, they must support the demands of others or compromise, that is, give up some of their demands in order to secure others. If the bargaining is successful, everyone should gain some of what they are after. If one or more players press their demands too far, the process might break down and no one will win anything. The cooperation is not a result of the fact that the players of the game agree on everything—they may agree on very little—but because each recognizes that their success depends upon the actions of others.

Members of the United States Senate have been known to get together and trade votes on matters of direct concern to them. The senator from Arizona asks the senator from Michigan to support his new irrigation project bill in return for support on a bill to limit the number of imported cars; and both promise to vote for increases in price supports for tobacco if their colleagues from North Carolina and Virginia promise to support their causes—and so the process goes. The result can be a series of decisions, no one of which is in the interest of a majority of the senators involved, but each one of which receives a majority of votes because of the trading of support. None of the decisions could be made without the recognition, by each senator that unless he supports the others' bills, they won't support his. Here then is a classic positive non-zero game; every player ends up a winner.

Another reason for the incidence of positive games in politics is the fact that the players are often competing for different prizes—they are in the game for different reasons. Consider the presidential elections of 1968 and 1980, both of them unusual among American presidential elections because each had three serious candidates. A superficial appraisal would lead to the conclusion that in each of these two elections, one candidate won and two lost. Since only one person can be elected President, when there are three candidates the result must be a negative game. This interpretation overlooks the possibility that not all of the candidates are in the election to win the presidency. This may sound strange: don't all of the candidates in an election want to win? The commonsense answer is yes; but a more realistic conclusion might be, all candidates would like to be elected, but some realize that their chances are slim. It is sometimes the case that those in the latter category have as their goal the making of a decent showing—receiving a certain percentage of the vote, for instance.

This is the strategy of a third-party candidate such as George Wallace in 1968 or John Anderson in 1980, who wants to establish himself and his policies as viable forces in the political system. The hope is that if such a candidate receives, let us say, 10 percent of the vote, it will demonstrate that the candidate is someone to be reckoned with in coming elections. The next time around, the leaders of the major parties may have to seek the support of the now established third-party candidate. This analysis probably comes close to describing the goals and strategy of George Wallace in 1968. He didn't really expect to become

President (although he no doubt would have accepted the job), but he did hope to establish himself as a credible alternative for the next election. The fact that he received more than thirteen percent of the popular vote and actually won the electoral votes of several states suggests that his goals were achieved. Conclusions about John Anderson's candidacy in 1980 are not so positive since he received only about six percent of the popular vote and no electoral votes. The conclusion that should be drawn from all this is that positive games can result from situations which on first examination appear to allow for only one winner; this is because so many political situations involve participants who have different goals.

The **game model** provides us with many important insights about the inner workings of politics; it gives us a feel for the basic process by which individuals, groups, and nations compete and cooperate with each other in order to achieve their goals. If politics is that process which decides who gets what, the game comparison helps us understand how. Another model, the systems model, complements the game model by giving an overall structure to our conception of politics. It is the subject of the next section.

POLITICS AS A SYSTEM

Most of us find it easy to visualize politics as a system, since systems exist all around us: automobiles, computers, human bodies, the solar system. The main objective of this section is to demonstrate that each of us is a part of several political systems—cities, states, nations, nation-states, the international system. This leads to another point which is central to an understanding of politics, that politics does not exist in a vacuum. The making of political decisions is the result of interaction between the political system and the rest of society. While the discussion of politics as a game identifies some of the essentials of politics, it might have left the impression that the game of politics has little to do with the larger society. This is clearly not the impression that one should have, and the best way to dispel it is to look at politics as a system.[8]

Two questions must be answered if we are to understand the systems model of politics. First, What is a system? and second, Why should we think of politics as a system? In order to answer the first question, let us consider the characteristics of all systems. Every system is made of a set of elements. An automobile has its engine, transmission, and suspension; a human body, its heart, lungs, and brain; the solar system, the sun and the planets; a political system its citizens, leaders, parties, interest groups, and government institutions.

But it is clearly not just any assortment of things that constitutes a system. The elements must interact with each other in such a way that when one of them is changed, the others are changed. This is true of machines, living organisms, physical systems, and political systems. Each is made up of a number of parts that together constitute the system. The system functions as it does because of the way its elements relate to each other. As the speed of an automobile engine increases, the automatic transmission shifts to a higher gear. Likewise, within the American system, when Congress takes action to increase its power, the President reacts to maintain his. At the level of the international system, if the Soviet Union develops a significant new weapon, the United States will no doubt take counter measures. In each case we are talking about a set of interdependent parts—we are talking about a system. It should be clear that the notion of an interdependent set of elements is closely related to the game of strategy in which players must consider the moves of opponents. Thus, the game model and **systems model** are complementary.

Now, the second crucial element of the systems model comes into play. We would like a model which enables us to relate the process of politics to the rest of the society—to make it clear that politics does not exist in its own independent world. After all, the central point of this text is that the political process performs essential functions for society. The systems model provides a way to illustrate how this is done. The idea is that the political system sits in the middle of the society (see Figure 2.1) and receives **inputs** from it, does something with the inputs, and then produces **outputs** which go back into the society. Let us describe more fully how this process is supposed to work.

According to the systems model, the political process gets rolling when individuals and groups make **demands** (the first kind of input) on the government, asking it to satisfy needs and desires—for more freedom, economic security, or police protection, to name only a few. The decision makers examine the various demands, consider their own interests, and make their decisions—executive orders, legislative acts, or court decisions. These become the outputs that are sent back into the society, and backed up with the power and authority of the decision makers. At this point, the demanding groups and individuals find out, through the **feedback** process, how the system has handled their demands.

If the system has acted to satisfy the demands, the process pauses for the time being. If, on the other hand, the system has not satisfied the demands, the demanders have several choices: to accept the decision because the decision makers are able to enforce it; to try again

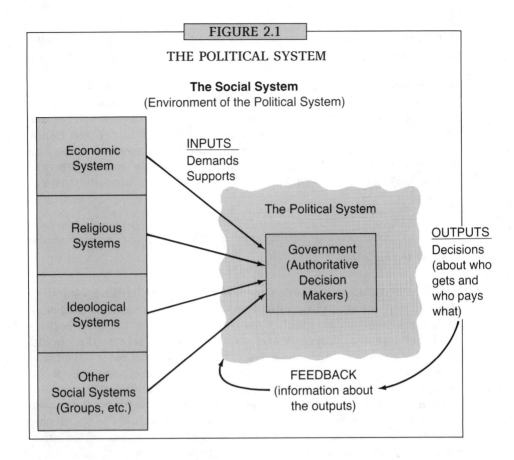

FIGURE 2.1

THE POLITICAL SYSTEM

The Social System
(Environment of the Political System)

Economic System

Religious Systems

Ideological Systems

Other Social Systems (Groups, etc.)

INPUTS
Demands
Supports

The Political System

Government (Authoritative Decision Makers)

OUTPUTS
Decisions (about who gets and who pays what)

FEEDBACK
(information about the outputs)

with more moderate demands; to work through another part of the political system; to begin to withdraw their support from the decision makers or even from the system itself. When large numbers of people withdraw their support from the political system, major change (even revolution) can occur. After all, this reaction is really based on the assumption that the only way to make the system more responsive is to create a new system. Giving or withholding **support** is then the second kind of input and according to the model, it results from the way that the system responds to demands. And, it is now clear that support can be given or taken away from the individuals or party in control of the system, or from the system itself.

What then does the systems model add to our understanding of politics? One of its more important implications is that politics is a continual process in which inputs (demands and supports) affect outputs (decisions) and the outputs have an impact on the next round of inputs—and on it goes. In addition, viewing politics as a system opens our eyes to the contextual nature of the political process. The game of politics is not played in an isolated arena cut off from the rest of society. Rather it is at the center of things—it takes place within cultural, legal, ideological, and economic contexts, all of which interact with it and provide many of the rules of the game. In addition, and perhaps most important, the political system is the main determiner of who gets what.

We are now ready to state a definition of politics that synthesizes the central ideas of the first two chapters: politics is the process in any society which, operating as a system according to a set of rules, and operating through the institutions of government while involving the use of power, decides who receives the benefits and who pays the costs of society.

SUMMARY

The purpose of this chapter has been to provide a better understanding of politics by viewing the political process as a game and as a system. It makes sense to view politics as a strategic game because politics involves interacting players who devise strategies to achieve their goals. Like other games, politics has rules. However, political rules have many sources and are always subject to change. This leads to several special problems in analyzing the game of politics; most significantly, the rules of politics are often changed in the middle of the game by those who are playing the game. Still, one mark of political stability is the degree to which the participants in a political system accept a set of rules, especially rules that are found in a constitution.

The realization that politics is a game should not, however, leave the impression that politics is all conflict and competition. The distinction between zero-sum and nonzero-sum games brings to light the equally significant role that bargaining plays in the political process.

Viewing politics as a system emphasizes several important features of the political process, primarily that politics is a never-ending activity that is in constant contact with the rest of society. Thus, the systems approach meshes nicely with the "who gets what" definition of politics that this text uses. The systems approach enables us to begin to explain how demands are made by society on government and how the government responds to these demands.

NOTES

1. Game theory has become an important part of several fields of study, including economics, business administration, and political science. A recent readable example of how it can be applied to politics is Steven J. Brams, *Game Theory and Politics* (New York: The Free Press, 1975).

2. The writer is William Cowper and he wrote these lines in 1785.
3. Philip Roth, *Our Gang* (New York: Random House, 1971).
4. For a thorough study of the development of the British Constitution, see Bernard Schwartz, *The Roots of Freedom: A Constitutional History of England* (New York: Hill and Wang, 1967).
5. *Plessy v. Ferguson*, 163 U.S. 537 (1896).
6. *Brown v. Board of Education*, 347 U.S. 483 (1954).
7. One leading student of American government has written that "No place was made for the parties in the system, party government was not clearly foreseen or well understood, government by parties was thought to be impossible or impractical and was feared and regarded as something to be avoided." E. E. Schattscheider, *Party Government* (New York: Holt, Rinehart and Winston, 1942), pp. 6–7.
8. See David Easton, *A Systems Analysis of Political Life* (New York: Wiley, 1965).

3

THE STAKES OF POLITICS: BENEFITS AND COSTS

We have defined politics as a process that decides who gets what and who pays what in a society. Such a system is necessary because the things that people want (benefits) are scarce and/or costly. Benefits and costs are the stakes of politics. The benefits and costs of a political system are many and varied—too many to allow for a complete listing. Our main concern here is how they are distributed within and among nations. Here we are clearly dealing with the "who" as well as the "what." "Who" can refer to individuals (Jane Doe, Ronald Reagan, Reggie Jackson); social categories (black-white, male-female); groups (doctors, farmers, truck drivers); classes (upper, middle, lower); regions (North-east, Southwest); and nations (developed, underdeveloped, the United States, Ethiopia). Mostly, in talking about the distribution of benefits and costs, we are dealing with categories, groups, classes, and na-tions—usually called aggregate data—and not with particular individ-uals.

Most of us are probably interested in the salary of the chairman of General Motors or how much the President of the United States pays in taxes or how much wealth the Marcos family was able to accumulate in the Philippines. But the more important political questions are: Why in the United States, is the average income of blacks less than that of whites? Why are most military installations found in the South and Southwest? Why are there so few female members of Congress? Why is the per capita income in Switzerland $14,408 while only $117 in Ethiopia? Why do upper-income groups in Sweden have a larger tax burden than the wealthy in the United States? All of these questions (which of course constitute only a small sample) require political an-swers; they all have to do with the factors that determine the allocation of benefits and costs.

THE DISTRIBUTION OF BENEFITS

While most people would concur that government should play some role in the activities of a society, there is no universal agreement about what benefits the political system should control. Such services as police and fire protection seem naturally public functions (although during the nineteenth century, many American cities relied on private police and fire departments). And, in 1986, as part of his attempt to reduce the government's budget deficit, President Reagan proposed a program of "privatization"—selling almost $20 billion worth of government prop-erties to private buyers. If carried out, this policy would transfer from public to private hands such government assets as huge power stations and the National Weather Service satellites. Some commentators have

detected a more fundamental motivation for privatization: "a basic commitment to shrinking the size and power of government."[1]

When it comes to the more controversial question of the maintenance of the economic system itself, there is even less agreement. Some
support the principle of **laissez-faire**—the government should keep its
hands off the economic system. Others argue for varying degrees of government regulation, even ownership of most or all economic activities
and enterprises. These different points of view, or ideologies, are important in their own right because they significantly impact the way
politics is conducted in different nations. Thus, we will devote an entire
chapter to them.

Instead of trying to resolve this major controversy, a more fruitful
way to proceed is to note that some economic and social benefits are
directly allocated by the political system (e.g., aid to dependent children, subsidies for farmers, public health programs); and others are
indirectly allocated (the economic stimulation resulting, for example,
from a military base in a particular area). But whether direct, indirect,
or very indirect, in few cases are the benefits distributed in a society
unaffected by the actions of the political system. When the total federal
budget of the United States constitutes about 25 percent of the nation's
gross national product, it must have an impact. And, we should be
aware of the fact that this percentage has steadily increased over the
years, not only in the United States but in almost every country. As
Table 3.1 shows, in the United States it has gone up almost nine times
since the turn of the century. In short, the societies of the world have
become more and more politicized. Thus, it seems reasonable to assume
that while there are a range of viewpoints about what should and should
not be done by the political system, every government in the modern
world has a significant impact on its society's social and economic system, and therefore the distribution of social and economic benefits.

Several assumptions about the nature of benefits and how they are
allocated by the political system underlie our discussion:

1. There is a scarcity of most benefits—not everyone can be as wealthy,
   prestigious, or powerful as they would like to be. Thus, *distribution*
   is the key activity of politics and the central goal of most participants is **justice**—receiving what each considers a fair share.

2. In order to provide one individual or group with its benefits, others
   will probably have to receive less of theirs—not all government programs can be completely funded. Decisions must be made; trade-
   offs must occur.

3. Most benefits necessitate costs. In order for you to receive benefits,
   others will probably have to pay the costs; the result is a system of

TABLE 3.1

GROWTH OF GOVERNMENT SPENDING
(Percentage of National Income* Spent by Government)

COUNTRY	1890–1899	1920–1929	1950–1959	1975
UNITED STATES	4%	4%	18%	33%
SOVIET UNION	28	36	51	59
UNITED KINGDOM	8	25	23	48
FRANCE	15	21	27	41
GERMANY	7	21	17	49

*National Income is equal to GNP minus certain costs of production and foreign trade. Thus, National Income is somewhat less than GNP.

Source: *UN Statistical Yearbook;* and *Historical Statistics of the United States*, U.S. Dept. of Commerce, 1976, pp. 1114–1115.

transfer payments. If you receive more than you have paid, there is a net gain; if you pay more than you receive, a net loss. This applies not only to individuals but to groups and regions. It has been demonstrated, for instance, that in the United States the Northeastern and Great Lakes states tend to send more dollars to the federal government than they receive in the form of government benefits. The reverse is true of most of the Western states.

But it might be argued that one can carry this model of society and resulting competition too far, for some benefits, called **pure public goods**, are neither scarce nor too costly since they benefit everyone.[2] Those who use this concept would probably cite clean air as an example, since it can be consumed by one person without reducing the amount consumed by others. Some would add a social benefit such as education to the list of pure public goods. While it is often the case that some groups (suburban students) receive what is apparently a better education than others (inner-city students), in principle the entire society benefits as the overall level of intellectual skill increases, and there is no necessary limit to the amount of education that can be distributed.

Although it makes sense to argue that public goods benefit everyone in a society, the idea of pure public goods and benefits with no costs is difficult for many to accept. After all, even though everyone benefits from clean air, antipollution policies are costly. The money devoted to this purpose will therefore not be spent on other benefits; also trying to achieve a clean environment may make it more difficult to pursue a policy of rapid economic development. After all, a proliferation of factories leads to dirtier air. If factory owners are forced through government regulation to pay for the antipollution devices, they may decide not to expand (leading to a loss of jobs) or to pass the cost on to their customers (leading to higher prices). If government takes on the job itself, taxpayers will have to foot the bill. In either case, the achieving of clean air is costly.

The major point to carry away from this example is that very rarely can a benefit, even one as widely supported as clean air, be pursued without a consideration of costs and of other competing benefits. But this realization need not lead us back to the dog-eat-dog world of Thomas Hobbes. Remember the discussion of positive nonzero-sum games in the last chapter. While it is usually the case that not everyone can obtain everything they want, it is often the case that through bargaining and compromise, most can obtain some of what they want. Again we are back to the heart of politics.

And what about less tangible benefits such as freedom? Isn't it unquestionably the case that everyone is in favor of maximizing their freedom? Who could be against it? There are two points of reply. First, many would argue that if it comes down to a choice between freedom and social order, the latter must prevail. (They are assuming that too much freedom can lead to disorder.) Second, allowing some to maximize their freedom may mean putting restrictions on others. And we are not talking only of the obvious limitations placed on murder, robbery, rape, and reckless driving. No civilized society would consider these activities as worthy of protection under the banner of freedom.

Tricky political questions arise in the face of situations such as the following: a candidate for political office claims the right to ride freely through a neighborhood campaigning from a sound truck, while the residents of the neighborhood assert that their right to a quiet environment should take precedence; a reporter, claiming freedom of speech and press, writes a story about the private life of a celebrity, after which the celebrity demands a retraction on the grounds that his right to privacy has been violated. In each case, there is no way to maximize the rights of both sides at the same time; something has to give. It is usually the responsibility of the political system to decide how to resolve such situations.

How to bring order to our analysis of benefits? That is the question before us. One way is to make the straight forward distinction among **economic, social**, and **political benefits**. Economic benefits such as income and property are the most easily measured. Social benefits, such as freedom, equality, and security, are often less tangible than economic benefits, but no less real to the people who desire them. Political benefits are best thought of as those that allow people to have a hand in the allocation of other benefits. This follows from our definition of politics as the process of deciding who gets what. The most significant political benefit is **power**. Power is the fuel of politics—without it, the game of politics becomes very frustrating. In fact, power is so important that we will devote the next chapter to its clarification.

The Hierarchy of Benefits

There is another more systematic way to approach the question of benefits. Some social scientists have suggested that there is a hierarchy of human needs; that is, human beings have a number of basic motivations and some are more basic than others. Thus it is possible to arrange them in a rank order, or hierarchy. The most famous version of this theory was formulated by the psychologist Abraham Maslow.[3] According to Maslow, there are five main categories of needs: physiological, safety, love, esteem, and self-actualization. They constitute a natural hierarchy because until basic physical needs such as water and food are met, there is little thought of safety. Not until the individual feels the safety of an ordered and predictable environment does concern for love and affection become uppermost, and so on until the ultimate need of self-actualization is realized.

With a little imaginative revision Maslow's hierarchy of needs can be given a political interpretation, which might be very instructive for our purposes. We need not accept his ideas as completely true to recognize their usefulness as an organizational tool. In a society unable to adequately feed its population, the concern is food—people think of little else. Higher-level needs such as security and affection seem much less important. In the words of a political scientist who has studied this question as much as anyone, when "... people are constantly preoccupied with eating, staying warm, dry, healthy, and alive, they have not time to consider public policy."

The starving peoples of Ethiopia and Cambodia, for example, have little time for political activity; they are too busy trying to survive.

When basic physical needs are taken care of to such an extent that people do not spend every waking moment thinking about them, attention can turn to such goals as how to achieve an ordered society—how to protect those who wish to live in peace. This, it should be remembered, is the point at which Thomas Hobbes thought politics begins. Once order is the norm and people live lives of physical security they can begin appreciating the advantages of being members of a community or society. The main advantage is the affection, the feeling of belonging that results from close, regular association with others.

Finally, from physically satisfied and socially secure people develops the drive for self-esteem and self-actualization. In psychological terms this means more concern with their own individual hopes and dreams instead of mere physical survival. In a political system it means greater interest in the political system itself, in the nature of the decision-making process that determines who gets what. Thus, demands for a greater voice in the political process—that is, demands for power—come primarily from people whose most basic physical and social needs have been taken care of. Or, putting it another way, democracy—that form of government in which power is distributed to many people—becomes feasible only in those societies that have solved the basic problems of survival. Democracy will not yet work—in Ethiopia or Cambodia.

What we have, then, is a relationship between the major needs of people in a particular society and the development of its political system. It is not the case that every society whose citizens enjoy physical and social security will become democratic. But it does make sense to suggest that widespread interest and participation in the political process can exist only in such a society. Thus there does seem to be a hierarchy of political needs roughly corresponding to a hierarchy of individual needs. Now, let us reiterate that this does not mean that politics exists only in the most politically sophisticated societies. Politics exists in all societies, from the most impoverished to the wealthiest. In all cases benefits are distributed; the differences in political systems stem from the types of benefits and the number of people that participate in their distribution.

Physical Benefits. Let us use the hierarchy of needs model as a guide for describing the distribution of economic and social benefits. We will begin with basic physical needs and look at how they are distributed around the world. The most basic need is food. However one measures food consumption—calories, protein, or other nutrients—it becomes clear that the citizens of the developed nations have higher intakes than those of the less developed or Third World nations. The same could be said of shelters and their degree of sophistication (such as the existence of indoor plumbing and running water). In highly developed Western nations almost all residences have such conveniences, while in the most undeveloped, the majority do not.

Adequate food and shelter are important because they sustain life. A comparison of the healthiness of the people of various nations tells a great deal about how the basic benefits are distributed, since the ultimate benefit is life.

TABLE 3.2			
INFANT MORTALITY RATE (1980–1981)			
Nation	Infant Deaths (per 1000 Births)	Nation	Infant Deaths (per 1000 Births)
Afghanistan	185	Philippines	47
Nigeria	157	Soviet Union	30
Bangladesh	139	Cuba	22
Haiti	130	Poland	21
India	122	United States	13
Iran	108	United Kingdom	12
Brazil	84	Japan	7
Ethiopia	84	Sweden	7
Mexico	60		

Source: *The New Book of World Rankings* (New York: Facts on File, 1984), p. 330.

One of the most telling measures of the physical health of a society is the infant mortality rate; the numbers in Table 3.2 describe the proportion of 1000 infants who die within a year of birth. The difference between countries is perhaps more striking in this category than any other; for every infant death in Sweden there are 26 in Afghanistan.

Another measure of a nation's health, average life expectancy, is directly related to the infant mortality rate. Table 3.3, which compares the average life expectancy of people in a number of nations, shows almost the same rank order as that found in Table 3.2. Again, the difference between those at the top and those at the bottom of the list is striking.

These and other indicators establish one fundamental fact about the way physical benefits are distributed around the world. They are distributed unequally: there are definitely "have" nations and "have not" nations. In addition, it is clear that one of the basic sources of international disorder is this discrepancy in the allocation of the most basic benefits.

It is impossible to separate the basic physical benefits like food, shelter, and health from the distribution of economic benefits. After all, economic resources allow one to obtain the necessities or luxuries of

TABLE 3.3			
LIFE EXPECTANCY, 1980			
Nation	**Life Expectancy (in Years)**	**Nation**	**Life Expectancy (in Years)**
Afghanistan	40	Mexico	64
Ethiopia	40	Philippines	64
Bangladesh	45	Soviet Union	70
Haiti	45	Cuba	71
Nigeria	50	United States	73
India	51	Japan	75
Iran	58	Sweden	76
Brazil	63		

Source: *World Almanac,* 1986 (New York: Newspaper Enterprise Association, 1986), p. 662.

life. Thus, we will continue our examination of benefits by describing how those of the economic variety are distributed throughout the world and then at how they are distributed in particular nations.

Economic Benefits. Gross national product (GNP) refers to the total value of goods and services produced in a nation during the year. It is probably the best overall measure of a nation's economy and when observed over several years, serves as a good indicator of economic growth or decline. A rank order of GNPs indicates the relative size and economic power of the nations of the world, but the overriding message is that economic wealth is not distributed equally among nations: the GNP of the United States, now over $3 trillion, is 1000 times greater than that of Afghanistan.

GNP is an informative *macro*economic indicator. That is, it tells something about the economy as a whole. It does not, however, indicate how much of the nation's wealth each individual receives. This can theoretically be accomplished by dividing the nation's GNP by its population (to obtain a per capita GNP). A more widely used statistic is **per capita income,** which indicates how much the average citizen receives of the nation's total income. A glance at Table 3.4 demonstrates the huge spread in per capita income (and, thus, standard of living) in

TABLE 3.4			

PER CAPITA INCOME, 1986

Nation	Per Capita Income (in Dollars)	Nation	Per Capita Income (in Dollars)
Qatar	$35,000	Israel	$5,609
Kuwait	11,431	Poland	4,670
Switzerland	14,408	Mexico	1,800
Sweden	14,821	Brazil	1,523
West Germany	11,142	Kenya	196
Japan	8,460	India	150
United States	11,675	Afghanistan	168
United Kingdom	7,216	Ethiopia	117
Soviet Union	2,600	Bangladesh	119

Source: *World Almanac, 1986* (New York: Newspaper Enterprise Association, 1986) p. 622.

various countries. Without knowing anything else, the fact that the annual per capita income in Bangladesh is $119, while in Qatar it is over $35,000, tells us a great deal about the way people live in each country. Once again, we have evidence that the wealth of the world is not distributed equally.

But beyond this, both per capita GNP and per capita income show us that a huge GNP and reasonably affluent citizens are not necessarily synonymous; an apparently rich and powerful nation (in the macro sense) may have a very large population, thus its wealth must be spread around many more people. On the other hand, a nation with a lower GNP might have a small population and thus a much higher per capita ranking. Compare the People's Republic of China and Kuwait. China's GNP easily outstrips that of Kuwait, with $340 billion compared to Kuwait's $12 billion. But when population is taken into consideration, the complexion of the game changes; Kuwait has only 1,200,000 people to share in its wealth, while China has almost 1 billion.

While per capita ranking tells us more than a simple rank order of nations according to GNP, the important *political* question of how the wealth is distributed within nations has not been addressed. After all, it is a combination of high total GNP and small or moderate population that leads to high per capita numbers. But this still doesn't indicate who receives the wealth. Let us imagine two nations, each with a per capita income of $5000, an impressive figure in today's world. Nation A is composed of a very small, but very wealthy elite class, and a large, relatively poor peasant class. Nation B, on the other hand, achieves its $5000 average because of a large middle class, and few extremely wealthy or extremely poor citizens. All would agree that the two societies are very different, different because of the way that economic benefits are distributed. Here then we have arrived at the most important political question: who gets what?

Measures of income distribution are neither as straightforward nor easily calculated as rank orders based on GNP or per capita income, but there are several that are fairly easily understood. They are based on the commonsense idea that in an economic system that has realized perfect equality, each person would receive an equal amount of the nation's wealth. In a less than perfectly equal society, the degree of inequality might be determined by comparing the proportion received by those at the top and those at the bottom of the income ladder. The greater the difference, the greater the economic inequality.

Obviously, we can't come up with a list describing the incomes of every individual in a particular society. But information is available which enables us to statistically divide the society into income levels. Table 3.5 divides the United States into five income levels, from the lowest to the highest, each including 20 percent of the population. It then indicates how big a "slice" of the "income pie" each 20 percent has received in each of three years. In 1950, the poorest one-fifth of the population received 4.5 percent of the national income, while the wealthiest one-fifth received 42.7 percent. Thirty years later, the figures were 5.1 and 41.6, respectively—minor changes at best. We can conclude that there is a gap between the wealthiest and poorest segments of the American population and that over the last three decades there has been little change. It can of course be pointed out that with the significant rise in per capita income during this period (from $1501 in 1950 to $9521 in 1980), everyone is now receiving more. While this is true, it does not speak to the crucial political question of how the wealth is distributed. Again, the figures indicate that not much redistribution has taken place. An examination of other societies indicates that while there is some variation, economic inequality is characteristic of all of them.

So, there is statistical evidence to prove that the distribution of economic wealth is unequal; some people always seem to end up with more than others. But what if it is discovered that certain *types* of people usually receive more? We have already observed that the typical Ethiopian or Afghan receives much less than the typical Swede or West German. But what if we look inside a single nation? Will the now well-

TABLE 3.5

UNITED STATES INCOME DISTRIBUTION, 1950–1980
(PERCENTAGE OF TOTAL INCOME RECEIVED BY EACH FIFTH OF POPULATION)

Year	Lowest 20%	Fourth Highest 20%	Third Highest 20%	Second Highest 20%	Highest 20%
1950	4.5%	12%	17.4%	23.4%	42.7%
1970	5.4	12.2	17.6	23.8	40.9
1980	5.1	11.6	17.5	24.3	41.6

Sources: *Statistical Abstract of the United States,* 1978; and U.S. Bureau of the Census, *Current Population Reports,* series P-60, August 1981.

documented unequal distribution of wealth be related to ethnic background, race, sex, or region? The answer is usually yes.

Consider, for example, the United States. While in 1978 the median income of the male working population was $10,935; for white males it was $11,453, for black males $6861, and Hispanic males, $8380. Or compare the $10,935 figure for male workers with the median of $4068 for female workers. The differences are too great to be explained as coincidence. There must be underlying social and political reasons. They will capture our attention a bit later.

Social Benefits. As a society comes closer to solving its basic physical and economic needs, its attention can turn to the distribution of benefits which, while less essential, do seem to go hand in hand with a more fulfilling existence. In the language of the hierarchy of needs model, we are talking about the higher social needs. A good example is the ability to read and write. From the standpoint of the individual, literacy provides new awareness, new opportunities, and access to new ideas; from the standpoint of the society and political system, a high level of literacy provides the foundation for new forms of social and political existence, culminating in democracy.

Table 3.6 presents a list of nations arranged according to levels of literacy. The range is obviously great. If we refer to the data presented in earlier tables, it becomes clear that nations that rank at or near the bottom on measures of basic physical benefits also experience the lowest rates of literacy. The commonsense explanation seems to be that a nation that is still struggling to feed its citizens can devote few of its

TABLE 3.6			
LITERACY RATES, 1980s			
Nation	**Literate Population (percentage)**	**Nation**	**Literate Population (percentage)**
United States	99%	Zambia	43%
Soviet Union	99	Iran	37
Japan	98	India	34
Belgium	97	Bangladesh	22
Cuba	78	Afghanistan	12
Mexico	75	Ethiopia	6
Brazil	66		

Source: *Statistical Abstract of the United States,* 1985 (Washington, D.C.: Government Printing Office, 1985), p. 845.

precious resources to public education. Education and literacy are truly higher-level benefits.

Notice, however, the vicious circle that develops. Chances are, it isn't until the populace learns new skills that a society can really develop to the point that basic physical needs are no longer the chief worry. But, a nation experiencing problems satisfying such needs cannot afford the kind of educational system needed to begin the upward climb on the economic ladder.

Government Budgets and the Distribution of Benefits

We now know the kinds of physical, social, and economic benefits that can be allocated by a political system. The best way to see how they are allocated is to study the political system's budget.

A budget indicates in neat mathematical form the priorities of the political system. Let us quote one of the most knowledgeable students of public budgeting: "In the most general definition, budgeting is concerned with the translation of financial resources into human purposes. A budget, therefore, may be characterized as a series of goals with price tags attached. Since funds are limited and have to be divided in one way or another, the budget becomes a mechanism for making choices among alternative expenditures."[5]

There are two basic ways to explain the choices that produce a governmental budget. First, they might be viewed as the result of rational planning in which decision makers rank order all of the priorities of the society and then decide how to achieve the common good. The other explanation takes what many observers would consider a more realistic approach by emphasizing the many factors (in addition to consideration of the common good) that go into the construction of a budget. These include all of the things already mentioned, such as political culture, institutions, and the distribution of power. To quote our budget expert once again, "The victories and defeats, the compromises and the bargains, the realms of agreement, and the spheres of conflict in regard to the role of national government in our society all appear in the budget. In the most integral sense the budget lies at the heart of the political process."[6]

The Budget of the United States

The federal government of the United States spends more money than any other government, more than any other organization in the world. Thus it makes sense to focus our attention on who gets its hundreds of billions of dollars. The main purpose of this section is not to memorize a list of figures—the federal budget fills hundreds of pages—but to gain an understanding of the main categories of spending and to begin thinking about who benefits from them. After this experience, one can apply this thinking to the budgets of other nations and analyze them to discover who gets what.

There are a number of ways to make sense of the federal budget of the United States. First, one must attempt to comprehend its magnitude. The budget for fiscal year 1984 was about $848 billion (the fiscal year for the federal government runs from October 1 to September 30). The total for 1986 could hit $1 trillion. It is difficult for most of us to imagine one million dollars; it is nearly impossible to come to grips with one trillion. Maybe the following will help. If you spent $1,000,000 per day, every day, it would take 2740 years to spend a trillion dollars. Or, if you placed one trillion American dollar bills (each six inches long) end to end, they would go around the earth almost 4000 times.

Given the increasing politicization of societies around the world, it is not surprising that the federal budget of the United States has gotten bigger over the years, but it is easy to be overwhelmed with the rate of growth. Table 3.7 graphically demonstrates this. The growth is even more illuminating when we compare the size of the budget and the population of the country at various times. In 1790, there was a $4 million budget for a population of 4 million—$1 per person. By 1984, the population had increased to about 225 million but the budget stood

TABLE 3.7

GROWTH OF THE FEDERAL BUDGET
OF THE UNITED STATES, 1790–1984

YEAR	SIZE OF BUDGET (IN MILLIONS OF $)	YEAR	SIZE OF BUDGET (IN MILLIONS OF $)
1790	$ 4	1939	$ 940
1800	11	1943	7,936
1839	27	1950	39,544
1850	40	1960	92,223
1865	129	1970	196,588
1890	318	1975	326,105
1915	746	1979	493,100
1918	1,267	1981	661,000
1929	312	1984	848,500

Source: *1986 Information Please Almanac* (Boston: Houghton Mifflin, 1986), p. 65. Department of the Treasury, Financial Management Service.

at $848 billion—an average expenditure of $3768 per person. Since 1940, the point at which the billion dollar federal budget became a permanent part of the American political system, the population has not quite doubled while the budget has increased 848 times.

Where Is the Money Spent? Although the ever increasing budget clearly demonstrates the growing significance of government in the affairs of society, our main purpose at this point is to look at where these billions of dollars go. This, once again, is the primary reason for examining a budget. Table 3.8 lists the major categories of the United States federal budget and how much was allotted for each during 1984. The labels are fairly self-explanatory and give a good general overview of how the political system ranked the various needs of the society during that fiscal year.

The first and most significant fact that emerges is that the two areas receiving the greatest support (more than half the total budget), are income security (programs like Social Security and unemployment compensation) and defense. The other big-number categories deal with health and education. And, because more often than not the government runs a deficit (spends more than it takes in and thus must borrow

TABLE 3.8

BUDGET OF THE UNITED STATES FEDERAL GOVERNMENT, 1984

Budget Category	Amount (in Billions of Dollars)	Budget Category	Amount (in Billions of Dollars)
Income Security	$282.4	Transportation	$25.1
National Defense	245.3	International Affairs	13.2
Interest on Debt	103.2	Natural Resources and Environment	9.8
Health	90.6	Community and Regional Development	7.0
Education	25.3	Agriculture	12.1
Veterans Affairs	25.7	Energy	3.3

Source: *Statistical Abstract of the United States,* 1985 (Washington, D.C.: Government Printing Office, 1985), p. 305.

money), it must pay interest. The interest payment on the national debt in 1984 hit $103.4 billion, about eight times the amount spent on natural resources and the environment. Furthermore, the chance of this payment ending in the near future is unlikely since the total national debt has now passed the $2 trillion mark. In recent years, deficits have averaged $200 billion per year. This obviously means that the national debt has been and will continue to increase until spending and tax revenues are made equal. Given our main argument that budget making is a political process, we should not be surprised by the fact that deficits go up instead of down. It is usually easier for political decision makers to provide the benefits demanded by powerful groups and add to the deficit than to say no. In 1985, Congress attempted to deal with the deficit problem by passing the Gramm-Rudman-Hollings Act (named after the three United States senators who formulated it). It provides for automatic cuts in most government programs if the deficit reaches certain levels. Defended by some, it is viewed with cynicism by others who see it as a desperate move by politicians who should be able to cut the budget through the normal give-and-take of the political process. As of this writing, the Supreme Court of the United States is deciding whether the Gramm-Rudman-Hollings Act violates the separation of powers between the legislative and executive branches (and is thus unconstitutional).

Education is one of many categories to receive federal aid. Shown here is a Head Start classroom in Virginia.

Let's look beyond the numbers and speculate about who receives the economic benefits in some of the categories. Although we will touch only the tip of the iceberg, going beyond this brief analysis can be a very rewarding experience and it is enthusiastically recommended. Remember, our main objective is to get a feel for who gets what by examining the priorities of the biggest spender in modern society, the central government.

Each budget item is supposed to accomplish a particular goal—to maintain national security, support the prices of domestic agriculture goods, help provide adequate health care, pay off the national debt, and so forth. As a result, some individuals and groups gain more than others. For instance, who receives the more than $200 billion spent by the Defense Department? A great deal (about one-third) is devoted to buying and developing new weapons. (As of 1981 an M–1 tank cost $2.5 million, the latest Nimitz-class nuclear-powered aircraft carrier about $10 billion). Most of the billions go to a relatively small number of defense contractors and the hundreds of thousands of workers in their factories. Another large chunk, more than half, goes to pay military personnel and to operate and maintain the defense establishment. Thus, while it is an exaggeration that only a tiny segment of society receives the entire defense budget, it is true that the economic benefits resulting from defense spending are not distributed equally throughout society. Not only do the defense contractors and military personnel benefit directly, but the areas in which defense plants and military bases are located receive significant benefits as government spending filters through the community. Thus, the decisions of who gets defense contracts and where military bases are located are crucial political questions.

Guns or Butter? We won't go into all the other budget categories and their beneficiaries: farmers, the oil industry, cities, the unemployed, and so on. Only a more detailed examination of the budget—something we can't do here—can produce specific answers.

What we can do is make note of the classic choice that every political system seems to have to make, between **guns and butter**—between an emphasis on national security and social programs. Obviously neither can be totally ignored, but one can be given a higher priority—given limited resources, hard decisions in one direction or the other must eventually be made.

An example of the ups and downs of defense and social welfare spending is summarized in Figure 3.1. It traces the proportion of the federal budget devoted to each area over the last thirty years. In 1950, both items received about the same amount; the proportion allocated to social welfare increases very slightly while defense spending increases by 50 percent. Then, in 1960, defense begins a downward slide that lasts into the early 1980s; interestingly, the social welfare budget takes off at about the same point. What comes through this simple but informative diagram is a graphic demonstration of the priorities of the political system and how they can change, even reverse themselves over time. It would appear that the Reagan years have brought about a return to an emphasis on defense spending.

Comparisons with Other Nations. Let us now turn our attention to other countries. Are the priorities of the American political system out of step with those of the rest of the world? Table 3.9 indicates that when it comes to defense spending as a percent of GNP, the United States is just about average. But of course, 5.4 percent of a huge GNP equals a figure, as we have already seen, of more than $200 billion. Still, those who argue that the Soviet Union is replacing or has replaced the United States as the number-one military power are given some support by the table. It has been estimated that the Soviet Union's GNP is about 60 percent of that of the United States. But 13.3 percent of this amount is more than enough to close the gap. One is struck with the magnitude of some of the figures, especially those of Oman and Israel. Given the unstable political and social conditions existing in the Middle East, it is not surprising to find these and other Arab nations at or near the top of the list.

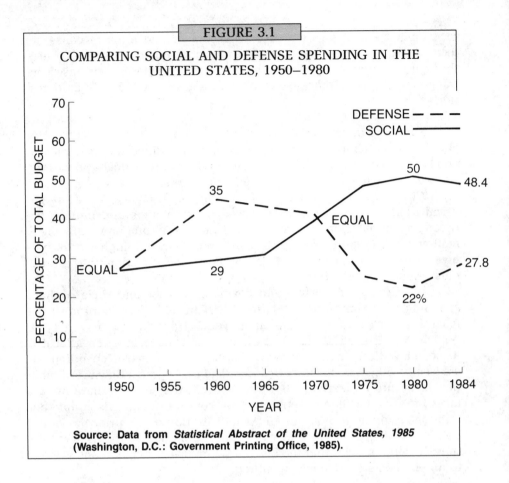

FIGURE 3.1

COMPARING SOCIAL AND DEFENSE SPENDING IN THE UNITED STATES, 1950–1980

Source: Data from *Statistical Abstract of the United States, 1985* (Washington, D.C.: Government Printing Office, 1985).

In regard to social welfare spending, we once again see a range of priorities. Table 3.10 compares a number of developed Western democracies in three areas of social spending. Sweden devotes almost 16 percent of its GNP to public health, public aid (usually called welfare in the United States), and old-age benefits; Japan, only 4.3 percent. While a full explanation of these differences can come only after a more thorough analysis of the political process, we can speculate that it probably has something to do with differences in culture and ideology.

THE DISTRIBUTION OF COSTS

Let us "turn the coin over" and look at the other side. We have been talking about benefits and who receives them. Equally important are the costs that must be levied by the political system and who pays them.

TABLE 3.9

DEFENSE SPENDING AS A PERCENTAGE OF GNP, 1977 AND 1982

NATION	1977	1982	NATION	1977	1982
World Average	5.7%	4.5%	United States	5.4%	5.2%
Oman	42.7	26.0	United Kingdom	4.8	4.8
Israel	28.2	29.8	Sweden	3.3	3.4
Saudi Arabia	15.7	22.4	Canada	2.0	1.9
Soviet Union	13.3	10.7	Japan	0.9	0.9
Iran	10.5	6.1	Mexico	0.7	0.5
People's Republic of China	9.4	6.7			

Sources: *Statistical Abstract of the United States,* 1985 (Washington, D.C.: Government Printing Office, 1984), p. 866; and *New Book of World Rankings* (New York: Facts on File, 1984), p. 87.

TABLE 3.10

SOCIAL SPENDING AS A PERCENTAGE OF GNP, MID–1970s

NATION	PUBLIC HEALTH	PUBLIC AID	OLD-AGE	TOTAL
Sweden	6.4%	3.5%	6.0%	15.9%
West Germany	4.6	1.0	7.6	13.2
Canada	6.6	2.0	2.4	11.0
United Kingdom	3.7	1.9	3.6	9.2
United States	2.7	2.5	3.4	8.6
Japan	3.4	0.6	0.3	4.3

Source: *Social Indicators,* 1980 (U.S. Department of Commerce), p. 406.

The point has already been made that few benefits are free; whether national defense or social welfare, someone must pay. Thus, political decisions must be made as to how the burden will be apportioned. Witness the tremendous battle that took place over President Reagan's 1981 tax cut proposals. Despite some initial discussion of the impact of the cuts on the American economic system, the debate soon turned into a battle between various groups, each arguing that its tax burden should be reduced. There were spokespersons for business, the wealthy, the middle class, the working poor. The Democratic leadership in the House of Representatives claimed that the President's bill was stacked in favor of business and the upper class, while the Republican leaders countered that their bill was the one that would really help the great middle class. The tax bill's final shape (any tax bill's final shape) was as much the result of the interaction and relative power of the concerned groups as of the philosophy of the President.

Human Costs

Before we go any further, let us make it clear that not all costs are economic. Important noneconomic costs must also be distributed in any society. They include physical and psychological burdens that some or perhaps all members of a society must bear; let us call them *human* costs. The most obvious and probably most important one is service in the armed forces of the nation.

National defense requires not only money but personnel. Two decisions must be made by the society: how large should the armed force be, and who shall serve in it? Both are political decisions of the greatest magnitude, at least as important as the nature of the tax system. Table 3.11 presents a list of nations and the relative human cost each has assumed to maintain its armed forces. the range is significant: the cost to the population of Israel, for example, is about twenty times as great as it is to the citizens of Japan.

But "how many" is only part of the equation. It is probably reasonable to assume that even with a high level of patriotism, most people would just as soon pass up the chance to serve in the nation's armed forces because it is viewed as a reduction of their freedom. Thus, if large numbers of personnel are needed, the political system must find ways to produce them. Two basic methods exist: one is to offer rewards in the form of such things as salaries, education, and prestige, in a magnitude great enough to overcome the reluctance of individuals. This produces a volunteer army. The other method is to use a system of compulsory service—in other words, a draft.

A volunteer force is not based on compulsion, but there is a good chance that those attracted will tend to come from the less privileged

TABLE 3.11			
ARMED FORCES PERSONNEL PER 1000 POPULATION, 1981			
Nation	**Per 1000 Population**	**Nation**	**Per 1000 Population**
Israel	44.6	Poland	12.3
North Korea	34.9	United States	9.6
Taiwan	27.5	Sweden	8.3
Syria	27.4	West Germany	8.0
Cuba	21.6	Saudi Arabia	5.7
Soviet Union	18.4	United Kingdom	5.7
South Korea	15.6	China	4.5
Oman	15.0	Canada	3.4
East Germany	13.6	Japan	2.1

Source: *New Book of World Rankings* (New York: Facts on File, 1984), pp. 83–84.

segments of the society. Thus, service in the military will not be distributed equally throughout society. If, on the other hand, a compulsory draft is the source of personnel, then some real decisions have to be made about the basis of selection. Will everyone be drafted or only those of a certain age or sex? Will college students be exempted until they complete their education? The questions go on and on but they must be answered. The draft system that emerges will be political since one way or another, everyone in the society will be affected either by being required to make a two- or three-year commitment of their life (even putting it in jeopardy), or by being exempted from this awesome responsibility.

Economic Costs: Taxation

Let us return to the question of economic costs that are distributed by political systems. It is clear that the most important and pervasive kind of economic cost is taxation.

Objectives of Taxation. There are two basic questions to ask of any tax system: What are its purposes? and Upon what principles is it based? While the second question is more relevant to our present concerns, the first also has important implications for politics.

Tax systems are created to achieve some or all of four objectives. The most obvious is to produce revenue to pay for the political system's spending programs. Often accompanying this objective is a more controversial one, the redistribution of income. Some enthusiastically support this function of taxation; others condemn it with just as much fervor. It is not difficult to see why there are strong feelings on either side.

The basic idea of redistribution is fairly simple; set up a tax system that takes a greater percentage of higher incomes and returns some of the revenue to those with lower incomes in the form of various social welfare and income maintenance programs. The result is a net gain for some and a net loss for others; consequently the gap between upper and lower incomes decreases.

A third role of tax systems is to function as a tool in the regulation of the nation's economic system. The accepted wisdom for several decades has suggested that during times of runaway inflation, an increase in tax rates will leave less money in people's pockets, thus giving them less to spend, and so prices will come down; during times of recession and unemployment, the opposite policy should be pursued—if tax rates are lowered, people will have more money to spend and thus demand will go up, factories will have to turn out more goods, and people will be called back to work.

What to do when unemployment and inflation are high at the same time is one of the real puzzles facing modern policymakers. One recent proposal suggests that a lowering of tax rates will result in more individual saving, which in turn will lead to more investment; thus the two evils will be combatted simultaneously.[7] We cannot resolve the theoretical dilemma; luckily we need not establish our basic point. Adjusting the tax rate has become an acceptable tool of modern governments, even if the results are not always predictable.

Finally, taxes are sometimes employed to regulate certain kinds of behavior that have been defined as socially undesirable; if a society decides that tobacco and alcohol are unhealthy, one way to reduce their consumption is to establish an additional tax. Or, if a nation's sources of energy are in short supply, a higher tax on their consumption may slow their depletion.

Some governments attempt to pursue all of these objectives; others only one, the production of revenue. Whatever the government's goals, its tax policies will have a significant political impact: the burden has to be distributed and some will invariably feel that they have been treated unjustly.

Principles of Taxation. No tax system can be completely understood without some knowledge of the principle or principles upon which it is based. Despite their lofty philosophical sound, such principles are political in nature for each seems to favor one group or another. Let us examine them in that light.

One way to ground a tax system is with the **benefits received principle.** It suggests, simply, that costs should equal benefits received. Thus, the tax I pay to the government should be proportionate to the benefits I receive from the government. If I receive more, I should pay more.

This principle can work in certain cases, but it doesn't seem applicable to those taxes that are the leading source of revenue for government's major functions. Fishing license fees and road tolls are based on the benefits received principle; these user fees are paid only by those who benefit from well-stocked fishing grounds and properly maintained roads. According to this argument, if you never go fishing or never drive on turnpikes, you shouldn't have to help pay for them.

However, once we move beyond these rather specific areas, the benefits received principle begins to break down. First of all, how do we decide how much each of us benefits from a strong national defense, a clean environment, or safe neighborhoods? The only reasonable answer seems to be, equally. These are examples of the power that results from pooling resources; some things could never be accomplished by individuals. And when we look at the other great area of government spending, social welfare, the benefits received principle makes no sense. These programs assume that there are some people who for one reason or another cannot provide certain services for themselves at an adequate level. The reason that people use food stamps is because they couldn't buy adequate food without them. To ask them to pay a tax equal to the amount they save by buying their food with food stamps is to defeat the purpose of the program—if they can pay the tax, they probably don't need the food stamps. A realist knows that such programs are subject to abuse. But all in all, the people who avail themselves of such programs are those who can least afford to pay for the benefits. Thus, while the benefits received principle can work in some specific cases, it would be self-defeating if used as a major source of revenue.

What, then, is left? Some would support the **ability-to-pay principle**. It would seem that this is the best way to raise revenue and to many it is obviously the fairest principle of taxation; those who earn more can afford to pay more. Naturally, those who would end up paying higher taxes often disagree with this taxation method. Thus, we have a classic political dispute about who pays what; lower-income groups supporting the ability-to-pay principle, upper-income groups rejecting it.

Upper-income groups are more likely to support the third tax principle, the **equality principle**. "What could be fairer," they ask, "than a system taxes everyone at the same rate?" The supporters of ability-to-

TABLE 3.12			
INCOME TAX RATES OF THREE HYPOTHETICAL COUNTRIES (as percent of income)			
INCOME (IN DOLLARS)			
Nation	**$5000**	**$20,000**	**$50,000**	**$100,000**
Nation A	20%	20%	20%	20%
Nation B	10	20	30	40
Nation C	40	30	20	10

pay counter with, "What could be fairer than a system that taxes more heavily those who can best afford it?" The answers to the questions require us to make a distinction between progressive and regressive taxes.

Types of Tax Systems. Tax systems based on the ability-to-pay principle are called **progressive**. Found quite commonly in the political systems of the West, the **progressive tax system** increases the tax rate as income goes up. Thus, a person earning $100,000 would pay at a higher rate (let us say 50 percent) than one earning $10,000 (20 percent). Note that it is insufficient to say that the upper-income person pays more in taxes; that would be the result if each taxpayer paid at the same rate. Twenty percent of $100,000 is more than 20 percent of $10,000. What makes the tax progressive is the fact the the *proportion* of taxable income increases. Table 3.12 describes the tax systems of three hypothetical nations. Because the rate is the same for each income level, the tax system of nation A is not progressive. The tax system of nation B is progressive.

Nation C has a **regressive tax system** because the rate decreases as income goes up. Thus, contrary to the progressive tax, those with high incomes benefit and those with low incomes suffer. It is not easy to find a tax as blatantly regressive as our hypothetical nation's, but slightly less obvious examples can be found. For instance, the Social Security tax of the United States is for many a regressive tax since individuals pay a flat rate (7.05%) of their income up to a cut-off point ($37,800). Thus, as Table 3.13 shows, Americans who earn more than $37,800 actually pay a smaller proportion of their income into the Social Security system than those earning less than $37,800 and, as income increases, the proportion continues to decrease.

Many social analysts argue that even if all Americans paid 7.05 percent of their entire income, the Social Security tax would still have

TABLE 3.13	
SOCIAL SECURITY TAX SYSTEM OF THE UNITED STATES, 1984	
INCOME	**PERCENT OF INCOME PAID BY EMPLOYEE**
$ 10,000	7.05%
20,000	7.05
37,800	7.05
50,000	5.32
70,000	3.80
100,000	2.66

to be considered regressive. They claim that all flat-rate taxes—that is, taxes based on the principle of equality—are regressive. The reason is that the lower the income, the less an individual can afford the tax; the greater the income, the less each additional dollar matters. Thus, returning to Table 3.12, nation A's tax system would be considered regressive because the individual making $5000 feels his 20 percent tax bite ($1000) much more than does his wealthy neighbor, whose $100,000 income requires a $20,000 tax payment. If this argument is accepted, then most flat-rate sales taxes, property taxes, and the like are regressive.

When the distinction between progressive and regressive taxes is pushed far enough, it seems to lead to the conclusion that all tax systems favor either lower- or upper-income groups. A society that uses progressive taxes exclusively would seem to be under the control of the less wealthy or a very benevolent ruling class. Likewise, if regressive taxes are the norm, the wealthy must have the upper hand.

The real world is usually not that neat. The tax systems of most nations are "mixed bags" of progressive and regressive taxes. In the United States, for instance, the federal income tax is progressive, but the Social Security tax is regressive, as are most state and local taxes. The only reasonable conclusion seems to be that a tax system is not the product of a single rational stroke but is instead the result of a long, endless process of give-and-take in which tax policies are added and subtracted as cultural values change and the balance of power shifts. Recent research has shed some light on this question. Perhaps the most interesting conclusion is that the less developed the society, the more reliance on regressive taxes; the more developed, the more the reliance on progressive taxes. It has even been shown that within the United States, less-developed states like Mississippi have more regressive tax systems.[8] It seems reasonable to conclude that as a society modernizes and as its political system becomes more open and democratic, the tax system is shifted in a more progressive direction. The commonsense explanation seems to be that democracy means a wider distribution of power, which in turn leads to the tax policies favoring the interests of the less wealthy but more numerous groups in society.

Let us complete this discussion of taxation by referring to Table 3.14 which demonstrates that tax burdens vary from nation to nation. In this list of Western nations, the most heavily taxed is Sweden, with more than one-half of its GNP going toward taxes, while in Japan the proportion is less than one quarter. Remember, however, that Japan also ranks at the bottom of the list in both defense and social welfare spending.) We will consider other implications of these interesting statistics in later chapters.

EXPLAINING THE INEQUALITY OF BENEFITS AND COSTS

If nothing else, it is clear from the discussion of this chapter that whatever the benefit or cost, unequal distribution is the norm. Some nations achieve more equality than others, but nowhere has perfect equality been realized.

To some, inequality, whether economic, social, or political is self-evidently bad; in their minds the only acceptable human condition is basic equality. To others, the unequal distribution of social and economic benefits is a perfectly natural consequence of the unequal abilities of human beings; some people are more intelligent or are more highly motivated. Thus they should receive more of the benefits of life.

Now, this debate takes place in the realms of moral philosophy and ideology. Fundamental human questions are being discussed. We will return to them in Chapter 7, where the nature of several ideologies is discussed in more detail. At this point, our attention is focused on the factors that have an impact on the distributive process, and, not on whether inequality is good or bad. Later, we will also be interested in the impact of inequality on the functioning of the political system.

TABLE 3.14					
TAX PER CAPITA AND AS A PERCENTAGE OF GNP, 1977*					
Nation	**Per Capita Tax (in Dollars)**	**Percent of GNP**	**Nation**	**Per Capita Tax (in Dollars)**	**Percent of GNP**
Sweden	$5061	53.4%	France	$2845	39.6%
Norway	4204	47.5	United States	2564	30.3
Denmark	3822	42.0	United Kingdom	1599	36.6
Netherlands	3557	46.3	Japan	1392	22.2
West Germany	3196	38.2	Italy	1304	37.6
Switzerland	3018	31.5	Greece	794	28.1
Canada	2831	32.0	Spain	710	22.5

*National, state, and Social Security taxes
Source: Organization for Economic Cooperation and Development, Paris, France.

The first explanation of inequality is really a restatement of the idea that people receive different amounts of benefits because they are endowed with different levels of ability and motivation. A more complex version of this theory adds the idea that if there were not different rewards for different jobs, many essential functions would not be performed. How many people would go through the long and difficult training required to become a physician if there were not economic and social rewards at the end of the road? Thus, the distribution of benefits is supposedly based on the relative significance of various functions performed in each society. Those who do the most important work receive the most benefits.

But, it can be argued, this assumes a near-perfect system of distribution in which there is complete agreement about who deserves what. The trouble is, such a system does not exist. Other factors, including luck, enter into the process and provide the bases for other explanations of inequality. As we saw in the last chapter, while politics is not considered a game of chance, the element of chance is part of the game. Being born with a $10 million trust fund gives one an initial advantage over someone who begins with nothing. In many societies, having a particular family name, aristocratic title, or class background puts one several paces ahead in the race for more benefits. Such factors are not the result of the individual's own abilities, yet they must be considered in any analysis of "who gets what." This generation's unequal distribution of benefits has a cumulative effect on the next generation.

Some players in the game of politics get a head start. At the international level, the random distribution of natural resources has a profound effect on the world political system. There is no doubt that the single most important source of power in the Middle East is oil. Its existence there can be explained by geologists, but politically its location in that part of the world must be viewed as a lucky occurrence for Saudi Arabia, Iran, Libya, and other Middle East nations. What they do with this resource and how they use it economically and politically is of course another matter, and much closer to the hearts of political scientists.

This leads us to a set of factors of special interest to political scientists: cultural values and ideologies that shape the distribution of benefits and costs; the type of political institutions that actually decide who gets what; and the distribution of power. Each of these broad factors constitutes a major section of this book.

We can assemble our ideas at this point by saying that the distribution of benefits is the result of a combination of the following: (1) the psychological characteristics of individuals; (2) random factors, which can be labeled luck or chance; (3) the cultural and ideological environment; (4) structural features of the decision-making process, such as the institutions of government; and (5) how power is distributed.

SUMMARY

Every society needs a process to decide who gets what and to help people achieve their goals. This process is politics. Politics is necessary because most of the things that people want (benefits) are scarce and/or costly. Thus, political systems must identify and rank-order the benefits that people desire and decide who will pay the costs; benefits and costs are the stakes of politics.

A number of generalizations can be extracted from how benefits and costs are distributed. One that stands out is that benefits and costs are almost always distributed unequally within and among nations. There are several partial explanations for this phenomenon. They include the distribution of power, the nature of governmental systems, cultural values, ideology, and the nature of economic systems.

There are many kinds of benefits, both economic and noneconomic. They can be arranged in a kind of hierarchy, from the most basic physical to social and political benefits. It is assumed that before a political system can really deal with social and political benefits, the basic physical needs of the society must be met.

The best way to see how a particular government is distributing benefits is to examine its budget. This provides an initial feel for the political system's priorities—social programs (butter) or defense programs (guns), for instance. In addition, the priorities that are expressed in a government's budget tell us something about the distribution of power in the political system and the dominant cultural and ideological values of the society.

It is also important to examine how a political system distributes its costs, both human (service in the armed forces) and economic (taxes). It is clear that the distribution of costs is part of the political process since political factors such as power, governmental systems, culture, and ideology are primary factors in determining who pays what.

NOTES

1. Hobart Rowan, "For Sale: One Government," *Washington Post: National Weekly Edition,* Feb. 24, 1986, p. 5.
2. Pure public goods as discussed in Robert Lineberry and Ira Sharkansky, *Urban Politics and Public Policy* (New York: Harper & Row, 1978), pp. 218–19.
3. Abraham Maslow, "A Theory of Human Motivation," *Psychological Review,* 50:370–96 (1943).
4. James Davies, *Human Nature in Politics* (New York: Wiley, 1963), p. 16.
5. Aaron Wildavsky, *The Politics of the Budgetary Process* (Boston: Little, Brown, 1964), pp. 1–2.
6. *Ibid.,* p. 5.
7. This is one of the principles of what has become known as supply-side economics, a main tenet of President Reagan's economic program.
8. Ira Sharkansky, *The United States: A Study of a Developing Country* (New York: McKay, 1975), pp. 56–57.

CONTEXTS OF POLITICS

4

THE ENVIRONMENT OF POLITICS: POWER

Everyone reading this book is affected by political decisions. That much is clear from the first three chapters. But now we would like to know what factors have an impact on the political process, on who gets what, and who pays what. Remember that the systems model suggests that politics does not take place in a vacuum. The chapters of Part II will discuss the environment of politics; its main components are cultural, ideological, and economic systems, and the distribution of power.

Imagine a series of concentric circles which together describe the politically relevant parts of society. Or, if imagination is not immediately available, a glance at Figure 4.1 will do; it is really a different-shaped version of the systems model found in Chapter 1. The center circle stands for the institutions of government where final political decisions are made. Moving outward, we come to the distribution of power (the subject of Chapters 4 and 5), then the economic and ideological systems, and finally the culture. The idea is that the largest circles describe the most general aspects of society. Each circle has a reciprocal (but not necessarily equal) impact on the other circles. Thus, to cite just one example, culture—the most pervasive element in any society—has an impact on the economic system, and the economic system has a return impact on the culture. We need not establish all the reciprocal relationships that exist in any society to get a feel for the influence that factors other than the government itself have on the political process. But government will not of course be ignored; after Part II's discussion of the environment of politics, Part III will look at the political institutions at the center of things.

This chapter deals with the classic political concept of power.[1] We will first define it, then discuss its various types and, finally, some of its sources. In Chapter 1 we referred to the importance that power assumed early in the history of political science. Remember how Machiavelli made it the cornerstone of his political theory. Since his time, many political scientists have carried on in the same tradition. They would agree that "Some concept of power underlies virtually every description of political interaction, domestic as well as international."[2] According to this view, nothing in politics is accomplished without power—those with the most power also tend to receive a greater proportion of the benefits of society. And without power, governments could not retain control of the decision-making process.

DEFINING POWER

Before we go any further we should define **power**. It is one of those concepts used quite often in everyday conversations but rarely defined in a rigorous way. However, cutting through the ambiguity uncovers a

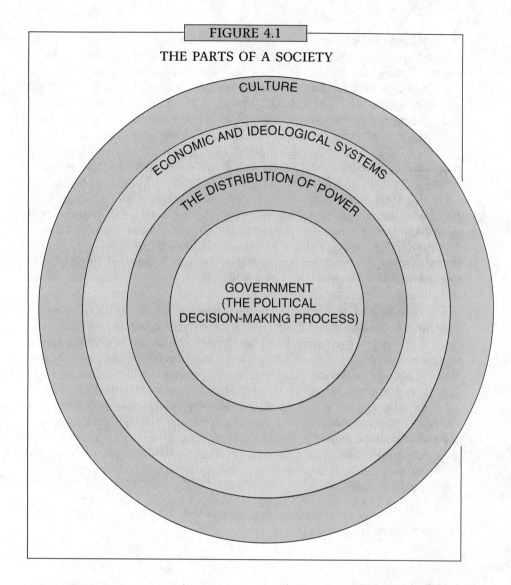

FIGURE 4.1

THE PARTS OF A SOCIETY

CULTURE

ECONOMIC AND IDEOLOGICAL SYSTEMS

THE DISTRIBUTION OF POWER

GOVERNMENT
(THE POLITICAL
DECISION-MAKING PROCESS)

core idea: power always involves controlling someone else's behavior. If your professor can get you to do something that you would not otherwise have done—read this book, for instance—it can be said that he or she has exercised power over you. This definition puts power on a one-to-one basis, a not uncommon situation: President Reagan vs. Speaker Jim Wright, Israeli prime minister Menachem Begin vs. Egyptian president Hosni Mubarak. But it is often the case that in politics, power is exercised at a distance. We know that our government is controlling our behavior, but not as the result of a visit from a bureaucrat or legislator. Or, consider the reverse situation, when voters wield in-direct power over decision makers by threatening to turn them out of office. Clearly, we must expand our definition so that it includes those who make decisions that eventually affect the lives of others, without one-to-one contact. When the Congress of the United States passes a law that regulates the automobile industry, it is an act of power, even though the impact is for many indirect and less than immediate.

It is clear from these comments that power is best thought of as *relational* and *behavioral*. Power exists when one person, group, insti-tution, or nation attempts to control the behavior of another; it takes at least two for power to exist. An individual cannot wield power unless he or she has someone to wield it over. And, power is something that exists only when it is used; it is a type of behavior. Later we will discuss the sources of power, things like wealth and military strength which, when used properly, allow one to control others. But power itself should not be confused with the sources of power. We will pick up the thread of this argument later in the chapter.

To come to grips with political power we should recognize that it can be both a *means* and an *end*. As a means it is, as we have said before, the fuel of politics, used to achieve the goals of those playing the game. Goals can be selfish (an increase in personal wealth or pres-tige) or social (achieving peace, reducing poverty), or a mixture of both. Whatever the case, power is instrumental in their realization.

As an end, power becomes desirable in itself; some people seek it the way others seek wealth. Psychologists have argued that there are people who have *political* personalities because of their great love of power. For them it is not what can be done with power so much as the inherent satisfaction they receive from wielding it.[3]

TYPES OF POWER

Because there are many ways to control the behavior of others, political power has a number of forms. We can identify five that are especially important: coercive, utilitarian, manipulative, legitimate, and personal. They are summarized in Table 4.1.

Coercive Power

The most obvious kind of power is **coercive**: when the President forces a senator to support one of his policies by threatening to campaign against him or her in the next election; when citizens pay their taxes because they are afraid of what might happen if they don't; or when a

TABLE 4.1

TYPES OF POWER: A SUMMARY

Type of Power	Typical Manifestations	Sources
Coercive	Threats	Military Strength, Force, Anything Feared
Utilitarian	Promises	Wealth, Anything of Value
Manipulative	Propaganda Socialization	Skill in Psychological Techniques-Mass Media
Legitimate	Authority	Governmental Office, Accepted Procedure
Personal	Influence	Charisma, Personality

small country gives up territory to a larger one after the latter has moved its troops to the former's borders. All are coercive because each involves the following relationship: A attempts to get B to do something that B would not otherwise do, by threatening to do something to B that B does not want to happen. Then it is up to B to decide what is less objectionable, doing what A wants or having A carry out the threat. If B does what A wants, the threat has succeeded; if not, A must decide whether or not to carry out the threat.

Let us refine our notion of coercive power by examining the case of the President and the senator. The President wants the senator to support an administration-sponsored tax increase; if the senator refuses, the President threatens to campaign against him or her in the next election. The senator must resolve three questions: 1. Is the threatened action worse than what the President wants me to do? (Voting for a tax increase may lose the senator more votes at home than would a negative campaign by the President.) 2. Does the President have the capability to carry out the threat? (The President obviously has the capacity to campaign in any congressional district, but his popularity may not be great enough to sway many voters.) 3. Does the President have the will to carry out the threat? (Is the threat credible?) (If the senator decides the threat is really a bluff, he or she will not give in. It is one thing to make a threat; it is something else to carry it out.)

Let us illustrate the importance of **credibility** in the exercise of coercive power by examining a historical example, the policy of *massive retaliation* formulated during the 1950s by the foreign policy leaders of the United States. The core idea of the policy was that, given the escalating cost of maintaining an effective defense and assuming the superiority of the American nuclear force, the United States should concentrate on strengthening its nuclear deterrent force. The result would be a strategy that said to all the world, "If you commit any aggressive act against the United States, it will be met with our ultimate weapon." Or in the less direct, but just as threatening, words of Secretary of State John Foster Dulles, the United States had decided to "depend primarily upon a great capacity to retaliate, instantly by means and at places of our own choosing."[4]

In theory, it sounded like a wonderful plan. The United States could decrease spending on conventional weapons, reduce its armed forces, and rely on a weapon so terrible that it would prevent any nation from taking aggressive action against the United States. But one central problem emerged over the next several years: the threat was not credible. Would the United States *really* respond to any act of aggression with a nuclear attack, knowing that its main adversary, the Soviet Union, had acquired its own nuclear arsenal? General Maxwell D. Taylor, then Chief of Staff of the American military, put it this way in 1957: it was "increasingly unlikely that any nation will deliberately embark on such a war (nuclear) with its prospect of reciprocal annihilation."[5] Thus, other nations concluded that while the American nuclear force would be used in response to the nuclear attack of others, it would probably not be employed against more limited actions; the cost to the United States would be greater than any resulting gains. The most terrible weapon in the history of mankind was not a complete source of power, because it was not a credible response to nonnuclear aggression. American policymakers began to realize this and so began the shift to a greater emphasis on conventional forces. However, it is commonly thought that the possession of nuclear weapons by both the United States and the Soviet Union prevents either side from using their ultimate weapon. The assumption is that neither could get away with a first strike; the devastation would be mutual. Thus, MAD (mutually assured destruction) describes a standoff: a balance of power based on a balance of terror.

Thus, an act of coercive power involves more than politicians hurling threats at each other. The threats have a purpose—to change behavior—and thus must be used with discretion, in the right amount, and with credibility. The objective is not to carry out the threat (sending in troops, firing an employee, withholding support from a fellow politician, going on strike) but to achieve desired behavior through the threat itself. However, because credibility is so important in the successful use of coercive power, it is sometimes necessary to do what is threatened just to prove that it will be done again. Force and power are not synonymous, but they are closely related.

Utilitarian Power

Utilitarian power is basically coercive power in reverse. Instead of controlling someone's behavior by threatening to do something they don't want, you *promise* something they do want. The structure of the situations are similar but the tools of power are different. Just as the President threatens to punish senators in order to obtain their votes, he might promise to reward others: a promise to place a new military base in a particular district in return for legislative support. This type of power is called utilitarian because it is based on the offer of something that is of utility, or useful to someone else. Among the things that have utility and are used as political rewards are wealth, position, employment, prestige, and power (remember, power can be both means and ends).

The object of utilitarian power must ask the same kinds of questions that occupy the object of coercive power. Imagine again a senator, this time considering the promise of the President to increase the defense contracts in his or her state in return for support of the President's tax legislation. The questions are:

1. Will the promised action more than make up for any losses suffered? (What is more important to my constituents, more government spending in our state or preventing a tax increase?)

2. Does the President have the capability to fulfill his promise? (Perhaps his promised action actually requires a series of complicated bureaucratic decisions, which might make the promise much more difficult to achieve than the President himself realizes.)

3. Can the President be trusted to make good on his promise? Is the promise credible?

It should be made clear at this point that in many real-world political situations, several political actors attempt to exercise power over each other. Rarely does one gain *complete* control; more often each settles for partial success, some more than others. The result could be a standoff, or a net power gain for some, a net power loss for others. The idea of net power is closely related to the nonzero-sum game. Again we catch a glimpse of the give-and-take nature of politics.

This is not to say that power is usually distributed equally. The last part of this chapter examines several theories, one of which argues that political power is *never* distributed equally.

Manipulative Power

To be controlled without being aware of it is to be manipulated. But how, you may ask, could that happen? In the case of direct coercive and utilitarian power, there is a conscious relationship between the controllers and the controlled. The former must communicate their threats or promises so that the latter can weigh the consequences of their actions. But **manipulative power** is not based on open communication. Instead, the power wielder attempts to change some or all of the values of others in a more subtle way.

This type of power assumes that if a person's attitudes can be reshaped, he or she can be made to behave the way another wants them to. If you could totally restructure someone else's attitudes so that he or she thinks the way you do, you would not have to threaten or reward; the person would behave the way you behave because he or she thinks the way you think.

Now, this type of total psychological restructuring is very unusual. But the reshaping of particular attitudes or beliefs is not; the techniques most closely associated with manipulation are brainwashing, propaganda, and socialization.[6] **Brainwashing** is the most specific and personal since it usually happens during times of war when one side attempts to break down the psychological resistance of captives and instill in them a new set of values.

Propaganda. Less spectacular but probably more important is **propaganda**, the intentional motivation of another through psychological techniques. Propaganda is really a type of advertising; in fact, many of the techniques used by political propagandists to sell candidates and issues are similar to the ones used to sell soap, beer, and automobiles. Actually, the meaning of the term *propaganda* has changed little since its inception in Europe about 300 years ago. It originally referred to the promoting of ideas and values through various persuasive techniques.

If you are a propagandist, your basic strategy is to identify some of the psychological and emotional needs and feelings of the targeted audience, and then to use them to create positive attitudes toward your candidate, policy, or ideology (or a negative attitude toward those who oppose you). This will require the use of such techniques as distortion or selective truth in which no lies are told but only some of the facts are presented.

Most political actors, whether individual or institutional, use propaganda but some are more successful than others. Much propaganda
fails because of its lack of subtlety—it is so heavy-handed that those
who are supposed to be affected are aware of the attempt and thus can
resist it. But there are other, much more subtle (and therefore effective)
examples that work because the connection between the propaganda
and the desired response lies below the level of consciousness.

In the realm of nonpolitical advertising, note should be made of
the long-standing strategy of the automobile industry to associate their
products with sex and glamour; or the recent campaign by several beer
manufacturers to convince their male customers that light beer fits the
macho life-style.

In politics, it is not uncommon to find the advocates or opponents
of a particular policy trying to forge a link in the minds of the public
between their position and something the public feels strongly about.
For many years, organizations like the American Medical Association
were able to prevent much movement on national health care legislation
by suggesting that it was really *socialized* medicine; the strategy worked
as long as it did because of the deeply imbedded antagonism that so
many Americans have toward socialism. And how many political leaders around the world have achieved their goals by associating themselves with the religious, cultural, and national traditions of their subjects? Witness Adolf Hitler's effective blending of the nationalistic
longings of the German people and his own political and social objectives.

Socialization. We learn most of our values through the socialization process. Since we will devote a good part of the next chapter to
this process, only a few comments will be made in this chapter. *Political
socialization* is defined as that process through which people learn the
political values of their society.[7] Although nearly all individuals
undergo the socialization process, isolating the concept of socialization
is very difficult because it is so pervasive.

What we can say is that families, friends, schools, clubs, unions,
employers, newspapers, television, and government all play a part in
the teaching of political values. Some do this intentionally but much
political learning is unintentional or autonomous, that is, the result of
ongoing processes that continue from one generation to the next without
really being under anyone's control. An obvious question at this point
is, If no one is really in control how can it be called manipulation?
This is a complex question and it is subject to several interpretations.
The best way to answer is to say that if one wants to think of autonomous socialization as an act of manipulation, the only way to do it is

to identify all of society or the culture as the manipulator and individual members of society as the manipulated.

Legitimate Power

In every political system political actors seek **legitimate power**. If they succeed, the result is perhaps the most precious possession of anyone active in politics, the *right* to make decisions for others. Having legitimate power means that decision makers are able to enforce their decisions without the need for threats, promises, or manipulation. The objects of power accept the **authority** of the decision makers.

On an individual level, authority is given to someone who seems to know more about a particular topic than others. This is what we mean when we call someone an authority—the physician, the economist, the scientist, the baseball historian. When someone is designated as an authority it means others will accept his or her judgments without the need for proof. Physicians do not have to provide most people with a detailed justification of their diagnoses; patients accept physicians' conclusions because they have already assumed that physicians know more than they do about their physical condition. Thus, true authorities have their decisions accepted *without question.* The more others ask for proof and explanation, the less authority they are entrusting to the authority.

Because more and more of politics is institutionalized, political authority is usually vested in institutions and processes. That is, when thinking of politics it is best to think of the authority of a world leader, such as Ronald Reagan or Margaret Thatcher. Putting it another way, the individual gains legitimacy (the right to make decisions for others) because of the office that he or she has assumed. What it boils down to is a distinction between the office and the person filling the office. In politics, authority begins with the former and flows to the latter. This means that it is possible to obey the commands of legitimate decision makers without liking either them or their decisions. This is what makes authority so crucial in any political system; it gives political leaders "breathing room" to make decisions that do not satisfy everyone without stimulating a revolution. This, in turn, gives the entire political system stability, for it means that support for the institution continues even as decision makers come and go. In fact, a good indicator of the amount of authority the institutions of a particular nation have, is to examine the amount of instability that generally exists in that nation's government. The less legitimate the institutions, the less likely the subjects of the system are to obey its decisions and therefore, the more likely its leaders are to rely on coercive, utilitarian, and manipulative power to stay in control.

Political leaders cannot simply take the authority they want. Instead, it must be granted by the people of the society. Neither presidents nor kings have the right to rule unless it is given to them. They may cite an ancient tradition, bloodline, or divine right to justify their claim, but only if their subjects accept the justification does their rule become legitimate.

Often a particular ceremony or process (which itself is considered legitimate) bestows authority on political leaders. In a legitimate monarchy the coronation ceremony provides the means for the orderly transfer of power. In a democracy, the electoral process decides who will be given the right to make decisions. It is important to emphasize the role of elections as legitimizers: Because the election itself is considered legitimate, the officials who are elected are granted authority.

Personal Power

Another name for personal power is **influence**. If authority results from the respect that people have for political institutions and processes, then influence results from the respect that people have for other people of a particular type. But what special characteristics lead to influence? Personality, intelligence, charm, knowledge—all can have an impact. Sometimes it is accomplishments in one field that lead to influence in others. How else to explain the employment of former athletes to sell products ranging from beer to popcorn makers? And, despite any potential they may exhibit as legislators, it is highly likely that senators Bill Bradley of New Jersey and John Glenn of Ohio initially derived influence over the voters because of their careers as a basketball star and an astronaut, respectively.

On a one-to-one basis, an influential person is able to control others with the force of personality. In politics there is a name for this quality, **charisma**. Originally an ancient religious term meaning "miraculously given power," charisma was transformed by the German sociologist Max Weber into a political concept.[8] It now refers to an almost superhuman quality that some people have, which causes others to blindly follow them.

Jesus, Mohammed, and other great religious leaders had an abundance of charisma in the original sense. Winston Churchill, Adolf Hitler, and Franklin Roosevelt would probably lead the list of charismatic twentieth-century leaders. In the contemporary era the scope of charisma has been broadened so that any politician who has personal magnetism is called charismatic. As long as the original link to superhuman, other-worldly qualities is kept in mind, this watered-down notion is acceptable.

Like all other forms of power, influence is relational. Thus, a leader has no influence unless there are others who can be influenced. This is an obvious but essential point. Some people exercise influence without realizing it. We have all known people whom we look up to for one reason or another, perhaps an accomplished relative, an understanding teacher, or a dynamic movie star. Without consciously attempting to, they affect our behavior when we use them as models.

But political influence always involves the conscious use of personal attributes—such as charisma—to control others. Thus, charismatic political leaders are aware of their special gifts and nurture them to the hilt. Consider, for instance, how the eccentric Libyan leader Colonel Moammar Khadafy maintains his image as larger-than-life man of the people; or how Fidel Castro continues as Cuba's revolutionary leader several decades after the revolution.

One more characteristic of influence should be mentioned. A political leader with influence does not need an official position to exert control over others. The source of control is the person, not the office. That is why we emphasized the institutional basis of authority in the last section; we can now make the distinction between obeying a leader because of the office he holds and because of the person he is. The two factors are often combined: Presidents Kennedy and Reagan have exercised influence because of their significant charm, but they also wielded great authority because of their office. Where influence begins and authority ends is not easy to discern. The point is that there is a difference. Perhaps the best way to see it is to make note of the fact that some political leaders have great power yet hold no official office. An example is Khadafy, who rules an oil-rich nation, yet holds no official governmental position. There is no doubt that Khadafy relies primarily on his charismatic—to his enemies, enigmatic—personality.

Combining the Types of Power

We have looked at the five types of power that are the most important in politics. They have been discussed separately in the interest of clear understanding. In the real world, however, they are often intertwined so that one leads to or reinforces others. No attempt will be made to provide a complete list of interrelationships. It will be enough to consider a few examples to develop the kind of appreciation for the complexity of power that is necessary for an understanding of politics.

One of the relationships has already been mentioned; coercive and utilitarian power are often two sides of the same coin. Another more complicated one is based on the fact that legitimate power is often the result of propaganda and the socialization process; people can learn to give authority to a particular political institution. This is probably a basic part of most political systems. Small children learn from parents, schools, and other socializing agents to respect the police officer, the President, and other authority figures. By the time children have reached adulthood, the institutions have gained sufficient authority to survive even the hardest times. Witness the continuing respect afforded the British monarchy, an anachronism in the midst of Great Britain's severe economic decline and social unrest.

Manipulative power can lead to legitimate power; and, interestingly enough, the reverse is also possible. Legitimate leaders (those who hold positions of authority) are more readily believed. Thus, the opportunity, or perhaps temptation, exists for them to use their position as a base for manipulation. Many citizens accept without question official government explanations of political and military events. In many systems this trust is no doubt well formed. But what if the officials gain more control through the use of selective truth or distortion? The 1978 movie *Capricorn One,* is based on an extreme version of this scenario. What if the American government, in order to maintain public support of its faltering space program, simulated a perfect mission in a studio and telecast it for public consumption? Could the government get away with this great deception? If so, what impact could it have on the setting of national priorities?

In our analysis of influence and authority, the distinction between the office and the individual was emphasized. Now, it should be made clear that it is not unusual for a charismatic leader to become so popular that he is able to endow an office, even a government, with legitimacy that lasts beyond him. George Washington surely had this effect on the young American nation. And in the People's Republic of China, Mao Tse-tung used his great personal influence to solidify a huge population and endow the new Communist regime with legitimacy. There are two ironic twists to this story. First, Mao actually feared the institutionalization and resultant deradicalization of his revolutionary movement. Second, Mao's retirement and death were followed by a public criticism of this larger-than-life national leader. But even while being blamed posthumously for many of the failures of the Chinese system, Mao must be given credit for grounding the political institutions of his nation with great charisma.[9]

SOURCES OF POWER

Political power is not created from thin air; it always has a source, something from which it is drawn. And just as there are many forms of power, there are many sources of power.

The military power of the United States was strong enough to overcome threats, in 1983, from the government of Grenada.

Wealth is the source of power that people can most readily identify with. Having a great amount of money, or control over someone else's, gives one a source of coercive and utilitarian power. The most blatant use of wealth is the classic political bribe. But most political money is used in above-board ways. As the price tag for electoral campaigns increases, access to money becomes essential to any would-be political candidate. Thus, those with money to contribute have a greater chance of exercising power.

Another classic case of economic power is **patronage**—the use of government jobs as a reward for loyal service or the threatened loss of such jobs for disloyalty. Some master politicians throughout history have relied on this significant source of power.

Numbers can often compensate for the lack of wealth, which is why political leaders usually attempt to win as much mass support as possible. In democratic systems this means promising electoral support or threatening to withhold it. In nondemocratic systems, numbers still matter: witness the upheavals in Iran and Haiti.

Military power is almost always coercive and its source is *physical strength.* If a nation has a small army, few tanks, and obsolete aircraft, its threats will likely have little impact on those it is trying to control.

We have already noted that *personality* and *charisma* are major sources of influence. Likewise it is obvious that holding office is the major source of authority for political leaders.

Two other related sources of power are *knowledge* and *skill.* As political actors and theorists have known for centuries, knowledge is power. A perfect example is the case of the oil industry in the United States and its political arm, the American Petroleum Institute (API).

Within the government of the United States, the Department of Energy has been given the job of regulating the oil industry in the public interest. In order to do this, it must receive a continual flow of information about oil production, reserves, and refining capacity. Where does it get this kind of technical information? Since the government has few sources of its own it must rely on the industry itself—the industry it is supposed to regulate. In the words of the API president, "If you want current information and statistics on the industry, you have to rely on ours."[10] This does not prove that the oil industry goes out of its way to mislead the government and the public, but it seems reasonable to assume that the API will present its data in the most favorable light possible. Until there is an independent source of information, we cannot really tell. So in effect, those with more knowledge (or in some cases, a monopoly on knowledge) are able to control the situation. That is why every government with designs on absolute power, attempts to gain control of the sources of information and knowledge.

The same could be said of the several types of skills that lead to political success. Again, the growing complexity of politics has to be taken into consideration. More and more political activities require skill and expertise, none more than power. Skill in using the mass media is an important source of manipulative power. Knowing how to make credible threats and believable promises takes skill and finesse. The point is clear: successful political activity is not a matter of brute force so much as skill and knowledge.

RATIONAL PERSUASION AND POWER

Even with its inclusion of skill and knowledge, the foregoing discussion may have left the impression that politicians spend all of their time trying to control each other. While this activity is basic to an understanding of politics, it does not exhaust the range of political relationships. As we have pointed out several times along the way, politics is as much a game of compromise and bargaining as conflict and confrontation. The typical positive nonzero-sum game often requires as much rational understanding as power. Thus, we must include rational persuasion as a legitimate part of the political world, especially in those situations in which two or more parties have common interests but are not aware of it because of a lack of knowledge, or because of the biases introduced by different cultures or ideologies.

Whether what we are calling rational persuasion—using facts and logic to win someone over to your side—is a form of power or not is an interesting question. Clearly it does not involve threats or promises and is apparently different from relying on one's personal influence or the authority of office. However, there is a fine line between the use of information to rationally persuade and the use of psychological techniques to manipulate. How, for instance, do we describe the typical political campaign? Is it manipulation or persuasion?

However, before we overcorrect for the impact of power, let us reiterate that if there is a central concept in the political process, it is power. Few political relationships are devoid of power. Even some that seem to be based on rational persuasion could just as well be characterized as acts of reciprocal utilitarian power. Legislative vote trading involves several people rewarding each other—getting each other to do things they would not otherwise have done.

So, we should come away from this discussion of power and politics with a balanced view. Power cannot be ignored, but neither should it be viewed as the only determinant of who gets what.

SUMMARY

A discussion of power is essential to an understanding of politics since power is at the center of every political system. If there is a central concept in political science, it is power.

Power—defined as the ability to control the behavior of others, to get them to do things they would not otherwise have done—is essential both for governments and citizens. Governments need power to enforce their decisions about who gets what—to make their decisions authoritative. Citizens need power whenever they want to increase their share of the benefits or reduce their share of the costs. Power is not only a means for securing one's ends; it can also be an end in itself.

There are many ways to exercise political power; thus there are several types of power. The most important are coercive power, utilitarian power, manipulative power, legitimate power, and personal power. Likewise, there are many sources of power, including wealth, numbers, and skill. While all of the various types of power are found in all political systems, there seems to be a relationship between the degree to which a government relies on authority (the degree to which it is legitimate) and the degree to which it is stable. Thus, political leaders who must rely primarily on coercive and utilitarian power are probably not as widely supported by their people as those leaders who rely more on authority.

NOTES

1. For a wide-ranging discussion of power, see Marvin E. Olsen, ed., *Power in Societies* (New York: Macmillan, 1970).
2. Harold and Margaret Sprout, *Foundations of International Politics* (Princeton, N.J.: Van Nostrand, 1962), p. 136.
3. The classic book in this area is Harold Lasswell, *Psychopathology and Politics* (New York: Viking Press, 1960).
4. Quoted in Walter Johnson, *1600 Pennsylvania Avenue* (Boston: Little, Brown, 1963), p. 308.
5. *Ibid.,* p. 309.
6. A good discussion can be found in J. A. C. Brown, *Techniques of Persuasion: From Propaganda to Brainwashing* (Baltimore: Penguin Books, 1963).
7. Richard Dawson and Kenneth Prewitt, *Political Socialization* (Boston: Little, Brown, 1977).
8. Max Weber, *The Theory of Social and Economic Organization* (Glencoe, Ill.: The Free Press, 1947), p. 324.
9. S. Schram, *Mao Tse-tung: A Political Biography* (Baltimore: Penguin Books, 1968).
10. Quoted in Frank Greve, "Knowledge Is Power for the Oil Lobby," in Bruce Stinebrickner, ed., *American Government 81/82* (Guilford, CT: Dushkin, 1981), p. 164.

5

THE ENVIRONMENT OF POLITICS: THE DISTRIBUTION OF POWER

TABLE 5.1

ARISTOTLE'S CLASSIFICATION OF POLITICAL SYSTEMS
Who Benefits from Power?

DISTRIBUTION OF POWER		ONLY THE POWERFUL	EVERYONE IN SOCIETY
	ONE	Tyranny	Kingship
	FEW	Oligarchy	Aristocracy
	MANY	Democracy	Polity

In the last chapter we talked about the nature of power. In this chapter we will take the next step and ask: Who has it? That is, how is power distributed in different political systems? This is an extremely important question because it helps explain the distribution of other benefits and costs. Our hypothesis is that those who have more power tend to receive more benefits and pay fewer costs. It is also a fascinating question. Most of us are interested in the powerful people, groups, and institutions of our communities because we sense that they "make things happen." So it is that when we look at national political systems, one of the first questions that comes to mind is, Who has the most power?

The great political philosophers have always been interested in the distribution of political power. More than two thousand years ago Aristotle developed a classification of political systems that is still considered useful by many political scientists. Aristotle's classification is very basic and uses two criteria: who has power and who benefits from the power. Aristotle claimed that power can be distributed to either one, the few, or the many. Second, he said that power can be used to benefit either the powerful or everyone. Converting this into a grid framework, we have Aristotle's classification depicted in Table 5.1.

In a *kingship* only one person has power and uses it to benefit everyone, while in a *tyranny*, the tyrant has a monopoly of power and uses it only for his or her benefit. When power is possessed by a few who use it for everyone, it is called an *aristocracy*; an *oligarchy* exists when the few use their power for themselves. A system in which many have power and use it for everyone is a *polity*, Aristotle's own personal favorite; when the many use power for their own benefit, it is called a

TABLE 5.2			
TYPES OF MODERN POLITICAL SYSTEMS			
TYPE OF SYSTEM	**DISTRIBUTION OF POWER**	**SCOPE OF POWER**	**TYPICAL EXAMPLES**
Authoritarian	Concentrated in hands of political elite	Mainly political	Military dictatorships, monarchies
Totalitarian	Concentrated in hands of political elite	Total society (most aspects of society)	Ideological communist regimes
Democratic	Widely dispersed among people and groups of society	Varies, but usually limits placed on what majority can do	Liberal democracies

democracy.[1] Aristotle's classification contains a normative dimension. That is, he is not only describing, but evaluating political systems. However, we do not have to accept Aristotle's judgments or his use of language (his equation of democracy with "mobocracy") to appreciate the value of this early attempt to get to the heart of the question of who has power.

Aristotle's ideas have set the stage for more contemporary sets of categories. The most common one distinguishes between democratic and nondemocratic political systems. In democratic systems power is widely dispersed so that the people, or a goodly proportion of them, control the decision-making process (see Table 5.2).

AUTHORITARIAN AND TOTALITARIAN SYSTEMS

Nondemocratic systems are just the opposite: a small minority has control of the political system—political power is concentrated in the hands of an elite. Actually, political scientists usually talk about two kinds of nondemocratic systems, the **authoritarian** and the **totalitarian**.[2] In the former the elite is satisfied with *political* control; they do not attempt to gain total control of the society. In an authoritarian regime, the everyday lives of average citizens may be relatively unaffected by the elite. The trade-off is that the power elite allows no one to threaten its political power. No one participates in politics except the elite.

A totalitarian elite takes it one large step further. Not only does it have all the political power, but it attempts to achieve total control of the society—what people think, do, watch, read, and listen to. There is an "official" everything. While authoritarian leaders want subjects who won't threaten their political power (in other words, political nonparticipants), totalitarian leaders use their power to control their subjects' hearts and minds. This requires a population of participants, not as decision makers but as totally loyal subjects, continually demonstrating their support for the ruling elite (thus, the high incidence of mass activities in such totalitarian systems as Nazi Germany and Communist China).

This also suggests something about the typical types of power used in each system. Manipulation is natural in totalitarian systems; the primary objective of totalitarian leaders is to resocialize their subjects, to turn them into new people totally supportive of the system. This process often begins with a highly charismatic leader, a Hitler or Mao Tse-tung, who is able to meld together his personality and the totalitarian values. The typical authoritarian elite is more dependent on coercive and utilitarian power. This is not to say that totalitarian regimes are short on the more visible types of power—Hitler was not only a master manipulator but an effective coercer. The point is rather that since in authoritarian systems power is not being used to reshape people, there is less reliance on manipulation. Of course in both systems, the ultimate objective of the elite is to gain legitimate power.

So, despite the fact that they are similar in concentrating power in the hands of the few, authoritarian and totalitarian political systems differ in several respects, most importantly in regard to the **scope of power** exercised by their elites.

Most political systems in the history of the world have probably been authoritarian. This includes monarchies (Saudi Arabia), military dictatorships (South Korea), and one-party systems (Egypt), among others. There have been many fewer totalitarian regimes; in fact, most historians point out that totalitarian politics is a modern phenomenon because serious attempts to reshape entire populations require the kind of communications technology that was developed only during the last century.

DEMOCRATIC POLITICAL SYSTEMS

The most obvious alternative to authoritarian and totalitarian power structures is **democracy**. This section will outline the main characteristics of the democratic power structure. The last half of the chapter will examine a theory that there really is no such thing as true democracy because all political systems are ultimately elitist; that is, political power always ends up concentrated in the hands of a small minority despite the system's democratic institutions and ideology.

The Nature of Democracy

Democracy is another one of those political words that is commonly used but rarely defined in any rigorous fashion. This is complicated by the fact that since the time of Aristotle (mainly during the last century), democracy has become a *good* word, a word that almost every nation and political leader wants to be associated with.

Looking around the world, we find a host of nations using "democratic" in their official title: the Democratic and Popular Republic of Algeria, the Democratic Republic of Afghanistan, the German Democratic Republic (East Germany), the Democratic People's Republic of Korea (North Korea). By tests used in the Western world, none of them can be considered democratic. To confuse matters a bit more, a number of other nations—all considered among the most democratic—officially call themselves kingdoms: Belgium, Denmark, Sweden, the Netherlands, the United Kingdom. What we seem to have here is a situation that needs clarification.

Let us try to straighten things out by making a basic distinction between the two most common usages of *democracy*. On one hand, there are the **people's democracies** found in the Soviet Union, the Eastern European nations, China, and Cuba, among others. In a people's democracy an elite has a monopoly on power, but its stated objective is to use power *for* the people. The leaders claim a monopoly not only on power, but on truth. Thus they know what is best for their people. The people themselves are not able, or not ready, to make such judgments themselves. It is a very paternalistic system; the typical leader of a people's democracy takes the same position that most parents do when dealing with their children; "We know what is best for you." To them, a true democracy is one in which an enlightened elite makes decisions for its citizens, not one in which the ill-equipped citizens make their own decisions. It is no accident that many of the self-proclaimed people's democracies are also totalitarian. After all, if the leaders know what is best for the people, they have the right to control every aspect of their lives.

The **liberal democracies** of the world (most West European nations, the United States, Canada, Australia, Israel, Japan, New Zealand, and Costa Rica) differ from people's democracies in one crucial respect.

In fact, the difference is so great that if one is a defender of liberal democracy, it is impossible to view a people's democracy as democratic. Pure liberal democracy says that if decisions are to be made *for* the people, then they must be made *by* the people; it rejects the notion that an elite knows what is best. It sounds a bit old-fashioned in this era, but Abraham Lincoln's "government of the people, by the people, and for the people" does as good a job of catching the sense of liberal democracy as any short phrase can. A liberal democracy emphasizes the "of" and "by," a people's democracy the "for."

In terms of distribution of power, it is clear that a people's democracy is elitist. Political power is retained by the leaders. How they use the power—whether for their own benefit or the benefit of the masses—is, as it was for Aristotle, a separate question. Here, then, we arrive at the heart of the matter: Only a liberal democracy is based on the principle of wisely dispersed power. If political power is defined as the capacity to have control over decisions that affect the lives of others, then a liberal democracy is based on the conclusion that everyone should share equally in this great responsibility.

One important implication of this analysis is that liberal democracy is best thought of as a *method* for making decisions, not a set of predetermined goals. There are, to be sure, certain values that seem to be associated with liberal democracy: freedom, equality, and justice. But they are really descriptive of the democratic decision-making process. The best way to put it is that a political system can be considered a liberal democracy, if it uses certain methods for making decisions, which give power to as many people as possible and in turn limit the power of the government.

We must clearly understand what the phrase "people making decisions" means in the modern liberal democratic state. To do this, the distinction between direct and indirect democracy ought to be mentioned. In a pure **direct democracy** the people *themselves* make all of the important political decisions—formulating budgets, setting tax rates, making defense policies.

The society that has come the closest to this ideal is ancient Athens. A leading student of democracy has written this about the nature of democracy in the city of Plato and Aristotle: "Athenian democracy was practiced in a small city-state, where the citizens themselves or a large sample of them could and did actually make many of the political decisions directly. Athens thus provides a working model of something close to the pure or extreme case of democracy. . . ."[3]

Comparing direct democracy in Athens with contemporary liberal democracy requires several qualifications. First, Athens was a very small society, at its peak not more than 300,000 in population. Secondly, since women, slaves, and foreigners were not considered citizens, the number of those who participated was much smaller—probably not more than 40,000. Even this was too many to participate all at once. Athenian records show, however, that almost all citizens did participate on a regular basis, and some meetings of the Assembly, the largest political institution, had 3000 to 4000 in attendance.

It should now be clear that the main difficulty of direct democracy is that it can work only in very small political systems. Once the population moves into the millions or hundreds of millions, direct democracy is impossible. Another, more philosophical objection to direct democracy is also worth noting. Even if it were possible to run a direct democracy with 10,000,000 people, it would not be desirable. As the world gets more and more complex, political decisions require more knowledge, expertise, experience, and time. These qualities are not likely to be found in any great abundance in a group of political amateurs. So, the argument goes, while the average citizen should have final authority, the important decisions must be made by professional, full-time decision makers.

The time has come to turn our attention to indirect democracy, in which the poeple exercise their power indirectly by electing leaders who will make decisions for them. Thus, according to the theory of indirect liberal democracy, the government and the people share power: governments make the day-to-day decisions, but the people hold the ultimate source of power: the right to turn them out of office.

All modern liberal democracies are indirect. This is not to say that direct methods are never employed. The use of the **referendum** in a number of states within the United States indicates that there still is a place for direct democracy. In a referendum, a policy issue—increasing or decreasing a particular tax, banning nuclear power plants, creating a state lottery—is placed on the ballot and accepted or rejected by the voters. It can be thought of as short-circuiting the indirect legislative process. In fact, some referenda are formulated and supported by groups who have not gained satisfaction from the normal decision makers.

The main criticism of this modern method of direct democracy takes us back to a previously cited argument. If the problems that modern political systems must deal with are getting more and more complex, then they must be handled by those who have the required time and expertise. Policy choices cannot be rationally analyzed and debated in the ambiguous and emotional atmosphere that hangs over so many electoral campaigns, so the argument goes; thus we have another classic political controversy. Should liberal democracies rely exclusively on indirect democracy or can direct techniques like the referendum be introduced on a limited basis?

The Elements of Liberal Democracy

Liberal democracy has several requirements, or characteristics, that give it meaning. **Popular control** and **majority rule** are in their basic form really fairly straightforward. The first refers to the central idea of liberal democracy, that power must be widely dispersed so that ultimate control falls into the hands of most of the people. The second describes the decision-making rule to use when deciding the outcome of the game of liberal democracy. Let us now examine each one.

Popular Control. Popular control is an ideal rather than an actuality; that is, there is no such thing as perfect popular control, only different political systems, some of which come fairly close to the ideal and others that fall short in varying degrees. Only the former can be considered liberal democracies.

In order for popular control to exist, a political system must have four characteristics.[4] To the extent that any or all are not present, the system must be considered less than a perfect liberal democracy. The first characteristic is probably the most important for it gets right to the central idea: *Every adult citizen should have the right to vote in a liberal democracy.* Voting is the major source of power for the citizens because it enables them, through their combined numbers, to decide who their leaders will be and allows them to vest the leaders with the authority they need to carry on the business of government. This is why we describe such a system as a functioning liberal democracy: the people have the ultimate authority. But voting is important for a second reason; elections not only put people into office, they also remove them. So, the threat of being turned out of office instills a sense of responsibility in prudent officeholders.

The right to vote is not preordained. While many see it as a self-evident right, in the real world of historical liberal democracy, it has been extended only after periods (sometimes long ones) of political conflict and compromise. It is not difficult to see why. Attempts to introduce voting into a nondemocratic political system will probably be viewed unenthusiastically by those in control, since they are being asked to give up some of their power. And movements to extend the right to vote to more people in a partially democratic system will not succeed unless those who hold the power can be convinced that their power will be preserved or even increased.

Let us illustrate these ideas with an example from American political history.[5] Since voting is a source of power and power is a political benefit, it is also a good indicator of how benefits are distributed. For the first thirty or forty years in the United States, voting was open only to white male property holders or taxpayers. As a result, a majority of

In a liberal democracy, the right to vote gives citizens the power to decide who their leaders will be and how the system should function.

the population could not vote. As the nation developed and moved west, one state after another dropped the land ownership requirement. Why? There are three possible reasons.

First, the new American nation began with a significant (for its time) commitment to **human rights**—the language of the Declaration of Independence was not mere rhetoric. As years passed, some individuals and groups developed moral arguments showing that this commitment implied a broadening of popular control. Thus, as the nation matured politically, its democratic ideals were extended to more of its citizens. Second, those who had gained the upper hand in national politics— members of the Democratic party of Thomas Jefferson and Andrew Jackson—saw that if they extended voting rights to less privileged classes, such as urban workers, these new voters were likely to vote for them, thereby increasing the Democrats' power base.

A third reason is linked to the second. America was moving West. The original thirteen United States had by 1820 become twenty-three. Because of their egalitarian frontier values and the need to attract settlers, states like Ohio, Kentucky, Louisiana, and Indiana entered the Union without property requirements. The older Eastern states realized that they were in competition for people and so the game of utilitarian power resulted in the removal of property restrictions throughout the nation. Thus, economic barriers to voting were eliminated through the playing out of the American democratic ideology plus some very hard-headed decisions by party and state leaders about how to hold onto and even increase their power.

The other two great expansions of the American electorate, suffrage of blacks and women, resulted from the same kind of interplay of moral persuasion and political power. It can be added that various combinations of these factors have led to the expansion of the voting public in other liberal democracies.

Let us reiterate. The right to vote is the element of popular control that comes first. If in a particular nation a large proportion of the adult population is not eligible to vote, then it is impossible to call it a liberal democracy.

The second requirement is that *elections must provide a real choice,* otherwise the vote is meaningless. An election with only one candidate is not really an election. We can agree with these sentiments while realizing that elections can serve other purposes, especially in nondemocratic systems. In the Soviet Union, for instance, elections are conducted regularly to legitimize the decisions of the ruling Communist Party and to make the people feel that they are part of the political process. But since the Communist Party alone slates candidates for office, a real choice is not available.

So, we can say that while elections are held in many political systems around the world, only in some are they used to choose between alternative candidates or policies; these of course are the liberal democracies.

But this is not the end of it. Some critics argue that even in a liberal democracy like the United States, the choice may not be as great as it seems to be. This argument is based on the assumption that while American voters usually have two parties to choose from, Democratic and Republican policies are usually so much alike that the choice is more apparent than real. This is a controversial position and we will examine it more fully in a later chapter. At this point we should be aware that the degree of political choice is easier to talk about than to measure, because it is a question of relativity. In some systems there are no elections and thus no choice; in others, elections but no choice; in still others, the choice is limited; finally, there are the wide-open systems with a multiplicity of choices because of a multiplicity of political parties. Only in the latter two cases can we talk about popular control.

It is one thing to have several viable candidates from which to choose. It is something else to know enough about each one so that a meaningful choice can be made. This is how we come to the third element of popular control: *adequate information.* Some authoritarian political systems allow opposition parties to exist but limit their ability to present their ideas to the public. This of course is due to the fact that the ruling elite controls the newspapers, radio, and television stations and they know that an opposition candidate without the capacity to convey his or her message to the people poses no threat. Here, then, is another example of "knowledge is power"; those who control information have the upper hand; those without it find it difficult to break into the system.

Although less blatantly obvious than in authoritarian regimes, the problems of obtaining adequate information in democracies can also be significant. In a modern complex industrial society, it is difficult for the average citizen to sort out the good information from the bad, and it is becoming more and more evident that because of its tremendous cost, gaining access to the mass media, especially television, is beyond the means of many would-be political participants. So, those who can afford television time have a much better chance of getting their message across.

Some critics of the mass media go further and argue that the media themselves have become one of the most powerful forces in politics. Thus the game is taken out of the politicians' court; it is no longer just a question of who can gain access or who can afford television time. Now, television and newspapers themselves shape the public's knowledge of political events. Although this claim is clearly debatable, one fact seems indisputable: The sources of public information are becoming fewer in number and more concentrated. Although there are more than 600 television stations in the United States, most of them are affiliated with one of the major networks, NBC, CBS, or ABC. In 1920, 42 percent of all the cities with newspapers had more than one. By 1978, this number had decreased to 3 percent. This means that in 1978, 97 percent of all American cities and towns had only one newspaper as their source of political news.[6] Since that year more newspapers have gone out of business. When in the summer of 1981 the *Washington Star* shut down its presses for the last time, our nation's capital was left with only one newspaper.

This discussion is not meant to imply that the American people, or the people of any liberal democracy, are at the mercy of the mass media. But it does raise some important questions about the sources and quality of the information used by the public for its political decisions.

Having the right to vote, to make a real choice with adequate information, means nothing if the elected officials ignore those who vote for them. Thus the fourth requirement is *elected officials must represent their constituents.* If the decision makers in liberal democracies behave as they wish, without a thought to the needs of their constituents, the whole democratic process is undercut. In examining real-world political systems, we thus look beyond the election itself to its impact on those who are elected. Only in a society that accepts the assumptions of limited government and political responsibility can democracy work. In short, elected officials must take seriously their responsibility to the voters; this results from a democratic culture and a political process that actually gives voters the power to remove leaders from office.

What does the key word, *represent,* mean? How are elected officials supposed to represent their constituents in a liberal democracy? Two theories explain how it can be done. According to the **delegate theory**, an elected representative does not use his or her own judgment, but should act as the people at home would if they were making the decisions themselves. It is clear that this is really a restatement of the classic theory of indirect democracy—elected officials hold office because there are too many people in the society to make direct democracy work. The problem is that in many cases the people at home do not speak in a single voice. Thus, according to the **trustee theory**, the representative must ultimately make his or her own decisions and must figure out what is best for the people, or at least what decision will displease the fewest number. The representative becomes a trustee, doing what he or she thinks is best.

Although this approach is often adopted for practical reasons, it is sometimes given a philosophical justification, one we have met several times: Professional decision makers can make better decisions than the mass public. Thus, true indirect democracy should follow the trustee theory. Representatives should not be unthinking reflections of the people.

Majority Rule and Minority Rights. If a political system allows all of its adult citizens to vote, gives them a reasonable choice, provides adequate information, and elects responsible officials, the requirement of popular control has then been met and the system has taken a giant step toward becoming a liberal democracy. But there is one more requirement to consider. It specifies the rule according to which decisions will be made—how the political system is to decide which candidates and policies win and which ones lose.

Common sense suggests the rule. If the whole point of liberal democracy is to give the people the ultimate power, then **majority rule** is the most reasonable approach. To allow a minority position to dictate to the majority would be patently absurd.

Majority rule stands on an undeniably solid foundation; one might think it is an unarguable principle. Yet, as it turns out, it is a bit more complicated. For while a liberal democracy cannot do without majority rule, it must be balanced against the principle of **minority rights**. If this is not done, an **unlimited majority rule system**—a political system characterized by a majority that can do anything it wants—develops. Under this system, a simple majority (50 percent plus one) can vote to ban all other points of view, or decide what the nonmajority should read, wear, or do. In short, because there is no protection for those who take positions opposite to the majority, the system begins to resemble the totalitarian regimes already described. The only difference is that totalitarian government is marked by its elitist structure. Remove that characteristic and the rest is the same; one segment (this time, the majority) attempts to totally control the other segments (the minority).

There are few good long-term historical examples of unlimited majority rule, but historians think they have found a few that come close, at least for short periods of time. They have usually occurred during periods of revolutionary change and when an authoritarian regime is being overthrown by the masses. The French Revolution seems to fall into this category; a student of this great world event has even called the political system that emerged a **totalitarian democracy**.[7] (Perhaps this is what Aristotle had in mind when he equated democracy with mob rule.)

So the question is, How does a liberal democracy achieve limited majority rule? That is, how does it grant the majority the authority to make decisions while at the same time protect the rights of minorities? There is no perfect answer; there is no way to achieve both at the same time. The more power the majority has, the less protection the minorities are given, and vice versa. This is the dilemma of liberal democracy. The more successful liberal democracies aim at a rough balance between the two, realizing that the balance can shift as power and values change.

Two basic methods can be used to limit the majority, and both are found in the Constitution of the United States. First, a distinction can be made between two levels of decisions that are allowed in the system: those that require a **simple majority** (50 percent plus one) and those that require an **extraordinary majority** (⅔, ¾, or any number more than a simple majority).

The first category includes the day-to-day decisions, such as electing public officials and passing bills in Congress. The second identifies a small number of decisions thought to be more important or fundamental. In the American system this includes ratifying an Amendment to the Constitution (¾ of the states), ratifying a treaty (⅔ of the Senate), and overriding a presidential veto (⅔ of each branch of Congress). These requirements of extraordinary majorities rest on the assumption that there are some decisions that are so important to the political system that they should not be left to simple majority approval.

There are several reasons for this assumption. First, obtaining an extraordinary majority is obviously much more difficult, and thus such basic changes will not be made indiscriminately. Second, when such a decision is made, it should have the support of the overwhelming majority of the population if it's going to work. A fundamental change in the Constitution should not be made by only 51 percent of the states, for example, since if 49 percent oppose it, the potential for severe conflict increases. Third, and speaking directly to the question of minority rights, decisions that could change some of the most fundamental rules of the game should require as large a majority as possible so that the number of those who might be adversely affected is as small as possible. This is not perfect protection, and there are some questions about requiring an extraordinary majority so large that it becomes almost impossible to get anything done. However, it does make it more difficult for the majority to always get its way at the expense of minorities.

There is another, more thoroughgoing, way to limit the power of the majority. This is to identify, as the American Bill of Rights does, the decisions that not even an extraordinary majority can make. Prime examples are decisions restricting the freedom of speech and religion. The intent of such basic constitutional provisions is to establish that there are certain kinds of human activities that are so important to the individual that not even a 99 percent majority can take them away.

Thus in a liberal democracy, unpopular ideas can be expressed and debated because small minorities, even a minority of one, can feel secure. Some political thinkers have argued that protecting minorities in this fashion is not only good for minorities but good for the entire society as well. After all, innovative solutions to societal problems are likely to come from those who do not conform to the dominant views of the society.[8] And, today's majority might very well be tomorrow's minority. Perhaps, therefore, it is a good idea for everyone to support the right of everyone else to think and speak freely.

In the real world, there is no such thing as a perfect right. For example, if in speaking freely an individual endangers the well-being of others, that individual's words are not protected. No one has made this point more clearly than Supreme Court Justice Oliver Wendell Holmes, when he wrote, "The most stringent protection of free speech would not protect a man falsely shouting 'Fire' in a theater and causing a panic." So, decisions must be made about how to balance the various rights that are claimed and protected within the system.

The Social and Economic Conditions of Liberal Democracy

Liberal democracies don't develop just anywhere. A combination of particular social and economic conditions must exist first. Since this combination is difficult to achieve, the number of liberal democracies in history is relatively small.

When one talks about the social and economic conditions of democracy, it must be made clear that this is not a simple one-to-one relationship. That is, there are no grounds for saying that a nation with conditions A and B will always become democratic. Some nations may reach this stage of social and economic without becoming democracies, but this is unusual. However—and this is the main point—all nations that have democratic political systems also seem to have passed a certain threshold of social and economic development.[9]

This threshold level is a combination of three main ingredients: (1) a decent standard of living, (2) a high level of literacy, and (3) a pluralistic society. First, in order for liberal democracy to catch hold, the economic system must move beyond the point where the main concern of the people is physical survival. That is, *a decent standard of living* must become the norm. Only when the citizens don't have to worry about their basic needs can they turn their attention to the question of popular control. In this sense, democracy is a political luxury, possible only in the more economically developed societies.

We can look at this requirement from two political standpoints. For a group wishing to achieve democracy in a nondemocratic system, it means nothing can be achieved until the society develops economically. For authoritarian leaders who want to retain their power, it means keeping people below the poverty line.

As an economic system develops, not only are more of the people's basic needs taken care of, but wealth is usually more equally distributed. This also seems to be related to the maintenance of liberal democracy. If wealth is a major source of power and power must be widely dispersed for popular control to exist, it seems to follow that not until the economic resources are fairly equally divided can democracy take root.

A second condition for liberal democracy is a *high level of literacy.* A population of illiterate people can be more easily manipulated by authoritarian and totalitarian leaders. And, looking at the other side of the coin, since democracy involves citizens using information to make choices, the greater the number who can read and write, the more democratic the system can become. Once again, we see that knowledge is power. Literacy by itself does not ensure liberal democracy. (Table 3.6

confirms this point.) But without a literate population, it is difficult to imagine the kind of informed citizenry needed in a liberal democracy.

To many students of democracy, the third condition for liberal democracies is the most important. If the central requirement of liberal democracy is the people's right to choose from among alternative candidates and policies, then this can best be realized in a *pluralistic society;* that is, a society made up of a multitude of groups representing a wide diversity of interests. The result of pluralism is a society that gives political choices a social and economic grounding. As we have already noted, politically astute totalitarian leaders always try to create a single value system, a society without alternatives. The reason now becomes clear: the less pluralistic and more monolithic a society is, the weaker will be the opposition to the ruling elite. The more pluralistic, the less likely that power will be concentrated in the hands of the few.

However, it is not just a multiplicity of groups that provides the foundation for liberal democracy. A large number of groups with different interests and points of view can function together as a society only if they share some basic values. For a liberal democracy to exist, the society must agree on the democratic rules of the game—there must be a **democratic consensus**. All, or at least most, of its members must accept the legitimacy of the electoral system; that is, that the election bestows authority on the winner, even if the winner is the opponent. In short, speaking politically, the democratic process has a higher priority than any particular set of social or economic goals. On a more psychological level, there must be respect and tolerance for those who take positions opposite to one's own. One doesn't have to like the opposition to recognize its right to exist.

As we will see in forthcoming chapters, some societies have pluralism without any real consensus; there are no generally accepted rules of the game. These are **culturally pluralistic** societies. Because they are divided into distinct cultural groups, they cannot achieve democracy or any other stable form of government, for that matter. The various factions have not yet developed the trust in each other which makes for stable politics. So, it is important to make a distinction between social pluralism and cultural pluralism.

This brief discussion seems to suggest that while the conditions for a democratic political system cannot be reduced to a neat quantitative formula, there does emerge the image of a society within which the seeds of liberal democracy can grow: (1) an economic system that can provide for the basic needs of its people and is committed to some redistribution of wealth in an egalitarian direction, (2) a population that is, to a large degree, literate; (3) a society that is pluralistic yet based on a democratic consensus.

ELITIST POLITICAL SYSTEMS

We now know what characteristics a nation must have to be considered a liberal democracy and that few nations around the world have them. However, to some students of politics, the incidence of democracy is rare. To them, liberal democracy is at best an unrealizable goal, at worst an illusion leading to an unwarranted sense of power on the part of the people. Those who see the political world in this way are called **elitists**. They argue that if liberal democracy is characterized by widely dispersed power, then there can be no liberal democracies because power is always concentrated in the hands of a small minority, the *elite*.[10]

We have discussed the most obvious kinds of elitist political systems. Authoritarian and totalitarian societies are without a doubt elitist since they are always controlled by a small minority. But now we are considering a theory of politics which argues that the elitist model must be extended to cover even apparently democratic regimes. Since this is a tremendously significant and controversial position, its assumptions and their implications should be examined more closely.

The Nature of Elites

Take any area of human endeavor—music, sports, business, politics— and rank its practitioners. One will almost always find that some score higher than others; some play better, work better, or have more than others. Those who rank near the top of the list can be called the elite. Thus, there is an elite of popular music, an elite of professional football, and an economic elite.

Elite theory proposes that there is always another elite: that small minority of any population that possesses most of the political power. It is they who control the political process. It is they who make the important decisions. In the words of one of the fathers of elite theory: "In all societies—from societies that are very meagerly developed and have barely attained the dawnings of civilization, down to the most advanced and powerful societies—two classes of people appear: a class that rules and a class that is ruled. The first class, always the less numerous, performs all political functions, monopolizes power, and enjoys the advantages that power brings, whereas the second, the more numerous class, is directed and controlled by the first."[11] The universal nature of the elite concept is reiterated by two contemporary political scientists: "The discovery that in all large-scale societies the decisions at any given time are typically in the hands of a small number of people, confirms a basic fact: Government is always government by the few, whether in the name of the few, the one, or the many."[12]

So, the first characteristic of the elitist approach is that there is always a small group with political power. But it is not just the fact that power always seems to be unequally distributed; after all, perfect equality is an unrealistic expectation in any area of human activity. The political elite is also *cohesive.* That is, its members have shared values and a common background, know each other (or at least about each other), and even interact with each other to a certain extent. This idea is at the heart of elitist theory. It does not simply claim that some individuals are more powerful than others, but that a cohesive group is in control.

Many years ago, sociologist Robert Michels tested the elitist theory by studying the structure of European political parties and labor unions. He concluded that the development of elites is not limited to political systems but applies to all human organizations. Michels labeled this universal principle the **Iron Law of Oligarchy.**[13] (Oligarchy in his analysis means the same as elite in ours.) The principle's significance is the assertion that elites control even democratic political institutions.

The question is, how can this be? Our initial answer is found in the contention that the most visible political leaders are usually not the most powerful ones. That is, a student of politics should not be deceived by the formal rules and structures of politics. Take a democratic system, for instance. According to the elitist approach, below the surface of popular control and majority rule lies the reality of politics. Either the leaders of democratic systems are not really responsible to those who elect them, or there are other elites—economic, military, or religious— actually pulling the strings.

The Recruitment of Elites

Where do elites come from? How are they recruited? There are three basic answers. After considering each one, we will see that they can be combined into a single theory of elite recruitment. First, there are those who argue that becoming a member of the elite is a matter of individual skill and dedication. That is, those who are the best at playing the game of politics are the ones who end up controlling those who aren't. This is one of the conclusions that Michels drew from his research. He decided that elites develop mainly because only a few people in any organization have the time, interest, skill, and resources required for leadership. They naturally gain control, leaving the rest as followers.

While it is easy to see the relevance of this explanation, most students of elites view it as too simple. What is missing is a social and institutional basis for elites. One classic theory gets at this problem by grounding elites in the values of the society.[14] That is, the assumption is made that every society has a dominant culture and that the elite will always reflect its central values. So, in an economically oriented culture, the elite will be drawn from the top business leaders; in a society that emphasizes military activities above all else, the generals will be in charge; in a society caught up in a religious revival, the clergymen will rise to the top. There are several important implications to this theory. First, elites are rarely out of touch with the rest of society. It follows then that when basic societal values change, a new elite will replace the old one; this is what one would expect if, for instance, a traditional religious society develops a more modern economic system. All of this adds an important notion to elite theory: although all societies are controlled by an elite, it is unlikely that any elite will retain its power indefinitely.

A third modern theory of elite development emphasizes the institutional basis of modern society. That is, since in today's world everything of importance seems to be done by institutions, it follows that it is institutions that possess power. Thus, when searching for a society's elite, one should begin by identifying its dominant institutions, whether economic, military, religious, or political. The power of individuals is, according to this view, derived from membership in powerful institutions. In the words of C. Wright Mills, the most renowned contemporary theorist of elitism, "No one can be truly powerful unless he has access to the command of major institutions . . ."[15] The elite is made up of those who lead these institutions.

Actually, the institutional explanation of elites is closely related to the cultural theory discussed in the last paragraph. What does one discover as the most powerful institution in a modern capitalist society? Big corporations, of course. What institutions control a militaristic society? Obviously, the armed forces. In a religiously based culture, which institutions are at the center of things? The Churches. Thus, we can combine these two theories and conclude that the political elite in any society will be drawn from those institutions which best reflect and most effectively achieve the dominant values of the society. Then, to fill the explanation out, the "individual characteristics" theory can be added in a fairly obvious way: it is the most skillful and resourceful members of the dominant institutions who become the elite.

The Power Elite Theory of C. Wright Mills

The most famous version of elitist theory is the one formulated by C. Wright Mills in his attempt to describe modern American politics.[16] One of the things that makes Mills' analysis so important is that it shows how one might go about accounting for the existence of elites in apparently democratic political systems.

As shown in our earlier quote from him, Mills uses the institutional approach to elite recruitment, with a three-level model of power distribution. At the top is the **power elite**, that small group of leaders of dominant institutions who make the "life or death" decisions for a society. The institutions that Mills identifies as the most powerful are the big corporations, the military establishment, and the executive branch of the national government. Together, they constitute the **military-industrial complex**. Because they have interdependent interests, a strong defense, and a strong economy, they tend to support the same policies and of course almost always get their way.

One rung down on the ladder of power is Mills' **middle level**. Here we find the most visible political actors: congressmen, senators, party leaders, and lobbyists. The significance of this level to Mills' theory of elitism is that most people think that this is where the action is, where the power is concentrated. According to Mills, this is a mistake: "Commentators and analysts . . . focus upon the middle levels and their balances because they are closer to them, being mainly middle-class themselves; because these levels provide the noisy content of 'politics' as an explicit and reported-upon fact; because such views are in accord with the folklore of the formal model of how democracy works."[17]

Below the visible political system lies the largest segment of the society, the **mass public**. It is characterized mainly by a lack of power, but because the mass public selects many of those in the middle level and really believes that congressmen and senators make important decisions, there is a sense of indirect power. This of course is a democratic mirage, since behind the visible politicians lies the power elite, making the life-and-death decisions. So, according to Mills, the power elite in contemporary America bases its power not only on control of the dominant institutions, but on the effective manipulation of the other segments of society.

Methods of Elite Control

How does the elite actually control the political process? Even Mills does not answer this question, which could fill an entire book. In effect, it takes us to the heart of the governmental decision-making process, a topic which we will dig into several chapters from now. At this point, let us simply sketch in four possible answers.

First, the elite may already have its members entrenched in important decision-making posts. Thus, they naturally make decisions in their own interest. This is clearly what we would expect in authoritarian and totalitarian regimes. Witness the generals who always seem to take over the reins of government in military dictatorships, or the fact that all decision makers in the Soviet Union are members of the Communist Party. But it can also be true, according to elitists, in the apparently democratic systems. Consider the corporation presidents who have served as Secretary of Defense (Robert McNamara of Ford for example) or Secretary of the Treasury (Donald Regan of Merrill Lynch).

But, it is often the case, especially in the less blatantly elitist systems that the elite, not interested in holding official political office, works for the election of those who will look with favor on its interests; this is a less direct way to exercise control. Thus, it might be pointed out that many American presidents have not themselves been members of the economic elite. In fact, some have had rather humble origins, such as Harry S. Truman and Richard M. Nixon. But elitist theory suggests that such political leaders are supported and "bankrolled" by the economic elite to such an extent that upon taking office, they find it difficult to make decisions contrary to the elite's interest.

The next method of elite control is one step removed from the previous one. If there are political leaders who are not directly controlled by the elite, then the elite may use various political techniques to influence their decisions. Coercive and utilitarian power are probably most prevalent at this level. In a democracy such as the United States, economic elites can promise to make or withhold campaign contributions in return for favorable decisions. In authoritarian regimes, army leaders may threaten to withdraw their support from a recalcitrant political leader. In religiously oriented societies clergy can threaten to withdraw their religious sanctions from secular leaders. This was a main source of the Roman Catholic Church's significant power during the Middle Ages. In each of these cases, the elite puts pressure on political decision makers in order to achieve the benefits they are seeking.

Many defenders of elite theory argue that these methods do not get to the heart of elite control. It is clear that such methods describe how an elite can attempt to guarantee that decisions made by the political system are made in its favor. However, what if the elite gets its way much of the time by preventing many potential issues from ever getting into the formal decision-making process? If successful, such **nondecision making** can be the ultimate form of elite control. In the words of the two political scientists who developed the concept, "Nondecision making is a means by which demands for change in the existing allocation of benefits and privileges in the community can be suffocated before they are even voiced; or kept covert; or killed before they gain access to the relevant decision-making arena. . . ."[18]

As we have seen, every political system has rules. Sometimes they are based on the traditions or biases of the society. Nondecision making is more often than not a matter of mobilizing these biases. For example, the elite may attempt to link a potential demand for a redistribution of benefits or costs to an unacceptable societal value. If successful, the demand will never receive a fair hearing or gain access to the decision-making process. In fact, it may never be publicly articulated.

In the United States, labeling a potential demand "socialistic" or "un-American" is often the kiss of death. Thus, as mentioned in the last chapter, the American Medical Association and other groups opposed to a national health care system were able to keep proposals for such a system from getting off the ground by labeling them "socialized medicine." Likewise, in the Soviet Union and Eastern Europe political elites attempt to head off undesired changes by calling them "capitalistic," "imperialistic," or "revisionist." These are examples of manipulative power. When elites mobilize the biases of their society (biases which they have often helped shape) they are really conditioning the nonelites to oppose attempted changes in the status quo. If successful, the elites have to worry much less about controlling the political process through threats and promises.

Modifying Elite Theory

Although the basic idea of elite control is widely accepted by contemporary theorists, few use it in its pure form. Given the complexity of modern society it is rather difficult to believe that a single elite could gain control of any political system. Instead, it seems more realistic to view the distribution of power in terms of **multiple elites**. The assumption that power tends to be concentrated in the hands of elites is not rejected, only modified so that now it is assumed that there are several elites in most political systems.

It has been suggested, for instance, that in the United States two regional elites compete for national power. One is based in the Northeast and Great Lakes region, the other in the South and Southwest. The former (called by one author *the Yankees*) is the traditional American elite. Its source of power is the great industrial complex that made the United States the world's foremost industrial power. But after World War II new industries developed, centered around energy, defense, and electronics. They located mainly in California, Texas, and other Sun Belt states. This has become the base of power for the "cowboy" elite.[19]

According to the theory of dual elites, present-day American politics is characterized by a struggle for power between the Yankees and Cowboys, which by the way cuts through the more superficial conflict between Democrats and Republicans. The function of the people (the nonelite) is to decide which elite will be given temporary political authority. This has led some political scientists to develop the concept of

elitist democracy, a type of system that combines the control of elites and the electoral decisions of the people.[20]

Another step removed from the original elitist theory is one that sees not just two but a multiplicity of elites competing for power. What this means is that because power is more widely distributed, no single elite can ever gain control of the system. Instead, there is constant competition among the elites as they jockey for position and attempt to gain an advantage.

Some theorists suggest that the number of elite groups is so large that it is very difficult for any one of them to control the decision-making process. In fact, it is much easier to prevent a decision from being made. Thus is born the theory of **veto groups**—the assumption that it is much easier to block policies that run counter to your interests than to push through policies that achieve your interests. Thus, the elite model becomes one of negative politics as elites spend most of their time vetoing unacceptable proposals.

So, the various modifications of elitist theory seem to point in the same general direction. They retain the central idea of democracy—the general population is involved in the political process—but qualify it by suggesting that the main function of the people is to select the elites who will make the important decisions.

SUMMARY

Since power is a primary determinant of who gets what, it follows that one of the most important political questions is, How is power distributed in political systems?

There have been a number of classifications of political systems based on the distribution of power. The most basic distinguishes between systems where political power is concentrated in the hands of a few (elitist) and those where it is dispersed among many (democratic).

A further distinction is often made between authoritarian and totalitarian political systems. While both are considered elitist, in the former the elite limits itself to control of the political system, while in the latter, the elite uses its political power to control the total society.

In liberal democracies, power is widely dispersed, ideally, to give the people final political authority. The typical result is an indirect liberal democracy in which the people do not make policy decisions themselves but elect representatives to make the decisions for them.

Liberal democracy is realized through popular control and majority rule. For liberal democracy to develop, a society should probably be economically developed, its people should be literate, and the society ought to be pluralistic while at the same time supportive of the same set of democratic rules.

Some students of politics see all political systems, even democratic ones, as elitist in structure. They argue that all human organizations are controlled by small minorities. Some political scientists have attempted to bridge the gap by formulating a model of power distribution that falls between liberal democracy and elitism. Called elitist democracy, it suggests that in real-world liberal democracies, elites compete for the support of the people.

NOTES

1. Aristotle, *Politics, Book IV.*
2. Juan Linz, "Totalitarianism and Authoritarianism," in *Handbook of Political Science,* vol. III (Reading, Mass.: Addison-Wesley, 1975). Also see Amos Perlmutter, *Modern Authoritarianism* (New Haven: Yale University Press, 1981) and Carl J. Friedrich, ed., *Totalitarianism* (Cambridge, Mass.: Harvard University Press, 1964).
3. Giovanni Sartori, *Democratic Theory* (Detroit: Wayne State University Press, 1962), p. 135.
4. This discussion is based generally on Robert A. Dahl and Charles E. Lindblom, *Politics, Economics and Welfare* (New York: Harper, 1953), pp. 277 ff; and Robert A. Dahl, *A Preface to Democratic Theory* (Chicago: University of Chicago Press, 1956).
5. See Robert E. Lane, *Political Life* (Glencoe, Ill.: The Free Press, 1959), ch. 2.
6. *Who Owns the Media,* (Harmony Books, 1979).
7. J. L. Talmon, *The Origins of Totalitarian Democracy* (New York: Praeger, 1966).
8. A classic statement of this kind of argument is found in J. S. Mill's *On Liberty.*
9. See S. M. Lipset, *Political Man* (Garden City, N.Y.: Doubleday, 1960), chaps. 2 and 3. Also see Samuel P. Huntington, "Will More Countries Become Democratic?" *Political Science Quarterly* (Summer 1984), pp. 193–218.
10. For overviews of elite theory see T. B. Bottomore, *Elites and Society* (Baltimore: Penguin Books, 1964); and Kenneth Prewitt and Alan Stone, *The Ruling Elites* (New York: Harper & Row, 1973).
11. Gaetano Mosca, *The Ruling Class* (New York: McGraw-Hill, 1939). This book was originally published in 1896.
12. Prewitt and Stone, *The Ruling Elites,* p. 132.
13. Robert Michels, *Political Parties* (Glencoe, Ill.: The Free Press, 1949). This book was originally published in 1911.
14. Mosca, *The Ruling Class.*
15. C. Wright Mills, *The Power Elite* (New York: Oxford University Press, 1956), p. 9.
16. *Ibid,* p. 324.
17. *Ibid.*
18. Peter Bachrach and Morton S. Baratz, "Two Faces of Power," in *The American Political Science Review,* vol. 56 (1962), p. 947.
19. See Thomas Dye, *Who's Running America?* (Englewood Cliffs, N.J.: Prentice-Hall, 1983), pp. 227–235.
20. See Peter Bachrach, *The Theory of Democratic Elitism* (Boston: Little, Brown, 1967).

6

THE CULTURAL CONTEXT OF POLITICS

In Chapter 2 the point was made that politics does not take place in a vacuum; the political system is part of and is profoundly influenced by a larger social system. The most all-encompassing part of the social system is **culture**. Culture refers to the basic values of a society. For our purposes, culture is important at two levels. First is the level of **general culture**, those basic values, orientations, and behavioral norms accepted by the people of a society; a culture defines what is good and bad, valuable and not valuable in that society. In short, it provides a society with its most basic rules of the game. At a more specific level is the **political culture**, which refers to the basic feelings that the people of a society have about the political process; what they think it should be like and how they think it really works. Political culture will naturally be the main topic of this chapter but we will begin with a brief discussion of the more general culture.

GENERAL CULTURE

It is obvious that we can't examine the culture of every nation. What we can do is identify some of the most common cultural values found in societies around the world and consider how they affect the political process. Sociologists and anthropologists who study culture have formulated several classification schemes, that is, ways of sorting out the main cultural orientations of different societies. We will mention several that seem to have some relevance for politics.

The Influence of Environment

It has been noted that people learn to either submit to, cooperate with, or attempt to master their environment.[1] These three possibilities provide a neat set of categories that address some of the most basic of cultural orientations. Consider the case of Bangladesh, especially the area fronting the Bay of Bengal. It is here that terribly destructive cyclones regularly sweep in and devastate the countryside. The cyclone and resulting tidal wave that hit in 1970 killed an estimated 250,000 people. Another fifteen years later killed 10,000. It is not difficult to visualize a population that resigns itself to this terrible but unstoppable force. The significance of the environment thus goes far beyond its physical characteristics; it becomes the foundation of cultural orientations to all aspects of human existence. The implication for politics is fairly obvious. If the values of submission and resignation become deeply embedded in the minds of the people, it is very likely that they will submit to political authority; they will view government leaders and institutions as distant forces that must be accepted, even if they are not loved or understood.

In other societies, the environment is harsh but predictable enough to be adjusted to. The cultural values that emerge in such societies are adaptation and flexibility. Thus, while the geography and climate of Egypt make for a life dependent upon the whims of the Nile, Egyptians have learned to cooperate with the great river, working with it to sustain life. The Egyptian culture, it has been observed, reflects the values of compromise and the need to remain flexible. In the eyes of those from a different cultural background, these traits sometimes manifest themselves as a refusal to make lasting commitments.

A basic characteristic of modern industrialized societies is the belief that the environment can be mastered through the application of technical knowledge. This belief is reinforced with each technological success. Thus the United States developed in sometimes hostile but incredibly abundant surroundings, which fostered the attitude that through hard work and expertise anything could be accomplished. It is not surprising that a more optimistic and solution-oriented political outlook developed here. A political culture emerged which, while not necessarily making the government an object of affection, did view it as something that could be used to help achieve an increasingly more abundant existence.

Achievement Versus Ascriptive Cultures

Other sets of cultural values can add to the usefulness of this framework. One of the most widely used is the distinction between **achievement** and **ascriptive cultures**.[2] In the former, people tend to evaluate each other in terms of what they have achieved, or what success they have had. It is often argued, for instance, that the United States has an achievement-oriented culture because people are evaluated to a large extent in terms of their economic success. (The often-heard question, "If you're so smart, why aren't you rich?" comes to mind.) In another achievement culture, the ancient city-state of Sparta, military success was the key to a positive evaluation. The point is that whatever the dominant institutions of a particular society, an achievement-oriented culture emphasizes individuals' accomplishments rather than their families, their class background, or their title.

In an ascriptive culture, the latter list of factors is what matters. Individual achievement counts much less than a person's inherited social status. Individuals who have not been overly successful in their personal lives but whose family is of high rank will be evaluated more highly than the successful "commoner." This would describe a traditional culture with a long-standing class system that *ascribes* status to

	SUBMIT TO ENVIRONMENT	COOPERATE WITH ENVIRONMENT	ATTEMPT TO MASTER ENVIRONMENT
ASCRIPTIVE ORIENTATION	Bangladesh	United Kingdom Japan	
ACHIEVEMENT ORIENTATION			United States

TABLE 6.1

ASCRIPTIVE VERSUS ACHIEVEMENT CULTURES

the members of society. It might include a peasant class with low status, an upper class with high status, and a particular family within the upper class from which the society's leaders are always drawn. But elements of ascription are also found in more developed Western societies. Walter A. Rosenbaum points out, for instance, that British culture is to a large extent based on the widespread belief that differences in class and social background are important barometers of a person's worth: "Most Britons have accepted social inequalities as a natural, even proper, facet of life; with this has developed what is commonly called deference in British social and political life."[3]

The likely impact of these cultural traits on the political process is not difficult to imagine. One would expect a more competitive political system and more competitive political participants to emerge in an achievement-oriented culture. And, it seems reasonable to assume that politics in an ascriptive culture will be based more on class, social background, and other indicators of traditional status.

The several categories of cultural values can be combined in interesting ways to describe various societies more fully (see Table 6.1). For instance, it can be said that in the United States, the mastery of an abundant but often hostile environment has reinforced the achievement orientation that was put in place by the first colonial settlers. Or, in both England and Japan—geographically unimpressive nations—people had to learn to adjust to and make the most of their environment; this seems to go hand in hand with a more ascriptive culture, a culture emphasizing moderation and a respect for a hierarchical system of roles and responsibilities. This set of cultural traits has surely had something to do with the success of these two small island nations.

Other Dominant Influences

Another way to get a handle on a society's culture involves identifying, if possible, that segment of the society that seems to be dominant and then considering its impact on the values of the society. Typical dominant segments are religion, the military, the economy, and ideology. Thus, it is often argued that the culture of the United States reflects its capitalistic economic heritage: hard work, competition, economic success, and the profit motive have seeped into every aspect of American life, including its politics.

Iranian society since the fall of the Shah and the rise of religious elite has been marked by an emphasis on Moslem values; there is no doubt that the new elite is trying to create a pure Islamic culture that will shape every aspect of life. Its success will be dependent to some extent on the degree to which the more materialistic and secular values emphasized by the late Shah have taken hold in Iranian society.

Other societies, such as ancient Sparta and modern Brazil and South Korea, have been dominated by a military elite and their cultures have relfected this dominance. The fact that these societies have been ruled by a succession of military leaders shows that their cultures have taken on militaristic values. (In South Korea, after eighteen years of rule, General Park Chung Hee was assassinated in 1979. He was soon replaced by another general, Chon Too Hwan.) Other societies such as the Soviet Union and Communist China are influenced by a dominant ideology.

POLITICAL CULTURE

Enough has been said about general cultural values to appreciate the claim that the political process does not exist in a vacuum. But we are more interested in the political culture itself, the orientations that people have toward their political system. There are different elements or levels in any political system and a political culture includes orientations to each of them. And, the fundamental assumption is that the sum of these orientations provides the starting point in our attempt to understand the environment of politics.

Orientations

Political culture can be thought of as a multidimensional phenomenon. People orient themselves to three basic levels of the political system: (1) the government, (2) others in the political system, and (3) themselves.[4]

The most obvious dimension of a political culture is the feeling that people have about their government: to what extent do they support it? Do they see it as a distant source of command, a benevolent source of help, or a partner in creating a better life? Support can be given to or withheld from the government or regime (those processes and institutions established to govern the system) or the particular leaders who have gained control of the government. The former is of course more significant. Presidents, prime ministers, and legislative majorities come and go, but when large numbers of people fail to support the political institutions of a society, questions must be raised about the ability of the system to survive. Although President Carter was defeated in his bid for reelection in 1980, the American political process continued on, as power transferred peacefully to a new President. Even when governmental change takes on a less-routine pattern, as in the removal of President Marcos from the Philippines after a national election that he attempted to manipulate, the Philippine system survived. In Lebanon, however, questions remain about the continued existence of a political system that is split into such hostile factions.

The second dimension of every political culture describes how people feel about others in the political system. "Others" refers to individuals and groups with different ideas and interests than oneself. While some cultures are more homogeneous than others, every real-world society is made up of a variety of political, economic, social, racial, and/ or religious groups. The question is, To what extent do they trust each other with political power? In the United States, what do Democrats do when a Republican is elected President? What do whites think when a black is elected mayor of their city? In Northern Ireland, how do Catholics feel about Protestant political leaders? In Nigeria, to what extent have the Ibo, Yoruba, Hausa, and Fulani tribes been willing to work with each other in the political process? The questions always come back to the element of **trust**. In some political cultures there are high levels of trust for others; in some, there are lower levels. The point is, the level of trust has a significant bearing on what can and cannot be done in the political system. Is everyone willing to play the game of politics according to a set of rules that allows others to win?

The third dimension of political culture is the perception that each member has of his or her own role in the political system. Is it to be one of active participation in the decision-making process or uncritical acceptance of the commands of a distant government? The key to this dimension is the concept of **efficacy**; how important do individuals think they are in the political process? Will their participation make a difference? Does it matter if they become politically active? This dimension has obvious political implications. We would expect those political cultures with higher levels of efficacy to also have higher levels of political participation. Or, looking at it from a different angle, in those political systems that encourage widespread political participation, more people have a higher sense of efficacy.

So, every political system exists within a political culture, a set of orientations that helps shape the political process. In saying this, it must be made clear that while there is always a range of orientations within any society, many societies are characterized by a **modal** political culture. Statisticians use the concept of *mode* to describe that item which is found the most frequently among a set of items. For instance, if 100 cars in a parking lot include 45 Chevrolets, 20 Fords, 17 Plymouths, 10 Toyotas, and 8 Volkswagens, the modal automobile is the Chevrolet. The concept can also be used to begin our analysis of political culture: it suggests that we look for those political orientations which seem to be the most prevalent in each political culture. Let us suppose that in nation A, a majority of the population feels that it can influence government decisions. We could say that the nation's political culture has, among other things, high levels of efficacy.

To carry out this kind of analysis more systematically, we can take the three dimensions of political culture and combine them in different ways to construct a typology of political culture. Each category of the typology is based on the relative degree of support, trust, and efficacy found in different societies.

Types of Political Culture

The Civic Culture, a major study of five nations (the United States, England, Germany, Italy, and Mexico), discovered three basic types of political culture: **parochial, subject,** and **participant**.[5] This threefold typology seems applicable to countries beyond the five studied and so will serve as the basis for our analysis. Table 6.2 lists the concepts described in the next several pages.

Parochial Culture. A **parochial culture** is characterized by little support for, and sometimes little awareness of, the central government. For example, "The remote tribesman in Nigeria or Ghana may be aware in a dim sort of way of the existence of a central political regime. But his feelings toward it are uncertain or negative, and he has not internalized any norms to regulate his relations to it."[6] Along with low support is a low sense of efficacy. If the government is perceived by most citizens as no more than a distant object, then it is not surprising that a parochial culture is also characterized by low levels of efficacy. People cannot be expected to feel politically important when they have no psychological attachment to the government.

A primary reason for the low levels of support and efficacy in parochial cultures is the fact that most of them are found in decentralized societies, that is, those that are divided up into groupings of people who belong to and identify with particular tribes, ethnic and language groups, religions, or regions. In such a society, the typical citizen has parochial attachments—he feels closer to his tribe, region, or ethnic group than he does to the "nation," if, indeed, he has feelings about the

| | TABLE 6.2 | | | | |

TYPICAL RELATIONSHIPS AMONG TYPES AND ELEMENTS OF POLITICAL CULTURE

	Level of Support for Government	Level of Trust for Others	Sense of Efficacy	Fragmented or Integrated	Impact on Government
Parochial Political Culture	Low	Low to Medium	Low	Usually Fragmented	Government can do very little
Subject Political Culture	High	High to Medium	Low	Integrated	Government has legitimacy and control
Participant Political Culture	High	High	High	Integrated to Moderately Integrated	Most likely to be liberal democracy
Revolutionary Political Culture	Low	Low to Medium	High	Fragmented	Government in danger of being overthrown

latter at all. It would seem to follow that there would be relatively little trust among the various groups in a parochial culture. After all, there are few if any rules of the game that all accept. Thus, there is a reluctance to trust members of other groups with political power or authority.

Subject Culture. The second type of political culture, the **subject culture**, differs from the parochial culture in that the typical orientation toward the government is one of greater awareness and, usually, support. In more down-to-earth terms, citizens in a subject culture view themselves as members of a political system with a legitimate government at its center. Whatever other group loyalties (religious, ethnic, regional) exist, they are secondary to loyalty to the national political system. However, the accepted role of the citizen is to be a subject, not a participating member of the political system. Political decisions are made by elites, not influenced by the masses.

On the other dimension of political culture, there is probably more trust among the groups in a subject culture than one would expect to find in a parochial culture. After all, most people have come to accept the authority of the central government and so they all have something in common; they are all citizens of the same nation, even if this only means obeying the commands of the same political authorities.

Participant Culture. The third type of political culture is the **participant culture.** It is similar to the subject culture in its recognition and acceptance of the legitimacy of government. But something important is added: the widespread belief that people should take an active role in the affairs of government. In other words, the level of political efficacy is higher. In addition, trust for others will probably be fairly high in a participant culture. If most members of the society accept the same rules for gaining and transferring power (through elections, for instance) and if loyalty to the nation is more important than more specific group loyalties, they will be more likely to trust each other with power.

Because high levels of support for government and high levels of efficacy define the political culture of liberal democracy, it is natural for the peoples of Western nations to assume that they always go hand in hand. As a matter of fact, it is possible for one to be high while the other is low. We have just seen that in a subject culture, support is high while efficacy is quite low.

Revolutionary Culture. The reverse is also possible—high efficacy existing alongside declining support for the government. The result can be a **revolutionary culture,** in which many people believe that the government should be changed, even overthrown. At the heart of a revolutionary culture is an ironic twist. There is withdrawal of support from the government because it is viewed as unresponsive to the demands of the people; thus, there is low efficacy *in regard to the government.* But this very distaste for the existing regime leads some to believe that only through concerted and probably violent action can things be made better—there is high efficacy in terms of assumed ability to change the system. This is really a definition of the classic revolutionary who emerges from such a situation. A large number of revolutionaries in any society will constitute a revolutionary culture.

Several basic facts about political culture should now be fairly obvious. First, when we talk about the political culture of this nation or that one, we are referring to modal traits. Second, these traits refer to the psychological orientations of people, how they feel about their political system. Putting these two facts together suggests that in no society will all people have exactly the same cultural orientations. However, some will have a single dominant culture, in other words, a set of cultural values that most people accept. Other societies will be split up into any number of cultural groups.

Integrated and Fragmented Cultures

This is a point that deserves more attention and so we will develop another set of concepts which describe the extent to which the people of a society share cultural orientations. On one hand, there is the **integrated culture**, which is characterized by widely shared orientations. In other words, most people have the same basic set of values, and speaking politically, view the political system in much the same way. On the other hand there is the **fragmented culture** which, as its label indicates, is divided into two or more distinct cultural groups, each with its own set of values and orientations.[7]

The relevance of all this for politics is fairly clear. In an integrated culture the governmental authority finds it easier to function since most members of the political system have come to accept the same rules of the game. In a fragmented culture, members of particular groups have not come to accept the same set of cultural values; therefore, what central government does exist will find it very difficult to exercise political control. More specifically, the central government will have little formal authority.

To get a better feel for the differences between integrated and fragmented political cultures, let us look at several examples. Compared to most nations, Japan has what must be considered an integrated culture. It is a relatively old nation with intricate patterns of tradition and custom and a homogeneous population. The Japanese people are remarkably similar in ethnic background and language. The rapid growth of the mass media in Japan has made the population that much more homogeneous. One of the most knowledgeable students of Japanese politics has gone so far as to say that "Probably no other country of comparable size and population has achieved so high a degree of homogeneity as contemporary Japan."[8]

The United Kingdom's population is less fragmented than many other nations, but its four national traditions (English, Welsh, Irish, and Scottish) plus a significant number of recent citizens from the old British colonies make it less homogeneous than Japan's. Its degree of integration is more a result of centuries of historical development, which have produced the framework for British politics, than the very homogenous population of Japan. Having gone through a series of critical stages, the British political system has reached its maturity with widespread support for its basic institutions and processes. It can truly be said that social groups in the United Kingdom are playing according to the same rules of the game. This is not to say, of course, that there is no disagreement within the British political system, nor that everyone accepts all of its policies: witness the continued violence that takes place in Northern Ireland. But most Britishers accept the authority of their government and the legitimacy of the rules of the national political culture. Note, for instance, that in the United Kingdom, criticism itself has been institutionalized and legitimized in the form of the "loyal opposition." This means that the party that has not gained control of the government is expected to take on the job of regularly challenging the policies of the governing party.

There are several good examples of fragmented cultures in today's political world. Northern Ireland and Lebanon come readily to mind. In these two strife-torn societies, most citizens identify more with a parochial cultural group than with the national culture. In Lebanon, the split between Moslems and Christians results in a national government that finds it very difficult to maintain order, let alone provide the other basic social and economic benefits taken for granted by the citizens of modern political systems. In Northern Ireland, continued conflict between Catholics and Protestants makes it nearly impossible to integrate the country with the rest of the United Kingdom. In neither political system is there a single dominant culture; there is not enough cultural integration to provide a set of basic rules within which the peaceful resolution of conflicts can take place.

Culture and Political Institutions

One of the most important questions we can ask about any political culture is, How does it relate to the political institutions that exist alongside it? The answer may seem so obvious that one may wonder why the question has been asked in the first place. Isn't it clear that the political culture and political institutions of each political system must be congruent? It isn't always obvious because sometimes they grow out of touch with each other. When this happens, the political system is in trouble and either the institutions or the culture have to change if the system is to regain its stability.

Let us consider several of the destabilizing situations summarized in Table 6.3. Imagine, for instance, what would happen if a young, benevolent, and newly crowned king in a very traditional subject culture decided to institute a democratic electoral process. The people view their proper role to be nonparticipating subjects of the government, but the new democratic institutions depend upon mass participation. As long as low efficacy grounds the culture, a democratic political system will not work. Only when the political culture changes from subject to participant can a democratic political process take root.

TABLE 6.3		
THE RELATIONSHIP BETWEEN POLITICAL INSTITUTIONS AND POLITICAL CULTURE		
	DEMOCRATIC INSTITUTIONS	**AUTHORITARIAN INSTITUTIONS**
PAROCHIAL CULTURE	Not Congruent	Congruent
SUBJECT CULTURE	Not Congruent	Congruent
PARTICIPANT CULTURE	Congruent	Not Congruent

The reverse situation is also possible: an authoritarian regime taking over a formerly democratic system attempts to institute more authoritarian processes which, of course, deny the people the right to participate in the making of political decisions. The problem is that the people see themselves as important participants in the process of deciding who gets what. They have a high sense of efficacy because of their democratic heritage and experiences. Once again, either the cultural values or the institutions must change if political stability is to be restored.

We can conclude that while it is possible for the political culture and political institutions of a particular political system to get out of "synch," this situation cannot last for any period of time. More than two thousand years ago, Aristotle noted that revolution, the most massive type of political change, is usually a result of the reaction of important segments of a society—sometimes the masses and sometimes the elites to a constitution (government structure) that no longer fits their notion of fairness and justice. In other words, the government and political culture have moved in opposite directions so that the culture no longer justifies the government.

Sources of Political Culture

Now that we have described a political culture and have identified some of its many varieties we can turn our attention to an equally important question: Where does a political culture come from? Why does one society have a subject culture and another a participant culture? Why is one integrated while another is fragmented? Why is one based on achievement while another ascription?

There are several ways to approach this question. One is to go back in time and examine certain historical periods during which dominant institutions and value systems developed. The assumption is that these institutions and value systems have been so influential that they have shaped the cultures of particular nations ever since. To take just one example, consider how West European culture was shaped by the coming together of the Industrial Revolution and the rise of Protestant religions.[9] The cultures of such nations as England, Germany, and Sweden still reflect the institutions and value systems that were produced during the sixteenth, seventeenth, and eighteenth centuries. More specifically, the capitalist economic system, emphasizing free competition and the profit motive, seemed to have an affirmity with the work ethic of Protestantism. Thus, many aspects of the political cultures of nations within which they developed can be traced back to the birth and maturing of these dominant economic and religious systems.

Cultural orientations of the present can be linked not only to historical periods of long duration such as the Industrial Revolution and the Protestant Reformation but also to more specific historical events of shorter duration, such as revolutions, civil wars, and economic depressions. Examples include the Chinese and Russian revolutions, the great worldwide economic depression of the 1920s and 1930s, and World War I and World War II.

One interesting example—and to some, not quite as well-known—is the Mexican Revolution of 1910–1917, which involved widespread destruction and violence. It also led to some significant changes in Mexican economics and politics. The power of the dominant landowning elite was broken and the foundation for reform was constructed. Internal and external critics of ensuing political regimes argue that they have not pushed economic and social reform far enough; Mexico still has one of the most unequal distributions of wealth in the world. Whether this is true or not, the fact remains that the revolution has had a lasting psychological impact on the people of Mexico, not just those who actually participated in it but also those who came after.

Comparative studies of political culture usually show that Mexican citizens have high levels of pride in their nation, even while demonstrating much less support for the actual performance of the Mexican government.[10] The factor that seems to explain this apparently incongruous result is the continuing significance of the revolution as a national symbol. Mexicans are proud of their revolution and what it stands for. They see it as an ongoing process that has not yet reached fruition. To quote from what is still the most thorough comparative study of political culture, "This pattern of high system affect (support for the political system) coupled with rejection of the actual performance of the government is . . . what one might expect in a nation characterized by a continuing attachment to a set of revolutionary ideals. Such a pattern of attitudes is what one might expect from a people suddenly drawn into politics by a revolutionary appeal."[11] Throughout the political system, the legitimizing function of the revolution is obvious: more than a half century after the revolution, the dominant political party is called the "Institutional Revolutionary Party." The political elite is still called the "Revolutionary Coalition" even though its members are, for obvious reasons, no longer drawn from those who fought in the revolution.

POLITICAL SOCIALIZATION

There seems to be little doubt that historical periods and events are related to the cultural orientation of those who experience and live through them. But underlying such broad historical explanations is another level of explanation based on the question, Why do people learn to think about society and politics in a certain way? The key word is *learn,* because the implication is that a culture is not something that people are born with. Instead, they acquire it from other people. This process of learning social values is called **socialization.**[12]

We can say that in any society the culture—political and otherwise—is a product of that society's socialization process. People learn to be achievement-oriented, to support their government, to trust other political groups. When we say that a political culture has been changed because of a civil war, devastating economic crisis, or revolution, we are really saying that people have learned a new set of cultural values and orientations. The concept of socialization acts as a bridge that links the individual to the larger society, including the political system. It is the concept we use to explain the existence of different cultural orientations in different societies. And, without such a concept we could not account for the fact that it is not just those who go through a tradition-shattering experience who are socialized, but also those who are born into later generations. This suggests that the latter must learn the culture from the former. Referring back to the Mexican Revolution, although few original revolutionaries are left, because of the effectiveness of the socialization process the ideals and psychological atmosphere of the revolution are still present in Mexican hearts and minds.

If political culture is the result of learning, the obvious questions are, How? and From whom? Actually, the two questions are closely related because in order to answer the former we must eventually get to the latter.

Directed or Autonomous Socialization

Sometimes we learn political values because someone wants us to (**directed socialization**); sometimes we learn them simply because of where we are and with whom we associate (**autonomous socialization**). With directed socialization, someone (a political leader) or something (a television network) tries to instill in people a particular set of values. After a successful revolution, one of the first things the political elite does is attempt to change the basic political values of the people, to reorient them toward the new regime. This can be seen in all its significance in such nations as the Soviet Union and China. Since their revolutions, one of the most important ongoing tasks in those countries has been education of the people (*education* here means the use of a number of psychological techniques to create a mass public supportive of the basic principles of Marxism).

It should be made clear that directed socialization is not limited to Marxist political systems; it is found in political systems of all types throughout the world. We mention the Soviet Union and Communist China only because directed socialization seems to be more evident and more essential to the functioning of their regimes.

Some students of liberal democracy argue that directed socialization is often product of nongovernmental groups such as the mass media. Sometimes, it is argued, television and newspapers themselves attempt to create an atmosphere favorable to a particular political point of view, liberal or conservative. At other times, they are the hired propagandists for political, social, or religious groups. In either case, directed socialization is taking place.

Anything that is "autonomous" automatically runs itself—it is self-perpetuating. Thus, once a thermostat is set for 70 degrees, it will turn the furnace on and off to keep its environment at the desired temperature. Likewise, autonomous political socialization is self-perpetuating; it is learning that takes place without anyone intending it to. None of us completely escapes the autonomous socialization process; in associating with parents, friends, teachers, and fellow workers, we come in contact with people, some of whose values and orientations rub off on us. They do not consciously attempt to make us liberal or conservative, supportive or unsupportive of the government; but because we are with them so much of the time, our beliefs and values begin to reflect theirs. All of this suggests that many values will be passed on from generation to generation with little conscious effort and, probably, some of the most important political orientations are acquired in this way.

So, what the concept of autonomous socialization does is makes us aware that much cultural learning is not the result of the conscious planning and manipulation of political elites. Autonomous socialization is a more pervasive process in which values are passed on to us by the people and institutions with which we come in contact daily.

The distinction between directed and autonomous socialization is not an either-or thing. Every culture is a result of a combination of the two, with an emphasis in some societies on one or the other. Let us pursue this idea and summarize our discussion with a set of generalization:

1. In ordered, more stable political systems, autonomous socialization becomes the main transmitter of political values.

2. Directed socialization becomes more important in times of crisis and change, in periods of revolution when existing values are being questioned by significant segments of the mass public, and/or when revolutionary elites are attempting to change existing values by re-socializing the population.

3. In such situations, autonomous and directed socialization come in direct conflict. What we have is a clash between the traditional culture (passed on from generation to generation) and the new culture (which the new elite would like to see replace it).

Agents of Socialization

To get a better grasp of this process we must turn our attention to the **agents of socialization**, those individuals, groups, or institutions from whom people learn their basic political orientations.

Family. Most students of socialization believe that the most formative learning takes place during the childhood years. This leads us to the first agent of socialization, the *family*. If most formative learning takes place in childhood, it seems to follow that the family is the most important socializing agent. In the United States and other Western cultures, "family" refers, more often than not, to the *nuclear family*, defined as "a small group composed of husband and wife and immature children which constitutes a unit apart from the rest of the community."[13] This is the first source of cultural values in most Western societies; mothers and fathers are the initial purveyors of a society's culture. In an integrated culture, this means most children learn to support the same basic rules of the political game. In fragmented cultures, different cultural groups will pass on their distinct views of society and politics through the family.

In many non-Western cultures, *family* refers to the *extended family*, a much broader social group that includes not just mothers and fathers

"My grandson, needless to say. is also pro-Reagan."

but grandmothers, grandfathers, uncles, aunts, and cousins. The members of such extended families can number in the hundreds. In fact, in societies that are divided into tribal groupings, the tribe and the extended family overlap to a significant extent. When this happens, the extended family continues to be the main socializing agent throughout a person's life. It is probably the case that most political learning that takes place within the family is autonomous.

School. Another socializing agent is the *school.* It is the next institution that most children come in contact with. In all societies schools do more than educate—that is, teach students how to read, write, and do arithmetic. They also (intentionally or unintentionally) expose students to a set of cultural values, either those of the dominant culture or of a particular cultural group within the larger society.

In some societies, including liberal democracies, schools tend to reflect the dominant culture, and so they function mainly as reinforcers of values already learned in the nuclear family. Once again, much of this socialization is of the autonomous variety. Teachers do not consciously set out each day to create a classroom full of loyal Australians, Americans, or West Germans. Instead, because teachers are themselves products of the culture and its socialization process, they unintentionally reinforce and add to the values that most children have brought with them to school.

As students move on through the educational system, the school does something else: it provides children with historical information that tends to support their value systems. This is not to say that history is intentionally distorted; the point is, rather, that beyond the occurrence of certain indisputable events, history is a matter of interpretation. Which of the multitude of events will be emphasized? Which historical figures will be selected as important and worthy of attention? How will wars, depressions, policies, and decisions be explained? It is not unrealistic to expect schools to select and emphasize the positive aspects of their nation's history and to ignore or at least deemphasize the negative ones. And when it comes to explaining events such as wars, it is not easy to accept blame or to admit guilt.

Even the more obvious socializing rituals that go on in the schools of most nations—singing national anthems and pledging allegiance to national symbols such as flags—are not as intentional and thus as directed as they might seem. In established political cultures, whether authoritarian or democratic, these activities become a normal segment of the day, a matter of habit. They are themselves a part of the culture and thus it is not so much what the song or pledge says (studies indicate, in fact, that many children have little understanding of their meaning) but the fact that the ritual is performed. The political values of both students and teacher are being reinforced and the legitimacy of the political system is being strengthened.[14]

In revolutionary cultures, schools are used in a more direct way by the new elite as agents of directed socialization. We again see the confrontation between the traditional culture, built over the years through autonomous socialization, and the new culture being created through directed socialization.

Peers and the Media. The importance of the *peer group* (one's circle of close acquaintances) as a socializing agent varies from society to society. In some it is probably the most important agent. But one of the main problems is separating its influence from that of some of the other agents. For instance, in school, do students acquire their values (or have them reinforced) from teachers or from their fellow classmates?

We often hear the argument that in today's electronic world, the *mass media,* especially television, are the main agents of socialization. It is very difficult to resist the assumption that as children spend more and more time watching television and less and less time interacting with their parents and other agents of socialization (the average school-age child in the United States spends more time in the course of the year watching television than going to school), television becomes the most important source of values. At this point, such assertions must remain assumptions, since few solid studies have directly tested them.[15]

In order to carry out what is at least reasoned speculation, we can make a distinction between two ways that the media might help shape the political culture. First, people may learn orientations toward the political system directly from television and newspapers. That is really what we have been talking about. Some critics of the media (especially television) suggest that people get most of their news from television; thus, the way that stations and networks interpret the news will directly shape the mass public's perceptions of and orientation toward the political system. Some versions of this theory make television stations an independent force in the political system, in competition with the government. Another version views them as agents of the government, interested not in objective reporting but in justifying the policies of the government.

Once again, there is no single truth. In many authoritarian and totalitarian regimes the mass media are under the control of the political elite. But, in liberal democracies, the situation is not so clear-cut. A free and independent press seems to be one of the cornerstones of a liberal democratic system. Yet there are times when reporters and decision makers develop too close a relationship for objective reporting. And, it is often the case that the media are dependent on the government for the information that is then transmitted to the public. American reporters whose job it is to cover the President often find that the only basis for that day's story is the information that the White House wants to release. In this way the President and his staff can color, to some extent, the way the American people evaluate his performance. This is one of the reasons for the furor behind the discovery that David Stockman, Reagan's first budget director, had carried on a candid—and often critical—discussion of his own administration's economic policies with a reporter.[16]

The media can also indirectly impact the political culture through their capacity to shape the more general culture. It has been pointed out that the political content of television is very low; other than newscasts and occasional news documentaries (which are usually watched by relatively few people), television programming emphasizes entertainment, not politics or public affairs. However, certain more general cultural values may be learned, values that ultimately help influence one's orientation toward politics. Perhaps the most controversial argument of this sort claims that in devoting so much time to violence and making it appear a natural result of human interaction, television may be conditioning a whole generation of political participants to see violence as an acceptable way of solving political and social disagreements.

Defenders of television have two replies. First, they say the critics of television exaggerate its significance as a socializing agent. Second, television programming simply reflects the values already present in the culture; television is big business and so television programmers strive to give people what they want to see and hear. Thus, at best, television is a reinforcer, not a creator, of culture. If violence is a common commodity on television, it is because the culture already emphasizes violence. Whether the mass media are reinforcers or initiators of cultural values, the conclusion seems to be warranted that here is an agent of socialization that merits further attention and closer scrutiny.

Government. What is the role of government in the socialization process? Can *government* itself be an agent of socialization? Our discussion up to this point seems to tell us, yes. But there are several complicating factors. First, as is becoming more and more evident, governments all over the world have become involved in almost every area of human activity. This suggests that the socializing functions of government will be difficult to sort out from other agents of socialization. We have just seen how difficult it is to keep the mass media and government separate, even in liberal democracies. And, where do we draw the line between the public school system and the government? Each is really part of the political system.

A second complicating factor is the fact that because of a wide variation in types of political systems, there is also a wide variation in the role of government as an agent of socialization. Some governments, especially those we have labeled totalitarian, take an active and conscious role in the teaching of political values. Since the time of Nikolai Lenin, the great Russian revolutionary, it has been an accepted tenet of Marxist theory and practice that other agents of socialization must either be resocialized or eliminated.

SUMMARY

Every political system interacts with and is influenced by a larger social environment. The broadest part of this environment is the culture, which refers to the basic values, orientations, and behavioral norms of the society. Those values, orientations, and behavioral norms that deal with politics constitute the political culture. The nature of the general culture, whether ascriptive or achievement-oriented, for instance, has an impact on the political culture.

More specifically, the political culture describes how the people of a particular society feel about their government, about others in the political system, and about their own role in the political system. The particular way that these orientations are combined will have much to say about the amount of authority that the government has, and the degree to which citizens participate in the affairs of their political system. There also seems to be a relationship between cultural orientations and the distribution of power. For instance, a subject culture seems to go hand in hand with the authoritarian type of political system, while the participant culture provides a foundation for liberal democracy.

Cultural values and orientations are passed on through the process of socialization. Political socialization refers to the process through which individuals learn basic political values. A distinction can be made between directed socialization (political values are intentionally instilled) and autonomous socialization (cultural values are passed on from generation to generation without direction). Political socialization is carried out by a number of agents including family, school, peer groups, the mass media, and, of course, government.

NOTES

1. See Florence R. Kluckholm et al., *Variations in Value Orientations* (New York: Harper & Row, 1961).
2. Talcott Parsons and Edward Shils, eds., *Toward a General Theory of Action* (Cambridge: Harvard University Press, 1951), pp. 76–91.
3. Walter A. Rosenbaum, *Political Culture* (New York: Praeger, 1975), p. 70.
4. This discussion is based on Rosenbaum, *Political Culture*, pp. 6–7.
5. Gabriel A. Almond and Sidney Verba, *The Civic Culture* (Princeton, N.J.: Princeton University Press, 1963), pp. 17–20.
6. *Ibid.*, p. 19.
7. See Rosenbaum, *Political Culture*, chap. 2, for a discussion of integrated and fragmented cultures.
8. Edwin O. Reischauer, "Japan," in Karl W. Deutsch et al., *Comparative Politics: Politics of Industrialized and Developing Nations* (Boston: Houghton Mifflin, 1981), p. 272.
9. Max Weber, *The Protestant Ethic and the Spirit of Capitalism* (New York: Scribners, 1958).
10. Almond and Verba, *The Civic Culture*, p. 103.
11. *Ibid.*
12. A good introduction to political socialization is Dean Jaros, *Socialization to Politics* (New York: Praeger, 1973). Also see Fred I. Greenstein, *Children and Politics* (New Haven, Conn.: Yale University Press, 1965).
13. G. Duncan Mitchell, *A Dictionary of Sociology* (Chicago: Aldine, 1968), p. 77.
14. David Easton and Jack Dennis, *Children in the Political System: Origins of Political Legitimacy* (New York: McGraw-Hill, 1969).

15. For some interesting ideas about the impact of television on children, see Kate Moody, *Growing Up on Television* (New York: Time Books, 1980).
16. William Greider, "The Education of David Stockman," *The Atlantic Monthly*, December 1981, pp. 27–57. For his own version, see David Stockman, *The Triumph of Politics: Why the Reagan Revolution Failed* (New York: Harper, 1986).

7

ECONOMIC AND IDEOLOGICAL SYSTEMS

This chapter continues our analysis of those factors that impact the political process. Perhaps nothing in the modern world is more obviously related to politics than economics. It often seems that most of the decisions made by government policy makers involve economic problems—fighting inflation, reducing unemployment, supporting farm prices, cutting the budget, lowering taxes, and/or strengthening the dollar. The intertwining of politics and economics appears to be an indisputable characteristic of every society. But in the present chapter we will go beyond this obvious fact and look at the impact that different kinds of economic systems have on the political process.

ECONOMIC SYSTEMS AND IDEOLOGIES

Looking around the world, we see that there are several ways that material values can be produced and distributed—that is, there are several types of **economic systems**. The best known are *capitalism, socialism,* and *communism.* The main question that a political scientist would likely ask about each is, How is the particular economic system related to its political system? More specifically, one might ask, what difference for the conduct of politics does the economic system make?

There is another factor, closely related to the economic system, that has an impact on the politics of nations all over the world. This is **ideology**. The concept of ideology has had a long and controversial history. It has been given a variety of meanings by a multitude of historians, philosophers, and political scientists; it has been portrayed as everything from the main cause of historical development to a mere reflection of the rest of society.[1] Our definition puts ideology somewhere in the middle of these two extremes. Simply speaking, ideology is viewed as one of the more important determinants of a political system's performance.

But what is an ideology? For our purposes it is viewed as a fairly coherent set of values and beliefs about the way the social, economic, and political systems should be organized and operated and recommendations about how these values and beliefs should be put into effect. Several crucial points emerge from this definition: ideologies are based on *ideal* pictures of human society; these pictures are constructed of *sets* of ideas that are supposed to hang together in consistent patterns; and they lead to real-world actions designed to put these ideas into effect.

We have already pointed out that economic and ideological systems are closely related. Let us see how. Most economic systems are based on or have developed from an ideology; in some cases, they are inseparable. For instance, socialism has at its heart a set of principles about the economic system and how it should be related to the other elements of human society. In short, "socialism" refers both to an economic system and to a set of ideological assumptions. In other cases, a particular ideology (liberalism, for instance) developed alongside an economic system (capitalism) so that one cannot be truly understood without reference to the other. A systematic analysis of both economics and ideology will be made easier if we think of an economic system as the actual way that a society produces and distributes things of material value, and an ideology as a set of beliefs about the way society, including the economic system, should operate. Thus, the ideology explains and justifies the political and economic systems. We are discussing ideologies and economic systems in the same chapter because they are so closely related, both in a philosophical sense and in a more down-to-earth, real-world sense. Each is important for an understanding of politics because politics and economics are intertwined and because both economic and political systems are usually based on a set of values that often takes the form of an ideology.

Another question might be asked, this time about the relationship between ideology and culture. The answer is fairly obvious: both deal with values. Thus, we would expect the political culture of a society with a dominant ideology to reflect that ideology. This is the case in Marxist-socialist societies such as the Soviet Union and China. The fit, of course, is never perfect; we have seen that the clash between a revolutionary ideology—one demanding changes in a nation's social, economic, and political systems—and the traditional culture—the result no doubt of centuries of development—is a normal and often violent occurrence. But, if the revolutionary ideology does take hold, it is reasonable to expect its basic values and assumptions to begin finding their way into the culture. And, in more stabilized societies, an ideology can serve as the basis of a culture. It could be argued, for instance, that the present-day culture of the United States is to a large extent a reflection of the capitalist-liberal ideology that was planted by the English settlers, and reinforced by two centuries of economic and political decisions. However, in Chapter 6 it was suggested that culture is a broader concept than ideology. A political culture includes a number of orientations to different parts of the political system that may or may not be part of an ideology.

Before we begin our analysis of specific ideologies and economic systems, let us make a distinction that should help this analysis. Ideologies can be categorized in a number of ways. One simple but very useful classification scheme is based on the distinction between radical and conservative ideologies. The difference is of crucial importance to an understanding of the functions of ideologies in modern politics. A **conservative ideology** justifies the existing system—since the existing system is closer to the ideal than any other possible system, it ought to be maintained. A **radical ideology**, on the other hand, criticizes or even rejects the existing system.

This means that a supporter of Marxism living in a Marxist society can be called a conservative. This might be contrary to our perception of what a conservative is supposed to believe in. After all, Marxists are revolutionaries; how can they also be conservatives? The confusion results from the fact that *conservative* is used in several different senses. It can refer to a particular set of substantive values (more about that later in the chapter) or to the fact that an ideology supports the existing political regime. The latter is what can be called the **positional sense of ideology**. Thus, in a society based on Marxism, capitalists (those supporting a capitalist system) are considered radicals. Everything turns upside down in a capitalist system, where the capitalists are the conservatives and the Marxists are radicals. Thus, the application of the terms *conservative* and *radical,* when used in the positional sense, is not to the substance of the ideology but to its position relative to the dominant ideology and culture of the society.

We are now ready to begin our analysis of the contemporary world's leading economic systems and ideologies. In each case, the analysis will move from a description of the basic values and assumptions of the original ideology or economic system to a consideration of how it has changed as implemented in the real world. In every case, it is fairly clear that changes have taken place; no political system based on an ideology has remained entirely true to the original ideals; adjustments seem to be inevitable. Likewise, economic systems have evolved into something somewhat different from—in some cases, quite a bit different from—their original forms.

A few fundamental dimensions of every economic and ideological system will be emphasized. We can structure our analysis around a very simple but incredibly significant question: What is the role of government in determining the outputs of the economic system? On the one hand, some systems emphasize central planning; that is, they operate from the assumption that an economic system functions best when decision makers coodinate the whole process of producing and distributing economic values. This is a political question because government always takes on the function of central planner. On the other hand, some systems are based on the assumption that economic systems work the most efficiently when they are free from governmental control, when decisions are made by the *market,* that impersonal mechanism of sup-

Do economic systems work more efficiently when they are free from government control or when government takes on the function of a central planner?

ply and demand. We will see that this distinction between government control and market control is crucial in understanding the differences between the major political-economic systems of the world.

CAPITALISM

Because of its impact on the development of Western society and politics, we will begin our analysis of economic systems with **capitalism**. While some Western nations no longer consider themselves strictly capitalistic, all have been profoundly influenced by this method for organizing economic activity.

Ideal Capitalism

The capitalist economic system revolves around a few simple principles, but their significance is far-reaching. They were first articulated in a systematic way by the eighteenth-century Scottish philosopher, Adam

Smith.[2] Just as Karl Marx can be called the father of communism, Smith can be called the father of capitalism. The principles laid out in his book *The Wealth of Nations,* published in 1776, still provide the framework for contemporary capitalism even though, as we will see, they have been reinterpreted for modern times.

Like most other economic theories, capitalism is based on a psychological premise, a simple assumption about human nature: it is that we are all self-interested; we naturally think of what is good for ourselves when deciding on a course of action. Uppermost in our minds is the desire to protect and even add to our private property. Thus, the desire for profit is the most basic of human motivations. We do what we do today because of the expectation of greater reward tomorrow.

But for capitalist philosophers like Smith, this is only half the story; there must be a way to explain how the interaction of a group of self-interested individuals can produce an efficient and just economic system. The explanation revolves around the concept of the **market**, the process through which **supply and demand** determine what and how much is produced and what it will cost.

The concept of market is fairly straightforward; most of us take it for granted. Put a number of self-interested people together in the marketplace and they will naturally seek to increase their profit, to sell high and buy low. If everyone behaves this way, the result will be the most effective system of deciding who gets what because no one can long afford to manufacture something for which there is little demand, nor charge a price that is greater than that charged by competitors. Thus, the interplay and resulting balance between demand and supply is what makes capitalism a just system. Prices should always fall to the lowest possible point and all basic demands should be met. There should be little unemployment since only fools would continue to manufacture something for which there is little demand. Manufacturers will move into high-demand areas and workers will move with them.

The key to the entire market system is *competition.* As long as there is wide-open competition among producers, the demands of consumers will be met. Another point to underline is the emphasis that the original theory of capitalism places on the *consumer.* It is interesting to note in this age of consumerism that the capitalist system articulated by Adam Smith is consumer-oriented. If no one demands a particular good or service, then no one will make or provide it. So, the ultimate determinant of distributive justice in the capitalist system is the nature of individual demands in the society.

What does government have to do with all this? Very little, Smith hoped. Since the market economy is self-regulating, it needs no help from public agencies. As a matter of fact, the more the government gets involved, the less efficiently the market works. Government regulations can only upset the balance between supply and demand. Thus, capitalism as espoused by Smith supports limited government. Government does not disappear; armies and police forces will still be needed to maintain external security and internal order. However, the economy can run itself as if, in Smith's words, a "great invisible hand" were controlling it.

To understand the relationship between government and economics in Smith's theory of capitalism, mention should be made of the economic system that preceded it. Throughout Europe, the dominant economic philosophy until the eighteenth century was called **mercantilism**. In the words of one historian, "Mercantilism consists essentially in the regulation of industry and commerce by the state government with a view to making the state more prosperous and hence more powerful in relation to neighboring states."[3] The growth of capitalism and its doctrine of limited government can thus be given a political explanation. The old mercantilistic system stifled free competition and free trade and thus restricted the growth of the new capitalist system, and the success of its main beneficiaries, the middle class. Those like Smith who defended capitalism saw that only if the role of government was decreased could their preferred system survive and flourish.

Contemporary Capitalism

Much has changed since the days of Adam Smith. Capitalism is the most representative of modern Western economic systems, but Smith might have some difficulty recognizing it. While the original principles of competition and the market are still at the heart of capitalism, the structure of capitalist systems has changed in significant ways.

One of the main reasons for change is the change in the size and number of producers, from many small ones to fewer large ones. The most characteristic element of modern capitalism seems to be the large corporation. Most industries are dominated by no more than a handful of these organizations. This is something that Adam Smith and the other early capitalists probably did not anticipate, although state monopolies were common during the age of mercantilism. When they wrote of the beauty of the market system and the wonders of supply and demand they had in mind a market of many producers. That is what gives the consumer the power to control supply and price.

Under capitalism, if a consumer doesn't like the price or quality of a certain pair of shoes, there are probably a number of other capitalists who are selling shoes more to his or her liking. But what happens if two or three large corporations are the only suppliers of shoes? Can wide-open competition really take place? It is highly likely that the price of shoes will reflect what these few companies want to charge more than the laws of supply and demand.

Something else has become obvious about modern capitalist systems. They are not immune from the evils of recession and inflation. People do lose their jobs and prices do sometimes rise to mind-boggling levels. In short, the capitalist system has its problems, many of them not unique to capitalism.

This has led many supporters of capitalism to advocate a revised version of their favorite economic system, with a much larger role assigned to government. Government is now accepted as a partner in the economic process. Among its main tasks are the maintenance of the market system and the moderation of economic upturns and downturns. In short, the capitalist economic system has become, to some extent, dependent on political decisions; the market is not left to run itself. Governments file **antitrust suits** in an effort to break up corporations that are reducing competition; they raise taxes to reduce inflation and lower them to combat unemployment. They buy farm surpluses to maintain the price levels of corn, milk, and tobacco. They establish tariffs on foreign goods. These are all things that Adam Smith would have considered examples of government interference.

The theoretical basis for this new kind of capitalism is usually traced back to the English economist John Maynard Keynes, who in 1936 wrote *The General Theory of Employment, Interest and Money,* a book which justified the crucial role that government ought to play in regulating the capitalist economy.[4] Almost overnight it became the bible of the "New Deal" policy makers of the Roosevelt administration as they attempted to pull the American economy out of a deep depression. Keynes's basic assumption was that economic depressions are not unnatural, as they were to Smith. There is nothing strange about unemployment and inflation because supply and demand are not always balanced. The conclusion is obvious: government must play a major role through its spending and tax policies in restoring whatever balance is possible.

Keynes's ideas not only provided a theoretical basis for the policies of President Roosevelt, they quickly became an ideology of sorts, justifying the growth of government in capitalist societies. The Reagan policies of the 1980s can be put in historical perspective if we view them as attempts to slow down, even reverse, Keynesianism. However, this much is clear: original and contemporary capitalism share the same values but the attitude toward government has changed.

The government in modern capitalist systems has assumed another role: to maintain certain social programs, such as unemployment compensation to help those who are temporarily dislocated by twists and turns of the economic system. We can call this tendency **welfare capitalism**.[5]

There is a never-ending debate about the size and scope of these programs. Some say they have gone too far; others, that they have not gone far enough. But the capitalist world seems to accept—albeit grudgingly at times—the government's role in providing what has become known as the "social safety net" for its citizens. A quote from one of the most influential modern capitalists, IBM president Thomas B. Watson, makes the point very clearly: "Much as we may dislike it, I think we've got to realize that in our kind of society there are times when government has to step in and help people with some of their more difficult problems. Programs which assist Americans by reducing the hazards of the free market system without damaging the system itself are necessary, I believe, to its survival. . . ."[6]

The growth of government in capitalist nations can thus be attributed to two factors: the need to regulate the economy so as to maintain a competitive and stable market system and to provide a minimal standard of living for those citizens who have suffered because of the downturns in the economy. But the basic values and assumptions of capitalism have not changed; the profit motive, competition, and the market are still at its core. What has changed is faith in an "invisible hand." For a student of politics, the most important implication is the greater significance of government in capitalist systems.

LIBERALISM

It makes sense to think of **liberalism** as the ideological counterpart of capitalism.[7] While some of the main principles of liberalism can be traced back to a time prior to the development of capitalism, liberalism as a political ideology really took off at about the time that capitalism became an identifiable economic system. This does not of course mean that one cannot exist without the other. There have been authoritarian political systems existing alongside capitalist economic systems, and it is possible to find liberal societies joined with nonmarket-oriented economies. The point is that capitalism and liberalism seem to have a natural affinity for each other. The emphasis on a competitive market of individual producers and consumers seems to be the economic equivalent of a political system in which individual citizens are each seeking to protect their own natural political rights. Thus the historical conjunction of "capitalism the economic system" and "liberalism the political ideology" is no accident.

We can say that liberalism and capitalism have undergone some significant changes through the years, so has liberalism. But let us begin with the early years of liberalism.

Early Liberalism

Liberalism became a coherent ideology near the end of the seventeenth century in the writings of the English philosopher John Locke.[8] Locke argued that individuals have certain **rights** simply because they are human; they are not granted them by government. These he called **natural rights**. The most important one is the right to property. The political implication of this is that government exists to protect these natural rights. What follows is one of the central principles of liberalism: governmental authority is derived from the people of the society and is limited.

What a change from other theories that had developed during the medieval period of European history! For instance, a number of kings, including two who reigned in England during Locke's own century, claimed that their power was based on **divine right**. This meant that authority was derived directly from God; thus, they could not be limited by and they were not responsible to the people. The unlimited and often irresponsible exercise of power that resulted from this kind of theory was the target of Locke's criticism. At the very time that Locke was publishing his great political book (1689), England was establishing a political system that recognized, once and for all, limitations on the power of government. Locke's political writings served as both a foundation for and justification of this new political system.

Thus, from the very beginning, the ideology of liberalism revolved around the ideas of individual freedom and limited government. The two ideas were tied together in a functional theory of politics; the political system exists to perform certain functions, primarily protecting natural rights such as property.

The fact that the most important function of government is protecting the individual's natural rights such as property says something important about early liberalism. It had a middle-class orientation; it was the ideology of a newly emerging class that feared the absolute power of upper-class-controlled governments. To middle-class liberals the concept of property meant more than real estate. Owning property is what allows one to exercise other rights; Locke realized that property was the main source of power.

This leads to another characteristic of liberalism—the belief that social, political, and economic change is natural. Such a position was to be expected from those who were attempting to establish a new ideology and political-economic system in a highly volatile and often hostile environment. It is no accident that Locke, the first consistent liberal, sanctioned the right of a society to revolt against an irresponsible government. And, the centrality of change in the liberal tradition was not lost on the philosophers of the American Revolution who, a century later, incorporated Locke's ideas in their own movement against what they viewed as political tyranny. Thomas Jefferson reduced it to a single phrase: "I hold it that a little rebellion now and then is a good thing, and as necessary in the political world as storms in the physical."[9]

Of course, liberals in modern Western political systems rarely advocate rebellion and revolution. After all, they have in some cases become the system. But even well-established liberals are still part of the tradition of change, even if it is change of a more moderate and gradual variety. Liberals who find themselves in authoritarian societies are often more likely to return to the more obvious radicalism of Locke and Jefferson in supporting the need for more drastic measures to obtain greater amounts of freedom in their societies.

Contemporary Liberalism

The great capitalist philosopher Adam Smith was also, not coincidentally, a liberal. One hundred years after Locke, capitalism and liberalism had been joined. And like capitalism, liberalism has remained true to its basic principles while undergoing some significant structural changes.

Modern liberals believe that government ought to play a major role in protecting individual rights. The major shift is toward the view that government is something to be used, not feared. This has led to what appears to be a contradictory situation; liberalism stands for limited government yet now liberals support big government. Racial, religious, and social prejudice and pressures toward conformity are the main threats and, according to the liberal, only a strong government can protect the individual from them. A good example is the liberal's support of government action designed to reduce discrimination against some segments of the society. This suggests that liberalism is no longer a middle-class ideology; it has now been extended to include a wider range of groups.

The enlarged role of government makes sense, however, only if government is to some extent democratic. Thus, in those times and places where government has been authoritarian or totalitarian, liberals have worked for less government. When the government is perceived as more popularly based, liberals view it as an aid to the expansion of freedom.

Modern liberals also support greater governmental activity in the economic system for many of the same reasons that modern capitalists do. Keynesianism is one of the ideological bases of liberalism, and even greater emphasis is placed on social programs designed to provide people with a minimal standard of living in times of economic instability. In fact, today's liberals would probably argue that many of these programs must go on a permanent footing since true freedom is possible only if some semblance of equality of economic opportunity exists. To critics of modern liberalism, this suggests a tendency toward economic leveling and an undercutting of the incentives that give the market system its momentum. The liberal replies that those who are placed at significant economic disadvantage by the inequalities of the system cannot compete equally.

So, liberalism has evolved from an ideology advocating limited government to one making government the main protector of individual rights and maintainer of minimal economic and social conditions. But, liberals argue, the central values laid down by John Locke are still at the heart of their ideology.

CONSERVATISM

In everyday political discourse, the two ideologies of liberalism and conservatism are rarely separated. In many Western democracies, political parties and participants are classified as either liberal or conservative, implying that these are the only two ideological choices and that everyone falls into one or the other.

Let us look at conservatism in light of this impressionistic background. We all have an idea of what conservatism is. It has something to do with defending the existing structure, usually called the **status quo**. This leads to the impression that conservatives resist change. After all, if what exists is good, why change it? These commonsense notions are on target, but we must dig into them a bit more to understand the role that conservatism plays in modern politics.

Traditional Organic Conservatism

There are actually several types of conservatism. Most historians mark the beginning of conservatism *as an ideology* with the writings of the late eighteenth-century English philosopher Edmund Burke.[10] Conservatives have existed in society in every historical period, but Burke is usually given credit for providing conservatism with a philosophical justification and turning it into an ideology that could have a powerful impact on real-world politics.

Burke's brand of conservatism was based on a reaction to changes that were going on around him. He saw the traditional social structure being altered and he did not like it; he saw the middle class becoming militant in its demands for more economic and political power and he did not like it; he saw a violent uprising in France in 1789 (which became the French Revolution) and he liked that least of all. All of these developments disturbed him because he saw society as an organic whole, made up of a large number of parts arranged in intricate patterns. Burke believed that no one can really understand the evolution of social and political systems; they simply develop over time. The society at any given time is good because it has developed and in doing so it might be said to possess the accumulated wisdom of the people of that society. There is no best society or political system. Here is where reformers and radicals go wrong, according to Burke; since no one can understand the reasons for a particular society or culture, then no one should attempt to change it. This can only lead to a tearing up of the social fabric that has been woven through the ages.

What all of this boils down to in less philosophical terms is a strong defense of *tradition*, the customs and values that have accumulated in a society. Burke believed that these should continue to provide the foundation for any political system not because they are ultimately good (no one can prove which values are ultimately good), but because they have lasted. Thus, conservatism becomes that ideology which defends, often in an emotional way, the existing traditions of a society and rejects any attempt to radically change the social fabric.

This is not to say that traditionalists oppose all change. Burke recognized that social, economic, and political systems evolve over a period of time. He was simply against the attempt of an individual or group to work for radical and abrupt change because of a presumed ultimate value such as freedom or equality. This, of course, was the basis of his criticism of the French revolutionaries; they were not only wrong, they were dangerous because in working for their perceived natural rights they were upsetting the basic order of European society.

Given the fact that in Burke's time European politics was still largely a game for the upper classes (although there had been some movement toward a wider distribution of power, especially in Burke's own England), it follows that his brand of conservatism had an aristocratic bias. The conservatives saw new classes emerging and realized that if they gained more power, the traditional rules of the game based on the principles of elitism were on the way out. Burke was definitely not a supporter of irresponsible political rule. He defended the existing British government, which had evolved into a system that recognized the right of Parliament to limit the power of the monarch. Burke himself was a member of Parliament, and it should be noted that he supported the American Revolution because he interpreted it not as an attempt to change things, but as the final move of a nation to establish its independence.

Still, the longing for tradition and the glorification of history made Burke a romantic. And so it is with today's traditionalists: they are really reacting to the rapid change that seems to have become part of modern society. They long for a slower-moving world that respects traditional social values.

Individualistic Conservatism: Conservative or Reactionary?

One of the problems of being a conservative is knowing what to do when a major change does take place. Do you swing over and become a supporter of the new system or remain true to the traditional values? If you do the latter, there would seem to be a real question about the purity of your conservatism. How can you be a conservative while defending a system that no longer exists? The traditionalists discussed in the last section might find themselves in this position as they continue to defend traditions that are fading away.

There is another contemporary ideological position, usually considered a conservative one, which is more obviously faced with this dilemma. Those who long for a return to a system which resembles the one that Adam Smith described are commonly labeled conservatives. But, if it is true that because of the growth of big corporations and their impact on the market, such a system no longer exists, then this ideology becomes **reactionary**; it proposes that we go back and recapture a system that works better than the present one.

The line between conservatives and reactionaries is often fuzzy, but it is no less significant because of its imprecision. Also, the term *reactionary* has unfortunately taken on negative connotations, wanting to return to the dark ages, so to speak. If one examines the reactionary position in a more neutral manner, it appears as a possibly reasonable ideological position: "I don't like the way things are today, and I wish we could go back to a better time." This is why modern social thinkers such as the Nobel Prize-winning economist Milton Friedman are called **nineteenth-century liberals.**[11]

The other confusing element in all this is the fact that this ideology (which is usually considered a type of conservatism) is virtually the same as original liberal-capitalism. Once we understand what is being said—a defense of individual economic and political freedom and a rejection of the increasing role of government—then the confusion appears simply as the product of multiple labeling.

Pragmatic-Positional Conservatism

Most of those who consider themselves conservatives would probably find Burke's reverence for tradition valid, if a bit too mystical and romantic. But most conservatives defend the status quo for more pragmatic reasons; they find that their own perception of "the good life" and the existing system correspond to each other fairly closely. This more pragmatic approach leads to **positional conservatism**, which gets us back to the commonsense notion of what conservatism is all about: defense of the status quo.

So, it follows that in contemporary Western capitalist systems like the United States, those who support the system as it has developed— an economy of large corporations existing alongside a large government—must be considered conservatives. This also helps explain why those who wish to return to a romantic past (traditionalists) or a truly free market (nineteenth-century liberals) might be considered mild reactionaries.

The positional notion of conservatism is ideologically neutral. That is, it refers only to the relationship between one's ideological position and the dominant values of the society. Thus, not only can there be corporate capitalist conservatives in the Western industrialized nations, but Marxist conservatives in the Soviet Union and Islamic conservatives in Saudi Arabia.

MARXISM-COMMUNISM

Communism is usually portrayed as the great alternative to capitalism. Although an oversimplification, this portrayal is not without merit. At the political level, much of international politics seems to be a confrontation between the liberal-capitalist nations of the West and the Marxist-Communist nations of the East. At the more philosophical level, communism really does present an alternative to liberalism and capitalism. It is based on a different set of assumptions and reaches different conclusions about what political and economic systems ought to be like.

Before going any further, the point should be made that **Marxism-Communism** is only one of several varieties of **socialism**. It is no doubt the most visible—but by no means the only—variety of that broad ideological tradition that began sometime in the early nineteenth century. Today, Marxism-Communism, democratic socialism, and Third-World socialism are considered the leading types of socialism. While all can be placed within a very broad socialist tradition, their differences, both philosophical and political, often outweigh their similarities. That is why we are discussing them in separate sections.

But let us not lose sight of the fact that all contemporary socialists can trace their ideas back almost 200 years to those who reacted negatively to the Industrial Revolution that was transforming European society. Thus, socialism was born as an ideology by those who viewed with dismay the development of a competitive economic system which led, as they saw it, to greater social and political inequality and greater hardships for the bulk of the population. Socialists naturally became the spokesmen for the emerging industrial working class (even though many socialist leaders were themselves members of the middle class). We can gain an interesting overview of contemporary ideologies by linking each to a particular class. In the eighteenth and nineteenth centuries capitalist-liberalism represented the increasingly powerful middle class, conservatism the endangered traditional upper classes, and socialism the ever-larger working class. All ideologies were reactions to the Industrial Revolution.

The crucial point about socialism is that it began as the ideology of the underdog, of the less well-off members of the society, and despite its many variations in the modern world it is still probably the call for *equality* that explains its appeal. Because of this simple emotional appeal, *socialism* has become a "good" word in many parts of the world. Thus, it is probably the case that many political leaders label themselves and their regimes socialist for propaganda reasons. Even so, the following statistics are very impressive: more than one-third of the nations of the world identify themselves as socialist; these nations control about two-fifths of the world's territory and population.

Original Marxism

All socialists of whatever stripe (including those who bitterly oppose the communist regimes of the Soviet Union and China) are indebted to the nineteenth-century German philosopher Karl Marx. He did not invent socialism but, more than any other socialist thinker, he formulated a coherent philosophical system from the bits and pieces of socialist thought. In this section we will summarize Marx's main assumptions and ideas; in the sections to follow, we will briefly consider how they have been applied to real-world societies.[12]

Marxism is both a scientific theory, allegedly presenting an accurate explanation of history, and a moral philosophy, indicating what in human society is good and bad. Marx himself viewed his work as a true scientific theory. He claimed he was not writing about how things *should be,* but what they were *really like;* he always viewed himself as an objective historian, not a moral philosopher. However, the implicit moral judgments are there and in many ways have proven to be the most influential aspect of his philosophy. It is also important to realize that much of what Marx wrote was a reaction to and a criticism of the liberal-capitalist ideology that he saw developing around him.

Marxism begins with several basic assumptions about human nature and society. First, humans are not naturally competitive and profit-motivated as capitalists believe. If people behave this way, it is because they live in competitive societies. This suggests that Marx and most other socialists are not individualists as liberals tend to be. The nature of the society determines the nature of the individual, not the other way around. This is why Marx assumed that there will ultimately be a society in which people cooperate; when the proper social conditions are present, the competitiveness that capitalists assume is natural will cease to exist.

Marx believed that the most important part of any society is its economic system (Marx called it the **mode of production**). All other parts of the society (the class system, state, and ideology) follow from the mode of production. Let us see how Marx applied this central hypothesis to the capitalist society. The capitalist mode of production (factories and machines owned by one group and operated by another) produces a class system (capitalists and workers), then a state (controlled by the capitalist class), and ideologies (that justify and legitimize the capitalist system). Several very crucial assumptions about the nature of politics are contained in this theory:

1. Politics is less important than economics.
2. All societies are divided into classes, with the ruling class always dominant.
3. The state or political system exists merely to help the dominant class retain its control (to Marx, it was self-evident that in a capitalist society, the state would represent the interests of capitalists).
4. Ideologies, religions, culture, and all other value systems exist to rationalize the power of the ruling class. (This is why Marx labeled ideologies "false consciousness" and religion "the opiate of the people.")

One of the features of Marxism that has made it such an impressive theory to so many people is its explanation of historical change. It is a dynamic theory; it predicts what will happen next. Marx saw history as a series of stages of development from the earliest, primitive communism through slavery, feudalism, capitalism, and finally communism. The movement from one stage to the next is inevitable, according to Marx, because historical change always follows a **dialectical process**. This means that in each society there will be class conflict.

As we have seen, every society is defined by a dominant class; the dominant class always produces its opposite, a class that it needs, yet must exploit. Thus we have masters and slaves, lords and serfs, capitalists and workers. The inherent relationship between each pair is dominance and economic exploitation; Marx saw no other possibility. Thus class conflict is inevitable, and from the conflict emerges a new class, which defines the new stage of history. This is how medieval feudalism developed out of the slave system of the Roman Empire and how, during the Industrial Revolution, capitalism developed out of feudalism. It must be stressed that Marx saw this dialectical process as an inevitable one; there can be no redoing of history. This is no doubt another reason for the popularity of Marxism: it is not to the Marxist a question of *whether* change will take place, but *when.*

The final touch in Marx's theory of history is what happens after capitalism. The answer is the last stage in history, **communism**. The communist society is different from all previous societies because it will be classless; the means of production, whether land or machines, will not be owned by one class. Instead, the economic system will be owned by the society and because according to Marx humans are not naturally selfish, there will be no exploitation. Furthermore, because class conflict—the fuel of the dialectical process—has ceased to exist, there will be no further historical development; history stops.

The most important political implications of all this is Marx's prediction that in the communist society, government and ideology will also cease to exist. Again, the conclusions are logical if one accepts the initial premise. If governments exist merely to help maintain the ruling classes, when there are no more ruling classes, there will be no more governments. Marx is a bit fuzzy about what this means. Does he mean that *all* government will wither away or just authoritarian central governments that help in the exploration of one class by another? Would he, for instance, allow the possibility of small-scale organizations of workers making decisions about what to produce in their factories? Whatever the interpretation, it is clear that Marx is describing a society in which economic power and the laws of supply and demand are replaced by social cooperation as the basis for policy making. Likewise, Marx argues that all ideologies and religions (remember, to him they are "false consciousness") will cease to exist since they exist only to further the interests of the ruling class.

An interesting question occurs at this point. Presumably, everyone in the final communist society will accept the principles of Marxism. Doesn't that make Marxism an ideology and thus no less false than other ideologies? Or, pushing history back a bit to Marx's own lifetime, why couldn't we consider Marxism an ideology since one of its main purposes was to defend the interests of the working class and to mobilize them in their opposition to capitalists? In this book, we are of course considering Marxism as an ideology, but Marx himself couldn't. His answer to these questions is at once logical and disappointing: Marxism is the first true scientific theory of history because it is the first theory to base its analysis on the final class in history, the working class. Since they will push history into its final stage, Marxism is not an ideology, but the ultimate scientifically certified predictor. Even many of those who find much of value in Marx's analysis resist the assumption that it is the *only* valid theory of history.

One more facet of original Marxism must be discussed, and to some it is the one with the greatest immediate impact. Marx was a *revolutionary* thinker. He believed that great historical changes take place only through violent confrontations between classes; the result is almost always a revolution. The cause of this violent conflict should now be fairly obvious: the exploited class finally has had enough **exploitation**. The capitalist continues to force the workers to work longer hours and then takes the product of this work and sells it for profit, so workers rise up and overthrow the ruling class. The revolution will be successful because by this time the capitalist system has become self-destructive. In the final stages of the capitalist period, the capitalist class, in its desire to increase its profits, attempts to pay its workers less and in so doing makes it more and more difficult for them to buy the very goods that allow the capitalist to make his profit. Thus, the revolution succeeds not only because the workers can take no more exploitation, but in addition, because the capitalist system is destroying itself from within.

The differences between capitalism and Marxism are obvious and striking. What is dearest to the heart of the capitalist, the market system, is the source of exploitation to the communist. While the capitalist values individual freedom above all else, the Marxist wants greater equality. But notice the interesting and ironic similarities. Both theories emphasize economics as the motivating force in society and each in its own way downgrades government. The capitalist worries about the interference of government in the free play of supply and demand, while the Marxist views government as the agent of the ruling class. The capitalist hopes government doesn't grow too large; the Marxist predicts it will go away.

Leninism

Because of Marx's firm belief that history must move through a series of historical stages, none of which can be skipped, he concluded that only those societies which had mature capitalist systems could experience communist revolutions. His own predictions were that England, the United States, and Germany would be first. A communist revolution is not possible in a society that is just beginning its capitalist stage because the necessary historical conditions are not yet ripe.

What do you do then, if you are a dedicated Marxist revolutionary who wants to apply the Marxist principles to your still largely feudal and only minimally capitalist society? This was the problem faced by the first successful Marxist revolutionary leader, Nikolai Lenin, when he analyzed his native Russia as it entered the twentieth century. His solution, really an updating of original Marxism, has had such a lasting impact on the original ideas that today, Marxists call their ideology **Marxism-Leninism**. The substance of his reworking also explains why communism has been a more popular ideology in the less developed areas of the world than in the industrialized West, its point of origin.[13]

Lenin did two very clever things to adapt Marxism to the Russian situation. First, he argued that the revolutionary transition into a communist society can begin to take place even before the workers are ready for it, even before a large working class has developed. The key is the existence of an **elite party** made up of leaders who thoroughly understand the principles of Marxism and know how to apply them. This elite party of professional revolutionaries will seize power in the name of the masses and reshape the society according to the communist blueprint.

This was a significant reinterpretation of Marxism for the master had always claimed that the communist revolution can occur only when the "objective" economic and social conditions are present. This means that to Marx, the revolution will be a mass spontaneous uprising of the working class. His disciple Lenin was suggesting a different route to the communist society. He thought he had a basis for his idea of an elite party in Marx's own writings. Marx had pointed out that after the revolution, there will be a period characterized by the **dictatorship of the proletariat** (*proletariat* means working class). The workers will take over the economic and political institutions and begin creating their new communist society. And, practically speaking, the workers may need ideological and political leadership for a time. Marxist intellectuals will normally perform this function. But this is a far cry from Lenin's concept of the highly disciplined, totally powerful, infallible Communist party, which actually pulls the workers through their revolution.

As time has gone by, every Marxist-Leninist party in every communist regime has used Lenin's theory to justify its totalitarian control. If only they know what is best for their society, then they should attempt to control every aspect of the society. Thus, the link between Lenin's concept of the Communist party elite and totalitarianism is clear.

Lenin's other important contribution was his theory of capitalist imperialism. Marx predicted that things would go from bad to worse in the capitalist world: more exploitation, longer work hours, lower pay, and finally the disintegration of the capitalist nations. Lenin came along a half-century later and found capitalism holding its own. His theory of **capitalist imperialism** explains why. Through the development of their colonies in Asia, Africa, and Latin America, the Western capitalist nations have opened up a huge new market; they have also discovered a huge new labor force. This keeps capitalism going for a period of time, but only makes its downfall that much more efficient. Now, instead of separate revolutions in each capitalist nation, there will be a worldwide conflict; workers, both Western and colonial, will rise up against the capitalists of the world and as international markets dwindle down to a precious few, the capitalist nations will fight for them. This will ultimately lead to world war and the cataclysmic destruction of capitalism.

The Present Status of Marxist-Leninism

If one were to summarize the present status of Marxist-Leninist communism, what could be said? There seems to be a wide discrepancy between the original goals of Marxism and what is being accomplished in those regimes that call themselves Marxist-Leninist. Most of them are controlled by an extremely powerful elite that seeks to strengthen its hold on society. We have seen the philosophical justification of this tendency contained in Lenin's theory of the elite party, but this does not make the regimes any less totalitarian.

In the Soviet Union, the first and still most important Marxist regime, a large bureaucratic state carries out the decisions of the Communist party. Soviet leaders point out that their nation is presently in its *socialist,* not communist, stage of development. Following Lenin, they argue that their society is still in a transitional period: the economy is not yet adequately developed, the workers are not yet ready to take over. These are the tasks of the Party. When the conditions are right, the workers will gain control and true communism will appear.

Another Soviet variation on original Marxism is the emphasis placed on building a powerful Russian *state.* This policy is most closely associated with Joseph Stalin, who succeeded Lenin in 1924 as head of the Soviet system. He justified a powerful national state with the following words: "Will our state remain in the period of Communism also? Yes, it will, unless the capitalist encirclement is liquidated, and unless the danger of foreign military attack has been eliminated. . . ."[14] According to Stalin, the Soviet Union had to make itself economically strong and militarily unbeatable to protect Marxism from the attacks of capitalists. Some critics suggest that Stalin was more interested in building a powerful Russian state than in furthering the cause of Marxism and functioned more as a traditional Russian czar than as a member of a communist party.

Most contemporary Marxist-Leninist regimes accept the necessity of a powerful communist party at their center, although some have criticized the Soviets for having created too powerful a state. This indicates that each national Marxist movement has developed its own interpretation and application of Marxism. Another important example is Mao Tse-tung in China.

After a long civil war, the Communist Party came to power in China in 1949, with Mao as its political, military, and ideological leader.[15] China was a vast peasant society, even less suitable from the standpoint of original Marxism for a communist revolution than Russia had been. But Mao probably saw Marxism as a theory with a special relevance to the lower classes, whether industrial workers or rural peasants. The most influential part of his theory is its reinterpretation of the communist revolution.

Mao argued that in a peasant society, emphasis must be placed on gaining control of the countryside and using hit-and-run tactics to wear down the army of the state. These **guerrilla tactics** describe the military aspects of the revolution. Equally important is the attempt to win the hearts and minds of the peasants through education, socialization, and propaganda. All of this will take time; in China it has taken several decades. But the result is a true change in the social and cultural foundation of the nation. This emphasis on cultural change can be seen in some of Mao's other contributions; the idea of a **permanent revolution** in which there will be a radical transformation of Chinese society. The "Great Leap Forward," as Mao labeled it, was put into place with the reorganization of the agricultural system from one of individual peasants to one based on highly regimented communes in which individuals were made secondary to the good of the society. This can be seen as the application of the military lessons of guerrilla war to the social and economic systems. But, in addition, it seems to be in the tradition of the original Marxist emphasis on the social rather than the individual and the central socialist goal of *equality.*

Mao and other Chinese leaders believed that if such a program were followed, China would "beat" the Soviet Union to the final society. It is, on the other hand, interesting to note that since Mao's death in 1976, there has been an attempt by Chinese leaders to moderate Mao's strategies and to move in the direction of a less radical interpretation of Marxism-Leninism.

When we look around the world, it would seem that Marxism-Leninism has made its greatest inroads in less-developed societies. The Russian and Chinese revolutions took place in nonindustrialized societies. Ongoing Marxist movements are the strongest in Asia, Africa, and Latin America. There is evidence that the established Marxist nations have had something to do with all this through their support of revolutionary groups in these areas. But the appeal goes deeper; it could be argued that most Third-World revolutionaries are less attracted to the elaborate theory and its long-range predictions than the very simple moral and emotional appeal of its underlying goals of economic justice and equality.

This is quite evident in the more thoroughgoing socialist nations. For instance, in South Yemen the socialist regime has attempted to achieve greater equality of salaries and severe limits on luxury goods. In Africa, Tanzania has been transformed into one of the more equalitarian societies in the world (it is still one of the poorest). But greater equality has been achieved thorough such policies as the forced relocation of peasants to small communes.

These examples bring us to what is perhaps the central ideological point. When Marxist-socialist goals are implemented in a thoroughgoing way, the result is a more *leveled* society, but not a *free* one. This is not surprising when we go back to the Marxist notion that the society comes before the individual. Social goodness is to be measured in terms of what is good for the entire society, not what is good for each individual. The assumption is, of course, that what is good for the society is good for each individual, but the result is not a maximization of personal freedom.

Perhaps we have come to the classic impasse between pure capitalist-liberals—who are willing to tolerate some inequality in order to maximize individual freedom—and socialists—who are willing to accept a decrease in freedom if it means more equality. The question yet to be answered is, Can a society have both at the same time?

One exception to the generalization that Marxism has had its greatest success in the less-developed rather than the more-developed parts of the world is the existence of Marxist-Leninist regimes in Eastern Europe. While as World War II ended there were well-established socialist parties in such countries as Czechoslovakia, Poland, Hungary, and East Germany, few students of this area would dispute the claim that their success in gaining control was mainly the result of the Russian Army. Let us quote one of the most respected students of Communism: "Once again, it should be stressed that these regimes did not conform to the hopes of the native communist leadership and were not really created by them. They were created by the Russians for purely Russian purposes . . . From the point of view of the countries transformed, the establishment of these client regimes undoubtedly was deplorable: if these were revolutions, they were revolutions gone astray, skewed in their development by outside interference."[16]

Thus, while there was some sentiment for socialism, we cannot explain the East European Marxist nations with any of the Marxist, Leninist, or Maoist theories of revolution. The high levels of unrest in Eastern Europe have forced the Soviet Union to move in its troops several times to restore order. The most important test facing East European Marxism is how the Polish situation finally works itself out. There we find the incongruous situation of a widespread labor movement. Solidarity, making demands on the Marxist government for more economic benefits, a greater voice in decision making, and more freedom. While the leaders of Solidarity claim they are not trying to tear down the socialist state, some observers see their movement as a swing in a more liberal direction.

DEMOCRATIC SOCIALISM

Marxist-Leninism is not the only type of socialism in today's world. We have seen that there are several variations on the Marxian theme; every Marxist nation seems to have developed its own particular characteristics. In this section we will examine a brand of socialism that has moved in a quite different direction—**democratic socialism,** the kind that is most evident in Western democracies such as Sweden, Norway, West Germany, and the United Kingdom.

The broadest values of democratic socialism can be traced back to Marx. It is fair to say that all socialists assume that people are naturally social and cooperative, that equality is the most important goal, and that justice implies preventing a single class from controlling the economic system. Also, socialists seem to have a warm place in their hearts for the working class.

To put this in historical perspective, it can be pointed out that during the last decade of the nineteenth century, Marxism became the dominant socialist ideology. But there were two interpretations of its basic ideas; each provided the basis for a particular type of socialism. First, there were the **radicals** who believed that revolution was necessary to achieve a classless society. This group (Lenin was its most famous member) tended to view Marxism as a scientific theory of history that produces infallible predictions. The other group, made up of those who became democratic socialists, saw Marxism more as a set of moral objectives whose realization was not as neatly predictable. They believed in the *evolutionary* rather than *revolutionary* development of socialism. The radical Marxists called the members of this group **revisionists** because they had allegedly revised the basic assumptions of Marx. The revisionists viewed themselves as more realistic socialists who realized that while Marx had made some telling criticisms of capitalist society, his predictions were not infallible.

The leading revisionist was a German thinker named Edward Bernstein who, in the late nineteenth and early twentieth centuries, laid out the basic principles of democratic socialism.[17] One of his revisions involved arguing that communist revolutions are not inevitable since economic conditions are not getting worse for the working class. Abuses still exist in the capitalist system, but because the power of the working class is increasing, such abuses can be corrected. Thus, he and the other early social democrats became reformers rather than radicals. This is the important point. Bernstein realized that the political systems of Europe and the United States were becoming more democratic. Average citizens, including workers, were gaining more power as the right to vote was extended to more and more people. Thus, he combined socialist values and democratic techniques and came up with *democratic socialism,* a socialist system achieved by working within the democratic system. This means organizing socialist parties, campaigning, and getting socialists elected to government office. It accepts the fact that socialist parties will compete peacefully with parties representing other points of view. Socialists must have faith that through political persuasion their ideas and programs will gain the support of a majority of the population. But this faith and the acceptance of the democratic system means that they will continue to work within the system even in the face of electoral defeat.

From Bernstein's ideas there have developed social democratic parties in most European nations and more recently in other parts of the world. It might be argued that in some, perhaps most of these parties, the democratic values have become more important than the socialist ones. The radical Marxists have from the very beginning viewed the members of such parties as liberal capitalists in disguise.

Social democracy also developed in England mainly through the Fabian Society. The Fabians formulated an interpretation of socialism similar to, but probably even more pragmatic than, Bernstein's version. Led by such well-known intellectuals as George Bernard Shaw, they took a practical, down-to-earth approach to socialist activities, advocating reforms of specific institutions and policies rather than a complete overhaul of the capitalist system. The Fabians worked closely with the increasingly important trade union movement and eventually became part of the British Labour party, which has taken the reigns of government several times in recent years.

What is it that democratic socialists are seeking? Once again, their ultimate goals are economic justice, equality, and at least a partial dismantling of the capitalist class system. Most early democratic socialists thought that the best way to achieve these goals was by nationalizing the economy; that is, by taking ownership of major industries out of private hands and turning them over to the socialist government. Here, then, is a marked difference between the support of the contemporary liberal for increased government regulation of the economy and the democratic socialist's more drastic proposal that the economy actually be publicly owned.

As a practical matter, most democratic socialist parties that have gained power in Sweden, Norway, West Germany, the United Kingdom and, most recently, France, have carried out less nationalization than their rhetoric might suggest. Such nations do have more public ownership than is found in the typical capitalist system, but usually no more than 10 to 20 percent of the economy ends up in public hands. As might be expected, the industries that are nationalized are the most basic ones: steel, transportation, energy, communications, and banking. But every democratic socialist government has left much of the economy in private hands.

Many socialists have come to place greater emphasis on the other important technique for achieving economic equality, the creation of a full-scale welfare state. We have seen some of this in modern liberalism, but the socialist advocates a much wider-ranging system based on what has become known as "the cradle to the grave" philosophy. It is the responsibility of the society, not each individual, to provide the basic components of a decent life: food, shelter, education, transportation, health care, and even burial. This is the best method for achieving greater equality: to combine a massive social welfare system with a very progressive tax system that redistributes the wealth in the form of free hospital care, college tuition payments, rent subsidies, and funeral allowances. Thus, we might say that in order to achieve high levels of benefits, the costs in the form of taxes must also be higher.

Now, there is a lack of unanimity among social democrats as to the function of the welfare state in the achievement of socialism. Some argue that the welfare state, while commendable, is not in itself socialism. A leading twentieth-century British socialist has this to say about the socialist welfare state: "What we have been doing is not to put people on an equal footing, but only to lessen the extremes of inequality by redistributing grossly unequal incomes. . . ."[18] His point is that the welfare state treats only the *symptoms,* not the *causes* of economic inequality. More drastic measures, including more public ownership, have been advocated as a more fundamental way to reduce inequality and the accumulation of private wealth. One result of this disagreement between the more moderate "welfare state" socialists and advocates of more basic changes has been the split in the venerable British Labour party. A number of leaders have left the party on the grounds that it has become too radical and have formed a new moderate socialist party called the Social Democratic party.

Despite disagreements within the social democratic movement it should be reiterated that all social democrats share a central value system. Economic and social equality is at its core and there is a firm commitment to the liberal democratic political process. In this sense, they are closer to the liberal-capitalist parties of the West than they are to the Marxist-communist parties of the Soviet Union and Eastern Europe. It should be noted that contemporary liberals and social democrats do not see eye to eye on all principles. While both accept democracy, they disagree on the question of what makes people economically "tick." Capitalists, even those who support large government, criticize socialists for removing the most important motivating factor, *profit*. If the system does not offer incentives for hard work, it simply won't work. Thus the capitalist is still a strong supporter of the *market*. The socialist replies that people are not as profit-motivated as the capitalists believe and that a pure market economy leads to unjustified inequality. So we are back to the classic philosophical debate over the relative merits of freedom and equality.

When we look beyond the philosophical debate and examine the capitalist and democratic socialist regimes that actually exist, it seems clear that in most cases the rhetoric of the dispute is more divergent than the actual systems. As we have already pointed out, no democratic socialist has nationalized more than 20 percent of its nation's economy. Thus much of the economy remains market-oriented. And every capitalist system has taken over the regulation of much of its economy. Democratic socialists support more extensive social welfare programs, but most capitalists support them on a smaller scale. Thus, one could conclude that there are differences in basic values but in the day-to-day world of politics and economics it is more a difference in degree.

As of this ninth decade of the twentieth century, two major definitions of socialism are apparent. On one hand, we have the Marxist-Leninist version: socialism is the stage of history prior to the final communist stage; it requires an all-powerful Marxist party which transforms the society into a totalitarian people's democracy. To the leaders of the Soviet Union, China, and all other Marxist-Leninist regimes socialism is the present, communism the future. On the other hand, there is the democratic socialist definition: socialism describes a society in which economic equality is achieved through a democratic political process. And it is fair to say that when democratic socialists visualize the good socialist society, they do not have in mind the stateless communism of Marx. They see a continued role for government as the coordinator of the economic system and provider of basic material needs for the population.

SUMMARY

In this chapter the relationship among politics, economics, and ideology have been sorted out and analyzed. Since the three are so closely intertwined, an understanding of politics is incomplete without an understanding of economics and ideology.

Economic systems produce and distribute material values. The best-known economic systems are capitalism, socialism, and communism. A crucial characteristic of each is the emphasis or lack of emphasis it places on the market (the laws of supply and demand). For political scientists, the main question is, What is the perceived role of the political system (should government play an important role or not?)?

Closely related to and often overlapping with economic systems are ideologies. Ideologies are sets of values and beliefs about politics, economics, and society. Ideologies can be classified as radical (critical of the existing system) or conservative (supportive of the existing system). The most important ideologies include liberalism, conservatism, and socialism.

NOTES

1. For a discussion of the concept of ideology and its role in politics, see Chaim Waxman, ed., *The End of Ideology Debate* (New York: Simon and Schuster, 1968). For good overviews of different ideologies, see Lyman Tower Sargent, *Contemporary Political Ideologies* (Homewood, Ill.: The Dorsey Press, 1984) and Roy C. Macridis, *Contemporary Political Ideologies* (Boston: Little, Brown, 1984).
2. For a readable account of Adam Smith and other great economic thinkers, see Robert L. Heilbroner, *The Worldly Philosophers* (New York: Simon and Schuster, 1953). For a thorough discussion of different kinds of economic systems, see Frederick L. Pryor, *A Guidebook to the Comparative Study of Economic Systems* (Englewood Cliffs, N.J.: Prentice-Hall, 1985).
3. Wallace K. Ferguson, *A Survey of European Civilization* (Boston: Houghton Mifflin, 1958), p. 455.
4. John Maynard Keynes, *The General Theory of Employment, Interest and Money* (New York: Harcourt Brace, 1936).
5. For a comparison of social programs in different Western nations, see Arnold J. Heidenheimer et al., *Comparative Public Policy* (New York: St. Martin's Press, 1975).
6. Thomas B. Watson, *A Business and Its Beliefs: The Ideas That Helped Build IBM* (New York: McGraw-Hill, 1963), p. 36.
7. The best introduction to liberalism is L. T. Hobhouse, *Liberalism* (London: Oxford University Press, 1911).
8. Locke's most famous political work is *Two Treatises of Government.*
9. Thomas Jefferson, letter to James Madison in Paul Ford ed., *The Writings of Thomas Jefferson* (New York: G. P. Putnam, 1892–99), vol. 4, p. 362.
10. Burke's most famous political work is *Reflections on the Revolution in France.*
11. Milton Friedman, *Capitalism and Freedom* (Chicago: University of Chicago Press, 1962).
12. A useful anthology of Marx's writings is David McLellan, *Karl Marx: Selected Writings* (Oxford: University of Oxford Press, 1977). For a summary of Marx's life and ideas see Isaiah Berlin, *Karl Marx: His Life and Environment* (London: Oxford University Press, 1959).
13. See Alfred G. Meyer, *Leninism* (Cambridge, Mass.; Harvard University Press, 1957).
14. See Isaac Deutscher, *Stalin: A Political Biography* (New York: Vantage Books, 1960).
15. For a first-hand account of the early stages of the Chinese revolution, see Edgar Snow, *Red Star Over China* (New York: Random House, 1938).
16. Alfred G. Meyer, *Communism* (New York: Random House, 1984), pp. 163–64.
17. A readable summary of Bernstein's ideas is Peter Gay, *The Dilemma of Democratic Socialism* (New York: Columbia University Press, 1957).

POLITICS FROM THE TOP DOWN: INSTITUTIONAL CONTEXTS

8

GOVERNMENT: FUNCTIONS AND LEVELS

THE BASIC NATURE OF GOVERNMENT

The Decision-Making Functions of Government

The Institutionalization of Politics

THE LEVELS OF GOVERNMENT AND HOW THEY ARE RELATED

Unitary Systems

Confederate Systems

Federal Systems

SUMMARY

We have now considered the most important elements in the environment of politics: the distribution of power, the culture, the economic system, and the ideology. Each has a significant impact on the political process. We are now ready to examine the government institutions that lie at the center of the political system.

THE BASIC NATURE OF GOVERNMENT

The word **government** is derived from the Latin *gubinere* and Greek *kubernan,* which mean "to direct or steer." This gets to the heart of what a government is supposed to do: steer, direct, or *govern* the society either because without government, life would be unbearably disordered (according to Hobbes) or because with government life can be made even better than it already is (according to Aristotle). In short, government acts as the final arbitrator, deciding who gets what, resolving conflicts, and mobilizing society to accomplish tasks that individuals are incapable of accomplishing. Plato, the first great Western political philosopher, must have had this in mind when he compared government to a ship. Just as a helmsman must steer his ship through storms and treacherous seas, so must the statesman steer the nation through political, social, and economic storms.[1] Since Plato's time the phrase "ship of state" has been used by countless writers and speakers to describe the functions of government.

A government can be found in just about every human society. To be sure, governments vary significantly in size and complexity. In the more developed nations, governments are divided into numerous agencies and bureaus, and government workers may number in the millions. As we move through the 1980s, one in every seventy-five Americans works for the executive branch of national government. In less-developed nations, governments are much less complex and the number of workers is smaller, but these variations in size and complexity should not make us lose sight of the fact that every society has a political system with a government at its center.

It seems clear that as society becomes economically and socially more complex, its political system becomes more complex. And, political institutions become more *specialized* as society develops; that is, each tends to perform a more narrow range of functions.[2] In the most primitive societies, the chief or perhaps a small group of elders perform all political functions along with most of the economic and religious ones. In fact, the three kinds of decisions may be indistinguishable from each other. For instance, Eskimo communities are led by the shaman and the headman. The shaman is the religious leader but in addition he makes sure that the customs and traditions that hold the community together are followed; he is the custodian of the culture, so to speak. The headman is the economic leader deciding such matters as where to hunt but in addition resolving disputes about who gets what. Thus, religious, economic, and political decisions are difficult to distinguish from each other.

What evidence is there to support the claims that government is at the heart of every political system? For one thing, as we saw in an earlier chapter, governments do more with each passing decade. In every society government has gotten larger, spending more money and employing more people, and this growth seems to be independent of ideology and economic system: it has happened in capitalist, socialist, and communist systems. We noted in the last chapter that each of these dominant ideologies has come to accept the role of a larger government. Capitalism and liberalism have shifted from a belief in limited government to the acceptance of a larger one. Marxist-Leninist regimes still predict the coming of the stateless society, but show little inclination to dismantle their powerful bureaucratic states. And, democratic socialists support a strong central government as the main source of economic justice.

Why this greater reliance on government? Can its growth be justified? The seeds of an answer can be found in the "ship of state" analogy. If anything can coordinate the varied activities of a society, it is the government. This does not mean that it will always succeed, only that nothing else can accomplish the goal. It must be admitted that the desire for more power and control by increasing the scope of their government's authority. But this tendency explains only a part of government's significance and growth.

The major reason lies in the fact that in almost all societies, only government has political *authority*. That is, government has been granted the right to make decisions that are binding on the entire society; rarely can a business corporation, labor union, or church make this claim. This is not to say that such institutions are considered illegitimate within their own sphere of activity, nor does it deny that they may wield significant power. However, we must remind ourselves that there is a difference between legitimate power (authority) and the other types.

Only government is given the right to make authoritative rules; in the language of games, government provides the rules within which the game of politics takes place. This is not to say that all governments are legitimate; some military regimes base their power on threats and coercion. We are talking about governments in general, and the thing that distinguishes government from all other institutions is its authority. It seems reasonable to argue that every society recognizes that there must be someone or something with final authority, an institution or set of institutions.

Its authority gives government a monopoly on *legitimate force.* Of course, even in the least violent societies, nongovernmental individuals and groups use force. But these acts of violence are obviously not considered legitimate. Only the government is supposed to maintain a police force and an army. When private armies do exist within a society, it is a good indication that the government has lost its legitimacy and civil war is at hand.

The Decision-Making Functions of Government

The institutions of government adopt procedural rules, formulate policies, and make substantive decisions. Although in the real world of politics the three types of decisions are closely related, they can be examined separately.

A **procedural rule** describes how the game of politics should be played—such things as who can get into the game, how decisions will be made, and how decisions will be enforced. Thus, laws that specify who can hold particular office and who can vote in elections fall into this category, as do rules that lay out the procedures for passing a law.

A **policy** is a governmental decision about how to achieve a particular goal. Thus we talk about energy policy or foreign policy, each of which of course is made up of a number of more specific proposals. It could be said, for instance, that the energy policy of the United States has as its main goal increased independence from foreign energy sources. Thus, the following specific decisions might be made: the decontrol of domestic oil prices, support for the further development of nuclear energy, and an increase in the gasoline tax. Each is a technique designed to make the United States less dependent on foreign oil.

A **substantive decision** specifies what concrete actions the government takes. The example of policy making just discussed includes several: raising the gasoline tax, putting more government money into the nuclear power industry, or removing price restrictions on crude oil. Several important points follow. First, such specific decisions always end up having an impact on the process of who gets what. If the gasoline tax is significantly increased, it will reduce consumption by forcing lower-income, but probably not higher-income, groups to buy less.

The second point is that many specific decisions about who gets what reflect a more general policy. The gasoline tax is increased *in order to* reduce the consumption of oil. Thus, when we talk about the policy-

After the accident at Three Mile Island, many citizens continue to question the need for further development of nuclear power.

making process, we are referring both to the formulation of general policies and the specific decisions that flow from the policies. However, it should be made clear that not every decision about who gets what is the result of a more general policy. Sometimes, a government finds itself reacting to a situation for which it is unprepared. Since it has not anticipated the situation, there is no policy to serve as a guideline. Students of the foreign policy-making process often cite this as a real shortcoming of many decisions. Thus, it is argued that nations react to crises, one at a time, without any policy framework. Likewise, political actors within nations often base their decision on immediate gain rather than long-term policy. Thus, legislation is just as often the consequence of bargaining and vote-trading as the reflection of a common goal, a policy, that all legislators are trying to achieve.

Another reason for questioning the assumption that all government decisions are the result of a general policy takes us back to the significance of power in the political process. Decisions often reflect the distribution of power in a political system at a given time more than any overall policy of the government. It might be argued, for instance, that a decision to increase government support for the nuclear power industry is the result of the relative power of that industry rather than a policy commitment to decrease the nation's dependence on foreign oil. To further clarify, it is very likely that the policy itself reflects, at least to a certain extent, the distribution of power within the system.

We now know that the outputs of government are rules, policies, and substantive decisions, but we can be even more specific. The policy-making process can be broken down into three basic steps: 1) making the policy, 2) administering it, and 3) interpreting it, if necessary. The first step is the most obvious one. It is what we assume legislatures in liberal democracies spend most of their time doing. When Congress or Parliament passes a law, a policy has probably been adopted or revised. In nondemocratic systems, policies are more often made by the chief executive, whether king or dictator.

It is obvious that after a policy or rule is formulated and officially adopted by the government, it has to be *administered* and *enforced.* This is usually entrusted to the executive or administrative agencies of the government. Thus, in the United States, if Congress passes a law increasing the income tax, it is up to an executive agency (the Internal Revenue Service) to administer it (decide how best to collect the tax).

Often in the application of a policy there will be questions about what it means, how it is to be administered and enforced. Thus, every political system has to devise a way to interpret its policies and rules. In a traditional monarchy this function may fall into the hands of the monarch and his or her chief advisers. The monarch makes the policies and tells the people what they mean—how they are to be applied in specific cases. In other systems, including many liberal democracies, the job of interpretation has been assumed by another agency of government, often the courts. In these nations, courts handle disputes that arise during the application of the government's policies; in resolving the disputes, they often have to interpret what the policy means.

The Institutionalization of Politics

At this point we know that governments carry out the function of making, administering, and interpreting rules and policies. But how do we explain the tendency for formal institutions to take over these functions? And why is it that these institutions become more and more specialized in the functions that they perform? One answer is very broad but difficult to refute. It is based on the observation that every area of modern society has become institutionalized—that is, dominated by large organizations. It has happened to business, labor, the military, athletics, religion, communications, education—no area seems exempt. So why should we be surprised when politics becomes institutionalized?[3]

But this is more of an observation than an explanation. The typical explanation for the tendency toward institutionalization suggests that as the world gets more complex, greater expertise is required to cope with it. And, greater expertise leads to a greater emphasis on the division of labor as each job requires more specialized skills. Thus, political decision making becomes so specialized and technical that only full-time decision makers can make them. This is reflected in the fact, mentioned earlier, that in the least-developed societies, politics is a much less specialized and institutionalized activity. Thus, economic and social complexity and the growth of governmental institutions seem to go hand-in-hand.

But there is another explanation for the institutionalization of politics, which concentrates not on the impact of the social and economic environment on politics, but on the institutions themselves. According to this argument, once established, institutions find ways to perpetuate themselves and even grow. We have already seen this argument used to explain the development of elites: leaders of an organization gain more and more political skill and knowledge and thus increase their power at the expense of the rank-and-file members. Now we are applying the theory to the organizations themselves. The point is that there are times when there is no functional payoff in the increasing size and power of an institution; perhaps the society could even do without it. But after a while, the institution becomes permanent because its power has increased to the point that it cannot be dissolved.

The increase in the significance of institutions in modern political systems is best explained, then, with a combination of these arguments;

governments are established, develop, and grow because they are needed and thus acquire authority, but also because they develop a vested interest in staying around and an impetus toward increasing their power.

Every modern society has institutions that perform the functions of making, interpreting, and administering political policies. But, with more than 160 nations in the world, it is not surprising that the types of institutions and thus the methods for carrying out these functions, vary widely. There are several basic distinctions that will help straighten out this confusing situation. For, as is often the case, the wide variation is more apparent than real, for the different types can be sorted out into a few basic categories.

In the remainder of this chapter, we will look at one important dimension of government: how power is divided between the central government and regional units such as states and provinces. In the next several chapters, the various ways that the three main kinds of institutions—legislative, executive, and judicial—are combined and/or divided will be the main topic.

THE LEVELS OF GOVERNMENT AND HOW THEY ARE RELATED

A quick examination of the nations of the world suggests that each one has a multitude of political units. In addition to a national government there are states, provinces, cantons, boroughs, counties, and townships, to mention only a few. In just one large nation they can number in the thousands. Instead of being overwhelmed by their number and variety, we should instead examine the relationships that exist among them, especially between the national government and the regional or local units of government.

A political theorist might argue that the perfect government would be one that could maintain adequate control of the political system while remaining responsive to the needs of the people, wherever they are. The first need suggests centralization (the more power it has, the easier it is for the central government to control the system); the second need suggests decentralization (the more power regional or local governments have, the closer government will be to the people). The problem is, in large diversified nations, the two needs may work at cross-purposes. Both perfect centralization and perfect decentralization cannot exist at the same time. There are three basic ways to work out a solution, each leading to a different type of political system.

Unitary Systems

A **unitary system** is one in which ultimate authority or sovereignty rests with central government. In other words, local units have no authority of their own. What they do, the central government allows them to do.

One of the most centralized of modern unitary political systems is that of France.[4] It has regional political units (departments) and local units (cantons and communes), but each is controlled by the central government. One of the ministries (divisions) of the French central government is the Ministry of the Interior. It is in charge of the administration of all the local units of government. Each of the departments has as its chief administrator a **prefect**. The most important fact about prefects is that they are appointed, and can be removed, by the central government. The prefect is superior to local officials such as mayors. He must approve the mayor's budget proposals and can even dismiss the mayor from office. What we see, then, is a political system in which governmental power radiates from the center, a unitary system at work.

It is interesting to note that after centuries of centralized, unitary government, socialist President François Mitterrand has attempted to begin decentralizing the system by giving more power to the local governments and decreasing the power of the prefects. Indications are that because a unitary government has been part of the French political culture for so long, decentralization will not be easy to achieve.

The United Kingdom presents another example of a unitary political system. There is a stronger tradition of local control than in France, but the British system is still unitary since the national government—specifically, Parliament—has ultimate authority. The difference is that the central government allows the counties, towns, and boroughs of England more flexibility than is the case in France.[5]

The use of France and the United Kingdom as examples makes an important point about unitary systems. While there seems to be a natural relationship between unitary and authoritarian governments (it is easier for a ruling elite to maintain control when it is working within a highly centralized government), we should not fall into the trap of assuming that all unitary governments are authoritarian. The cases of the United Kingdom and France prove the contrary. As a matter of fact, most nations in the world are unitary. Since most are also authoritarian, one would expect many political systems to be both. However, it must be made clear that we are talking about two different questions. Is power concentrated in the hands of a small elite or is it distributed widely throughout the society? This is the question of authoritarianism. How is power distributed among the various levels of government? This is the question of unitary government. Each question is of crucial importance but they must not be confused.

Confederate Systems

A **confederation** is the opposite of a unitary system.[6] Instead of a powerful central government with subservient and dependent local units, a confederation is made up of a number of sovereign states who have joined together to form a political system without giving up their sovereignty (the right to control oneself). If a central government is established, it exists at the pleasure of the individual political units; the central government may be given certain administrative duties, but it has no authority of its own.

At certain times, the only political system possible is a confederation. If several sovereign states find it necessary to unite in order to fight a common enemy, they will probably constitute themselves as a confederation since none is willing to give up its sovereignty. Each will cooperate as long as the others do and as long as the reason for cooperation exists. Thus, a confederation is inherently unstable. Its primary advantage—giving each unit control over its destiny—is also its main disadvantage; the central government can do nothing unless there is near-unanimous consent from the constituent units of government. Thus, a confederation either breaks up and reverts to its original condition of several independent states, or it strengthens its central government and becomes a federal system.

Before we turn to federalism, let us consider several historical confederations. It should be clear from what we have just said that there will be few confederations in existence at any given time.

The first government of the United States was a confederation.[7] An examination of its basic nature gives us a good idea of how confederations begin, what they are like, and what tends to happen to them. In order to fight their common enemy, Great Britain, the original thirteen states had to work together. Thus, they formed a political system. But in the process, no state gave up its sovereignty. A central government of sorts—the Continental Congress—was established, but it could not draft men for the army and could not force the states to pay taxes. In short, since it had no true authority of its own, it was dependent on the goodwill of the individual states. In the next section we will see what became of the American confederation.

We can go back even further in time to examine the Swiss confederation, out of which has grown the nation of Switzerland. In the fourteenth century, three small rural districts, or *cantons,* in the Alps banded together to defend themselves against the aggression of their larger neighbors. Thus was born the Swiss confederation. Over the next several hundred years, the number of districts increased to thirteen. Until the 1850s the Swiss confederation remained a true confederation; the cantons worked together on matters of defense but usually ran into disagreement when it came to internal issues. None was willing to give up its sovereignty. This attitude was reinforced by differences in language and religion. Some of the cantons were German, some were French, and some were Italian; some were Catholic and others were Protestant.

Federal Systems

The American and Swiss confederations each evolved into a **federal system**.[8] The structure of a federal system falls somewhere between the unitary and confederate varieties. Instead of making only the central government sovereign (unitary) or only the states, provinces, or cantons sovereign (confederation), a federal system divides authority between a central government and local units, and guarantees that neither can do away with the other; each has sovereignty.

Federal systems are often created from confederations. This is how the United States and Switzerland of today came into being. Each reached a point where it became obvious to many that if a nation was to survive, the central government would have to be strengthened. But, with strong traditions of local sovereignty, a unitary government was out of the question. The answer was a division of power; each level was entrusted with certain responsibilities and neither was given the right to dissolve the other. Typically, the central government was given control over policy areas of national concern—foreign affairs, national defense, postal service, a system of currency. The local units assumed such tasks as education and law enforcement.

No federal system has been free from jurisdictional disputes and in most cases the central government has become the dominant partner under the principle of "national supremacy." But there is, of course, a difference between a dominant central government in a federal system and a unitary government. In a federal system, the sovereignty of states, cantons, or provinces has to be respected by the central government. In the United States, the central government in Washington, D.C., cannot unilaterally change the boundary between Oklahoma and Texas, nor award the city of Toledo to Michigan. On the other hand, no state can unilaterally secede from the Union, a fact demonstrated once and for all during the American Civil War.

Why do federal systems develop? Again, the Swiss and American examples are instructive. In each case, the United States in the 1770s and Switzerland in the 1840s appeared unable to perform necessary functions—maintaining an efficient monetary system, for instance. A decision had to be made; it was to give more power to the central government.

Let us conclude our discussion of unitary, confederate, and federal systems with a brief overview of their incidence in the modern world and their relative advantages and disadvantages. Because of their inherent instability, there are almost no confederations. The best contemporary example is not a nation but an organization of them, the United Nations. There are a small number of federal systems, around twenty. They are either large nations with ethnic and regional diversity (such as the United States, Canada, and India) or nations that began as confederations (the United States and Switzerland). All the rest of the nations of the world are unitary.

The main advantage of a unitary system is its ability to effectively handle national problems. Its primary disadvantage is the difficulty that arises in administering its policies in diverse and remote areas of the nation. The advantage of the confederation is the opposite: the recognition of regional diversity. The main disadvantage is, of course, the formidable task of carrying out national policies without a sovereign central government. The federal system might be viewed as a happy compromise. Regional sovereignty is recognized, yet a strong central government is created to formulate and implement national policies. The small number of functioning federal systems is a commentary on the difficult and delicate balance that must be maintained to make federalism workable. Thus, we should expect the federal relationship to be in a constant state of flux.

It has been suggested, for instance, that the federal system of the United States has gone through several stages, including those in which the national government has been dominant and those in which the states have asserted greater independence.[9] Confrontations between the two levels have occurred (including a violent one, the Civil War), which established once and for all that a state could not leave the federal system. This implied that the national government is supreme. But, the theory of states' rights remains an important one. This theory argues that states should have more control over their own affairs. After decades of growth of the power of the central government, President Reagan announced the policy of New Federalism, based on the assumption that state governments should assume a greater role.

SUMMARY

A government can be found at the heart of every political system, making authoritative decisions. Throughout the world more and more demands are made on governments and so they tend to become larger and more expansive. This seems to be true in political systems of all types.

Governments make three kinds of decisions, involving procedural rules, policies, and substantive matters.

In all political systems there are different levels of government, from central to regional (state) to local; but there are significant differences in how these levels are related to each other. This leads to a set of distinctions among political systems. In the unitary system, central government is dominant. In the confederate system, regional governments are dominant. In a federal system, central and regional governments share power.

NOTES

1. Plato's *Republic,* translated by Francis Cornford (New York: Oxford University Press, 1945), p. 195.
2. See Samuel P. Huntington, *Political Order in Changing Societies* (New Haven: Yale University Press, 1968), p. 34.
3. See Samuel P. Huntington, "The Change to Change; Modernization, Development and Politics," *Comparative Politics* (April 1971), p. 301.
4. See Mark Kesselman, *The Ambiguous Consensus: A Study of Local Politics in France* (New York: Alfred A. Knopf, 1967).
5. See H. Finer, *English Local Government* (London: Methuen, 1950).
6. See Christopher Hughes, *Confederacies* (Leicester: University of Leicester Press, 1963).
7. See E. C. Burnett, *The Continental Congress* (New York: Macmillan, 1941).
8. See Ivo D. Ducharek, *Comparative Federalism: The Territorial Dimension of Politics* (New York: Holt, Rinehart and Winston, 1970); and William H. Riker, *Federalism: Origin, Operation, Significance* (Boston: Little, Brown, 1964).
9. Daniel Elazar, "The Evolving Federal System," in Richard M. Pious, ed. *The Power to Govern* (New York: Academy of Political Science, 1981), pp. 5–19.

9

LEGISLATIVE-EXECUTIVE INSTITUTIONS

Every nation has a political system, and at its heart is a government performing the basic functions of policymaking, administration, and interpretation. This chapter begins our detailed examination of the institutions of government. While they vary in size, structure, and complexity, all government institutions fall into three broad categories: legislative, executive, and judicial. In this chapter we will look at the first two with an emphasis on their role in the policymaking process. Chapter 10 examines bureaucracies, those executive agencies that have taken on the job of administering the policies of government and have become so important that to many political scientists they constitute a separate branch of government. In Chapter 11 our attention turns to court systems and their role in interpreting policies and rules and resolving conflicts.

LEGISLATIVE-EXECUTIVE RELATIONSHIPS

The first matter that must be taken up is the relationship between legislative and executive institutions. We will be examining only some nations, since not all have a legislature. Traditional authoritarian systems usually function without one. For instance, all policy decisions in Saudi Arabia are made by the king and members of the royal family since there is no legislature. In other nations, a legislative body exists but does little more than ratify decisions made elsewhere in the political system—by the king, the army, or the ruling party. The Supreme Soviet of the Soviet Union is a very impressive institution with more than 1000 members, but its only real function is to rubber-stamp decisions by those higher up in the Soviet government and Communist Party.

While we should not ignore such largely ceremonial legislative bodies—they are, after all, a part of some very important political systems—our attention must turn to the legislatures of liberal democracies; in the United States, the United Kingdom, and West Germany, to mention only a few, legislatures such as Congress, Parliament, and the Bundestag actually play a crucial role in the making of policy. In these nations, we find the legislature and the principle of popular control developed to their fullest extent, since the members of most liberal democratic legislatures are popularly elected.

The governments of liberal democratic nations are based on either the **separation of powers** or **fusion of powers** principle.[1] In the former, legislative and executive functions are divided and allocated to separate institutions—thus the label *separation of powers*. In the latter, the two functions are combined in a single institution—thus the label *fusion of powers.* In addition, the separation of powers almost always implies an independent judiciary. We will see later on just how significant this has been in the United States. However, since most liberal democracies—even those that accept legislative and executive fusion—assume an independent judicial system, we will concentrate on executive legislative relationships.

The oldest government organized according to the separation of powers principle is the United States. Several other nations, including Costa Rica, Mexico, and Venezuela, have followed their northern neighbor's lead. Since the chief executive in the United States is called the President, such a system is called a **presidential system**. In 1958, France adopted a new constitution that made major changes in the French government. The Fifth Republic (actually the twelfth government since the French Revolution of 1789) seems to reflect the American presidential system; in fact, so much power was given to the president that it is difficult to speak of the balance between the executive and legislative.[2]

Most liberal democracies have modeled themselves after the British fusion of powers system. Thus, the United Kingdom, Canada, Australia, other British Commonwealth nations, most Western European nations, and Japan have governments in which a single institution, the legislature, is dominant because the chief executive is part of the legislature. This is called the **parliamentary system.**

This suggests that there are two methods for separating, or fusing, the legislative and executive functions. One, of course, is by establishing separate institutions, each with its own authority, or by combining the functions into a single institution. The other has to do with how government officials are selected. If the legislators and executives are selected independently of each other, and if being a member of one branch precludes one from simultaneously holding office in the other, then a separation of powers system has been created. This was clearly the intent of the framers of the Constitution of the United States when they established different methods for selecting the President, members of the Senate, and members of the House of Representatives, and specified that one could not be a member of the executive and legislative branches at the same time. Thus, a senator who is appointed to a position in the President's cabinet must leave the Senate. Or, a member of the cabinet who is elected to the Senate must resign the executive post.

A parliamentary system is designed to institutionalize what the presidential system prohibits. The chief executive (usually called the prime minister) is selected by the legislature and remains dependent on the legislature for his or her authority. Unlike the President in the separation of powers system, the prime minister in a fusion of powers system serves only as long as there is support from the parliament.

Since the presidential and parliamentary systems are different in structure, one would expect them to be justified with quite opposite theories.[3] Supporters of the separation of powers system argue that their system prevents what is to them the greatest political evil, a concentration of power. No one has stated the case more directly than James Madison, one of the architects of the American system: "No political truth is certainly the greater intrinsic value . . . than that . . . the accumulation of all powers, legislative, executive, and judiciary, in the same hands, whether of one or few or many, and whether hereditary, self-appointed, or elective may justly be pronounced the very definition of tyranny."[4]

Supporters of the parliamentary fusion of powers system suggest that governments based on the separation of powers principle are less efficient and responsible than they ought to be. Because power is divided, it is difficult to translate goals into policies, and since no one is really in charge, it is easy to "pass the buck." Thus, in the United States, the President and Congress can blame each other when something goes wrong. In a parliamentary system such as the United Kingdom's, the one branch of government must assume the responsibility—there is no other to pass the buck to. And, when the government makes a serious mistake, the prime minister can be forced to resign, unlike the President (who can blame Congress).

LEGISLATURES

We will discuss in more detail the role of executives in modern political systems, particularly in the British, French, and American systems, later in the chapter. The following section will focus on the functions and structures of legislatures in both parliamentary and presidential systems.[5]

The Functions of Legislatures

What is a legislature? Most people think immediately of their own political institutions: Congress, Parliament, the Knesset, the Diet, the Storting. This makes sense insofar as each legislature has developed its own unique characteristics within a particular political culture. But all democratic legislatures perform four functions, in one way or another: (1) pass laws, or statutes; (2) serve as representatives of the electorate; (3) monitor the executive branch of government; and (4) provide a forum for the public discussion of policy issues. The first, and probably most obvious, is passing laws, or statutes. To most people, legislators are lawmakers. They seem to spend most of their time debating and voting on proposed laws. The fact that we call the results of this activity **legislation** indicates the close link between legislatures and lawmaking. If we recognize that laws are actually rules and policies, then it seems reasonable to view the legislature as the primary policymaker of the liberal democracy.

However, it is wrong to assume that policymaking is the only function of legislatures. They also perform a *representative* function. Since in an indirect liberal democracy the people elect others to go off to the government and make decisions for them, these "others" (called representatives) tend to be concentrated in legislatures. Actually, the policymaking and representation functions are closely linked. After all, a policy reflects a particular set of interests; some stand to benefit more than others. When a policy decision is made to beef up the nation's navy rather than the air force or the army, shipbuilders will benefit. Thus, it would not be surprising to discover that legislators representing coastal states that are dependent on this industry have worked hard to get the policy enacted. Thus, not only individuals but economic and social groups gain representation through the legislature.

Some legislatures were created or have come to represent broad social interests. Historically, the two branches of the British Parliament developed to represent different segments of the society. **The House of Lords** was composed of and reflected the interests of the nobility—barons, dukes, and earls, who inherited their seats. **The House of Commons**, on the other hand, reflected the interests of the middle-and, later, the working class.

Some legislatures are designed to help maintain federal political systems. Thus, the legislature—or at least one branch of it—is set up to give the regional units (states, provinces, etc.) representation in the government. The structure of the U.S. Congress is the result of a political compromise that led not only to a separation of powers system, but also to a federal one. The Senate was established to give every state equal representation in the new federal union. Each state, whether large or small, has two senators and since the Senate votes according to the principle of majority rule, the small states gain equal power with the more populous ones. Similarly in West Germany, the two-house legislature consists of the Bundestag and the Bundesrat. The members of the Bundestag are elected by the people, while members of the Bundesrat represent the Länder, the main regional political units, similar to the states in the United States. While it is less powerful than the Bundestag, the Bundesrat still has the authority to prevent laws inimical to the interests of the Länder from being passed.

Legislatures exist not only to make policy and represent individuals, groups, and regions, but also to *monitor* (and even restrain) *the executive branch of government.* In the separation of powers system this function is essential since the system works only if each branch is able to limit the power of the other branches. Even when there is a strong executive who initiates most policies, the legislature must give its approval. Most legislatures in separation of powers systems have the "power of the purse"; that is, only they can appropriate the funds that the government spends. Some of the most powerful executives in history have been slowed to a crawl by a cautious legislature.[6]

Another way that a legislature can check the activities of the executive is through its ability to monitor, investigate, and publicize the activities of executives. Let us look at just one policymaking area as an example. In every political system, the chief executive has assumed the role of foreign policymaker, mainly because it is very difficult for the legislature to take the lead in this complex and delicate area of policymaking, where a premium is placed on quick decisions. The legislature can, however, make the foreign policymakers in the executive branch justify their decisions by investigating them and requiring public explanations. While this may appear to be an after-the-fact sort of check and not likely to bring about immediate changes in policy, it might make the executive branch more wary and perhaps more responsible in the making of future decisions.[7]

In its own way, the parliamentary system provides for legislative checks on the executive. The executive is part of the legislative system, and usually controls the legislative work by setting its agenda. However, since the prime minister's success depends on the support of the legislature, the threat of a withdrawal of support can be a real source of control for the legislature.[8]

One of the most important elements in the British parliamentary political culture is the idea of the **loyal opposition**. The leaders of the major party that has not gained control of Parliament are expected to become full-time critics of the governing party's proposals; they push and prod the prime minister and other government officials to justify the government's policies. This is often cited as part of the genius of the parliamentary system: the recognition that while government needs direction, it must also rule in a responsible manner.

Tied to the idea of an institutionalized opposition is the use in most parliamentary systems of the formal question-and-answer period. Legislators in the British, West German, and French systems have the right to ask their governments (in other words, the chief executives and their assistants) to answer questions dealing with policy decisions and indecisions. This usually includes written questions and answers and, in the House of Commons and the Bundestag, a one-hour period at the beginning of each legislative meeting, during which government leaders can be asked to orally defend their policies. The fact that this activity is not taken lightly is borne out by the fact that in recent years the members of the House of Commons asked their leaders nearly 27,000 questions per year, while in the Bundestag the number is a more modest but still substantial 4000. That these questions and answers are made part of the public record makes them that much more effective as a check on the executive.[9]

A fourth, and closely related, function of legislatures is to *serve as a forum for the public discussion of policy issues.* Some critics of modern legislatures see them as little more than debating societies where time is spent on speech-giving rather than policymaking. This criticism usually goes hand in hand with the assumption that the executive has taken over most of the policy initiation function, making the legislature little more than a noisy rubber stamp. Even if the assumption were true (most political scientists view it as an exaggeration of the truth), the discussion of policy in the legislature can itself serve a public function. Alternatives are sorted out, options are identified, and the public is informed. Even the most powerful executive can be influenced by public opinion; and it is possible for legislators to have an impact on the formation of this opinion through their speeches and debates.[10]

How Legislatures Are Structured

Now that we have considered the basic functions of legislatures, let us examine some of the structural features of legislatures that have an impact on the policymaking process. The most important one has already been discussed and it will be taken up again in the last section of the chapter. This is the formal relationship that exists between the legislature and executive, fused or separate. At this point we are more interested in the internal structure of the legislative institutions.

The first, and most obvious, structural feature is whether the legislature is **unicameral** or **bicameral**. A unicameral legislature has only one house, or chamber. Examples can be found in Denmark, Finland, Israel, Costa Rica, and Sweden. A bicameral legislature has two houses. They can be equal in power, as in the United States Congress, where both the House of Representatives and Senate can initiate legislation and where both must approve of a bill before it becomes law. Or, the houses can be so unequal in power that one totally controls the legislative process while the other remains largely a remnant of the past. Such is the case in the United Kingdom, where even though Parliament is divided into two branches, in reality the House of Lords has been almost completely eclipsed by the House of Commons.

In still other bicameral legislatures, one house has become dominant but the other continues to perform important functions. In West Germany, for instance, the Bundestag is clearly the more powerful branch of the legislature. But the other branch, the Bundesrat, is not insignificant. We have already noted that the main function of the Bundesrat is to represent the Länder, the regional units of government in the federal government. Each Länder sends delegates to the Bundesrat who vote as a unit under the direction of their Land government. While the Bundesrat initiates few laws, its approval is necessary for the passing of major legislation. Thus, the interests of various regions of West Germany are represented.

A number of other structural features help shape the legislative process. One of the most important is the way that legislators are selected. The method of selection is a good indicator of what a legislative body is intended to do. It is interesting to note, for instance, that the more powerful houses among bicameral legislatures—the House of Representatives and Senate in the United States, the House of Commons in the United Kingdom, and the Bundestag in West Germany, for example—are elected directly by the people. It is equally true, on the other hand, that the legislative houses that are indirectly elected (such as the French Senate and the West German Bundesrat) or not elected at all (such as the British House of Lords) have less power. Is this a coincidence or a reflection of the centrality of popular control in liberal democracies? In fact, it is the latter; as political systems become more democratic, the democratically elected branch assumes more significance.

Another set of structural factors has to do with the way each house of the legislature organizes itself around such internal features as committees and political parties. We will have more to say about these factors later in the chapter when we examine and compare the policymaking process in several nations. For now, let us simply point out that in some legislatures—the American Congress being the prime example— the most important legislative work is done by a large number of standing committees (15 in the Senate, 22 in the House of Representatives) organized on a functional basis, that is, according to various subject areas: foreign policy, agriculture, defense, banking, and so on. A legislative proposal goes first to an appropriate committee where it is discussed, supported, reshaped, or rejected. It is usually the case that if the committee rejects the proposal, it is effectively dead—it will probably never make it to the full legislature for further consideration. If the committee supports the bill, chances are the legislature will accept its recommendation. What this all suggests is a very decentralized legislative system with power divided among the various committees and their chairmen.

Senator Bob Dole, left, the minority leader, and Senator Bob Packard, chairman of the Finance Committee, celebrate the committee's unanimous approval of a tax-revision bill.

The British Parliament presents a quite different picture of legislative organization. Instead of powerful subject-matter committees, Parliament has only eight non-subject-matter (and thus nonspecialized) committees. Instead of titles such as Foreign Relations Committee, British parliamentary committees are simply labeled A, B, C, D and so on. This suggests the reality of the situation: while bills are assigned to committees, the real legislative work is performed by the prime minister and his or her cabinet.

These quite different organizational tendencies are reinforced by the nature of political parties in each of the two legislative bodies. British political parties are highly disciplined. That is, they are well organized with control flowing from top to bottom. Thus, when party leaders in Parliament make a proposal, they can expect the members of their party to vote accordingly. In Congress, on the other hand, parties are not nearly as well disciplined. There is less cohesiveness and less control from top to bottom. Legislative leaders can be much less confident that when they announce the party's position, its members in the legislature will vote "the party line." Thus, in the United States Congress, the decentralized influence of the committee system is reinforced by relatively undisciplined parties; in the British Parliament, weak committees and disciplined parties go hand in hand. Later in this chapter, we will study their impact on the decision-making process.

EXECUTIVES

Having examined the functions that legislatures perform and some of the main structural features that provide the framework for legislative decision making, let us now turn our attention to the functions and structure of the executive institutions of government. (In the last section of the chapter, we will put the legislative and executive back together again by describing the policymaking process in several nations. This is not only the best way to get a feel for the way decisions are really made but also to gain an appreciation of the richness of the political process.)

Some have called the twentieth century the "age of the executive" because of the widely held impression that power in every political system has gravitated toward the executive branch of government.[11] In liberal democracies legislatures have gotten weaker, the argument goes, and executives have picked up the slack. If this impression is an accurate one—and there is reason to believe that it is—then this century is not the first age of the executive. The great political leaders of the past—among them Julius Caesar, Henry VIII, and Napoleon—have been chief executives.

This is surely to be expected since liberal democracy and its popularly elected legislatures have been with us less than two centuries. Thus, in pre-democratic political systems the executive has clearly been dominant. And, in contemporary authoritarian and totalitarian regimes (remember, most of the nations of the world fall into these categories), executives rule with little or no restraint from legislatures. But (and this is the most significant point) even in liberal democracies the executive has increased its power.

One reason is the high visibility of executives relative to legislatures. When we think of American politics, the names of Presidents come to mind; in the United Kingdom, it is Churchill and Thatcher; in France, de Gaulle and Mitterand. Executives are the "celebrities," the household names of politics because they are at the center of things, because they seem to be the ones who make things happen. More news reports deal with the comings and goings of Presidents and prime ministers than of the congressmen and members of Parliament. In the

United States the most prestigious beat for a television or newspaper reporter is the White House because that is where the action is.

The fact that executives tend to be the celebrities of politics does not necessarily mean, however, that they are more powerful than legislators. They may simply be more interesting to watch and read about. Appearances are often misleading; however, in this case, appearances lead one to the basic truth—perceptions of growing executive power are fairly accurate.

The question is, Why have executives increased their power in almost every modern political system? Some of the reasons are fairly obvious. Modern politics usually requires quick decisions, something that slower-moving and more deliberative legislative institutions are not particularly good at. Modern political decisions often require specialized knowledge, something that the executive branch usually has more of. Modern political systems always need some sort of coordinating force, something that compact executive institutions do better than large legislatures. And the trends in modern politics seem to point in the direction of an increasingly powerful executive. A student of European politics put it this way more than twenty years ago: "All government bodies have found their duties increasing in many respects. These duties, however, do not seem to have been evenly distributed. It has become commonplace to remark that parliamentary assemblies are ill-suited to the new responsibilities assumed by twentieth-century governments and that the larger share of these responsibilities has devolved upon the executive branch."[12] The common thread that seems to run through each reason is the need that every political system has for leadership, the kind of leadership that executives can provide.

Types of Political Executives

So we know that executives are supposed to be leaders, not because they are any smarter than other decision makers but because the complexity of modern politics has thrust them to center stage. Almost everyone has an idea of what an executive is, but most of us have difficulty coming up with a neat definition. When we concentrate on political executives, things get even trickier because presidents, prime ministers, kings, and dictators seem to do so many different things.

Actually, we can identify three basic executive roles that have to be filled in every political system: (1) chief administrator, (2) chief policymaker, and (3) chief of state. Sometimes these are combined into a single executive office; often, they are divided among several offices.

Political executives are supposed to be the *chief administrators* of their political systems. They are expected to administer, to execute the policies of their governments. The institutions that have been entrusted with the actual administration of governmental policies are so important that we will devote an entire chapter, Chapter 10, to them.

A second role of executives is that of *chief policymaker.* We have seen that in liberal democracies legislatures play a significant part in the policymaking process. The point here is simply that the executive's role is also important and usually dominant. The third basic role of the executive is to act as **chief of state**, that is, symbolic and ceremonial head of the political system. Together, administration, policymaking, and acting as the symbol of the nation define the political executive.

Before we examine the functions of modern political executives in more detail let us consider the different types of chief executives that might be found in the political systems of the world. There are two central questions to ask of each type: How is the executive selected and replaced? (Political scientists call this the *recruitment* process.) and To whom or what is the executive responsible within the social and political systems? In effect, these two questions define the scope of executive authority.

The first kind of executive is found as *leader of primitive tribal societies.* Because of the influence of the Western nations on less-developed areas, it has become more difficult to find examples, but they still exist and fortunately, some anthropologists have spent great amounts of time observing and describing the tribal executive. One such anthropologist, a student of African tribal societies, has said this about the chief of the Nuer tribe of East Africa: "He will not become leader unless his personality commands prestige; this he may gain from a reputation for his prowess in fighting in his youth, for skill in debate, or for ritual powers (which are believed to be inherited). A man who has gained prestige in these various ways may be able to build it up further by marriage alliances with similarly placed men in other villages; others may attain their position in the first instance through such alliances."[13] Thus, the chief's authority is a result of demonstrable leadership, ritualistic-religious powers, and political skill.

The Nuer leader, called the "bull," has one main function: to lead the tribe and its only source of livelihood (cattle), from camp to camp in search of water. Once he has established his authority, the bull is followed without question. However, while the bull's authority is to a large extent religiously sanctioned, his continued authority depends somewhat on his ability to make good decisions about when and where to move the tribe. Thus, he is in a sense responsible to the tribe.

It is clear that this kind of tribal executive, while obviously political, presides over what can only be considered a minimal government. Let us now consider executives who have authority in more complex political systems. The first is the **absolute monarch**, called by some a despot. The absolute monarch claims he is responsible to no one, except perhaps God. Thus, it is not surprising that many have claimed **divine right**; that is, their authority is granted to them by God and so they are responsible only to God. There have been examples of divine right monarchies in all eras from ancient to modern times, but the best examples are to be found in the annals of medieval European history. The most famous was probably Louis XIV of France, who reigned from 1643 to 1715 as the "Sun King." The status of the absolute monarch was simply stated when Louis said, "I am the state." Such an executive rules with unlimited power—no other sources of political authority are recognized and so one would not expect to find a functioning legislature existing alongside an absolute monarch. There is no doubt that he performs all of the basic executive functions: administrative, policymaking, and symbolic.

It is not inaccurate to view the absolute monarch as a further development of the tribal executive. The monarch has simply increased the scope of his power. It is thus no accident that one of the best examples of an absolute monarchy, the government of Saudi Arabia, was built on a tribal foundation. The present Saudi royal family reigns as the result of decades of military activity and political maneuvering during which the tribes of the Arabian peninsula were brought under the authority of the Saud family. Officially, the royal family has unlimited power. But, because there are more than 4000 princes, including several hundred who actually participate in the governing of the nation, decisions are often the result of a consensus-building process. However, and this is the most important point, the monarch who of course is the head of the royal family is the ultimate authority, responsible theoretically only to God and the Islamic religion. Realistically, he has to maintain the support of the tribes and the other powerful princes.

We can make several generalizations about absolute monarchies. First, most are sanctioned by (receive their legitimacy from) religious sources. Second, authority is usually inherited. The royal family is the source of authority—the eldest son at any given time is the representative of the family's claim. There can be changes in the royal succession as one royal family replaces another. This happened in medieval Europe and it happened in Arabia when the Saud family reclaimed their land from the rival Rashid family. But, once a family has established itself, authority is passed from one generation to the next.

A number of absolute monarchies have evolved into **constitutional**, or **limited, monarchies**. This means that while the monarchy retains status as the dominant executive office, its authority is no longer recognized as unlimited and divinely sanctioned. Instead, the monarch rules within the limits specified by other institutions, often a legislature. One of the key shifts in the political culture is the recognition that the monarchy is responsible to the society, that the monarch is not above the law.

This transition from an absolute to a constitutional monarchy took place in Great Britain in one century. At the beginning of the seventeenth century British kings were claiming divine right and the unlimited authority that that claim implies. Eighty years, and a civil war later, the British monarchy had become a limited executive office, sharing authority with a parliament and recognizing the restraints of a set of rules, a constitution. The authority of the constitutional monarch is inherited, but unlike the unlimited monarchy, ultimate authority is derived from the society through its constitution.

As the nations of Western Europe became more democratic during the nineteenth and twentieth centuries, their monarchies lost all real administrative and policymaking power. But, in most cases, they remain as the symbols of their nation; they still fill the role of chief of state. It is interesting to note that the constitutional monarchies of today—the United Kingdom, the Netherlands, Sweden, Norway, Denmark, Belgium, Japan, and Liechtenstein (which, appropriate to its size, has a prince instead of a king)—rank at the top of anyone's list of democratic nations.

This brings us to the next type of executive office, **the military dictator**. One recent study concluded that eighty-one nations have experienced an attempted military takeover during the twentieth century. Another study found that between 1946 and 1970, the military tried to take over the government in fifty-five nations.[14] Some of them were unsuccessful, but a significant number of existing governments have been established by the seizure of power by a segment of the military.

We call this seizure of power by a military elite a **coup d'etat**— literally, a "blow against the state." The military leaders who come to power in this fashion either set themselves up as political executives (often with a change of title from General to President) or designate civilian leaders and perhaps even allow elections, but retain ultimate authority through the power to veto any decision that they find unacceptable. In some cases, a military dictatorship evolves into a fairly stable regime in which power is passed from one leader to the next with minimal amounts of instability. In the process, the system moves from military rule to civilian rule with military support. This is what took place in Egypt.

In other cases, such as in Nigeria, the nation moves through a series of coups d'etat, as one group of military officers after another becomes dissatisfied with the existing military regime. This, of course, means long periods of instability. In either case, the military dictatorship must retain the support of the military if it is to retain its power.

Even though some military executives carry out social and political reforms and thus seem to feel some responsibility to their people, on a more basic level they are ultimately responsible to the military forces who put them into power and who have the potential to remove them.

Military dictatorships must not be confused with one other type of political executive, the **totalitarian dictator**. The two have some common features: the totalitarian executive sometimes takes power after a coup d'etat, but at other times results from a more massive uprising, a revolution. In either case, totalitarian dictators differ from military dictators because of their attempt to legitimize themselves by means of an ideology or religion and their attempt to gain total control of the society.

We discussed the nature of totalitarian systems in Chapter 5, so we need not go over that ground again. We are at this point interested in the kind of executive leadership that emerges in such systems. Again, they base their authority on a set of principles contained in a particular ideology or religion; the leaders claim that they have the truth on their side, and thus are entitled to administer the nation and make its basic policies. Good examples of totalitarian dictatorships are the Marxist-Leninist regimes of the Soviet Union and China. Likewise, the current system of Iran is dominated by clergymen who have proclaimed the existence of an Islamic republic, a nation based on Moslem principles and led by executives who gain their authority through their commitment to the "true" religion.

Transitions of power in totalitarian dictatorships are often as unstable as they are in military dictatorships. One of the reasons is the tendency toward the personalization of power. Thus Stalin, the Soviet leader who succeeded Lenin, became a ruthless dictator, more important than the Marxist ideology that legitimized him. Since his death, Soviet leaders have made a conscious effort to rely on collective leadership. The move toward collective leadership was punctuated with a program of **destalinization**, which began in 1956, three years after Stalin's death. Destalinization involved the removal of Stalin's name from thousands of buildings, monuments, and towns. The most striking change took place in 1961 when Stalingrad, a major city on the Volga River, was renamed Volgograd. The final act of destalinization came the same year with the removal of Stalin's body from the Lenin Mausoleum, where it had rested next to the father of Russian Communism.

However, executive succession within any totalitarian system is still more the result of a struggle for power than any institutionalized process. As of this writing, the Ayatollah Khomeini is still the chief executive of Iran, but because of his advanced age, we can assume that the internal struggle for power that will determine Khomeini's successor has already begun. And in the Soviet Union, we have seen the outward signs of the succession process as three chief executives died within a few years. All indications are that the present political chief, Mikhail Gorbachev, is doing a masterful job of consolidating his power.

The last two types of executives are found in liberal democracies. They are the **president** of the separation of powers system and **prime minister** of the fusion of powers system.[15] In both cases, they gain their authority from and are ultimately responsible to the people and a constitution that indicates the limits of the executive's power. In each case the executive is elected, serves a term in office, and then is replaced in a peaceful fashion with another election. Thus, it is the electoral process that actually legitimizes the democratic executive.

The most important differences between the President and the prime minister are the method of election and the relationship with the legislative branch of government. As we have seen, the President is elected directly by a vote of the people, the prime minister by a vote of the parliament whose members are elected by the people. This makes the prime minister more dependent on the legislature and at the same time more in control of the legislature. The President, on the other hand, in being independently elected does not have to depend on the legislature for power but is less able to control it.

There are several variations on the presidential theme. We have already discussed the President of the United States and will have occasion to, again, in the next section. The main points to remember are that even though it is a powerful office, the presidency is limited by the not-insignificant powers of Congress. In France, the presidential office created by the Constitution of 1958 is given even more powers than the presidency of the United States. The French society, searching for a resolution of their problems, turned to their World War II hero, Charles de Gaulle; a new constitution was written, custom-built for the new president.

Like the American President, the French president is elected by the people and is thus independent of the French legislature, but the French president is given the power to nominate the premier who leads the legislature; this means, in effect, that the president gains significant control of the legislative process. In addition, the president of France sets the legislature's order of business and can dissolve it (no more than once a year). The president can also assume even greater powers in times of national emergency and can bypass the legislature by taking proposals directly to the people in the form of referenda. A wise president does not use this power indiscriminately. But when used with discretion, the mere threat of a referendum can overcome the resistance of even the most stubborn legislature.

The powers of the French president do not stop here; perhaps the most significant one is the power to control the purse strings of government. The president draws up the budget and proposes it to the legislature, which in turn can make no changes; if it does not approve the budget within seventy days, the president's proposal becomes law anyway. (There must be times when the President of the United States dreams of such power.)

What we see in the French presidency is an American President with even more power and fewer limitations. The president is truly the center of the French political system. President de Gaulle said it best: "The president elected by the nation is the source and holder of the power of the state."[16] However, the French parliamentary election of 1986 indicates that problems can occur. A coalition of conservative parties won a small majority in the National Assembly, thus creating a unique situation for the Fifth Republic—a president of one party having to govern alongside a legislature of the other party. The power of the French president has never before been put to this kind of test.

Another presidential system that concentrates great power in the hands of the executive is found in Mexico.[17] There, the president finds it relatively easy to get policies accepted by a legislature even weaker than the French one. One of the main reasons is the existence of a political party system in which one party, the Institutional Revolutionary Party (PRI), is dominant. While the president and the legislature are elected independently, they are always dominated by the PRI. Thus, the Mexican president can always count on near-unanimous support in the legislature.

Another interesting feature of the Mexican presidential system has to do with the way that a successor is selected. This must happen every six years since the president is allowed to serve only a single, six-year term. An election is held, and even though other parties are allowed to participate, the PRI always wins (its presidential candidate received 94.4 percent of the vote in 1976). Thus, the real selection takes place when the PRI slates its next presidential candidate. After consultation with other party leaders, the incumbent president selects his successor. Thus, while the election serves a legitimizing function, the selection is mainly a function of the inner circle of the party.

Functions of Political Executives

Now that we have examined the main types of political executives, let us return to the functions that they perform. We noted that executives are administrators, policymakers, and symbols of their nations. We will now look at these roles in more detail by breaking them down into more specific categories. Thomas Cronin, a political scientist who is a student of the American presidency, has identified seven functions that the President performs.[18] With some adjustments, his categories can be used to describe the executives of all political systems.

First of all, there must be an executive office that serves as the symbolic head of the nation, and is given such ceremonial tasks as welcoming foreign dignitaries. This role, which we have labeled *chief of state*, exists in every political system. In some cases it is combined with the roles of policymaker and administrator. Thus, the President of the United States is all three. In other systems, the three roles are split in such a way that one executive is chief of state while the policy and administrative functions are performed by a second executive.

The best example of this system is found in the United Kingdom. The monarch is the chief of state, possessing only ceremonial powers, while the prime minister is the true political executive of the nation. Thus, it is Queen Elizabeth II who travels around the world representing her nation.

In the Soviet Union we find another, actually more flexible, arrangement. The structure of the Soviet political system is incredibly complex, with numerous governmental and party offices and agencies. In sorting them out, we can identify three important executive positions. The first and most powerful is the **General Secretary of the Communist Party**. This is the chief policymaking post in the Soviet system and its importance is an indication of the control that the Communist Party has over the political system. **The Chairman of the Council of Ministers** is the chief administrator of the Soviet government. He oversees the various ministries which are entrusted with the task of implementing the policies of the Communist Party. The third position, equivalent to the chief of state, is the **Chairman** or **President of the Supreme Soviet**. It must be reiterated that these are three separate executive offices and they are often filled by three separate individuals. Since it is largely a ceremonial post, the Chairman of the Supreme Soviet is usually reserved for an elder statesman of the party. However, Leonid Brezhnev filled the position while he functioned as secretary of the party.

In many other authoritarian politital systems the role of symbolic leader is thoroughly integrated with the role of policymaker. This is especially true in those nations that have been created or restructured through the leadership of a single strong personality—Mao Tse-tung in China, Fidel Castro in Cuba, or Moammar Khadafy in Libya.

Perhaps the function that has had the greatest impact on the growth of the executive in modern political systems, is that of *crisis manager*. The world has become more and more complex; social, economic, and political change occur at an ever-increasing rate. The result is a continual series of crises, both domestic and international. Thus, quick decisions are needed, which only a centrally located executive can make. The function of crisis management cuts across political systems. Prime ministers, presidents, chairmen, and kings have all been thrust into the role.

The basic policymaking role of the political executive is that of *priority setting*. In laying out the basic priorities of the system, the executive decides what can and must be done and ultimately, who will get what. The best indicator of the government's priorities is its budget, for it is the budget that translates priorities into concrete reality; and in most political systems, the executive has taken the initiative in budget-making. In the United States, Congress still plays an important role, but it is more that of reactor, reviser, and ratifier than initiator of budgets. The President and his executive staff have gained the upper hand. In France, as we have seen, the president can in effect write his own budget with little interference from the legislators. And, in the Soviet Union, the budget is the product of party and government leaders.

Once the priorities of government are devised, the chief executive must seek the support of others in the political system. It is at this point that *coalition building* takes place, even in the most authoritarian regimes, since no executive has complete control of the system. As many commentators have pointed out, the American President must be a skillful politician—he must be able to use power to get his policies accepted. This could be said of all executives.

This process of building support differs from system to system, but it goes on in all of them. In democracies it means gaining the support of the legislature, building a coalition of powerful groups (business and labor, for instance), and, finally, appealing to the mass public. The most successful presidents have been those who were good at all three techniques. In totalitarian regimes, executive leaders must constantly retain the support of other government and party leaders. In military dictatorships the dictators must retain the support of the military; many have found out the hard way just how crucial this is. We have seen that even in the classic monarchy, the monarch must actively seek the support of other family or tribal leaders if he or she is to retain control of the system.

Once the government's policies are adopted, they must be carried out. The function of *policy implementation* always falls to the chief executive under the role of chief administrator. We will discuss the implementation and administration of government policy more fully in the next chapter.

Closely related to the function of policy implementation is that of *government overseeing*. The chief executive is expected to monitor and coordinate the various activities of the government. These are very difficult (some would say impossible) tasks, but if anyone can do it, it is the executive. This also means that the chief executive must delegate a great deal of authority to subordinate executives.

The final executive function is the *recruitment of other executives.* No chief executive can do everything; some have tried, but none have succeeded. An executive who tries, usually gets so bogged down in detail that he loses the perspective required for big decisions. Thus, the mark of good political executives is the quality of the cabinet they appoint and the advisors they listen to.

One other point can be made in this regard. In some systems, one of the most important leadership-recruitment decisions made by the executive is that of selecting—or at least, influencing the selection of—a successor. In authoritarian and totalitarian systems the preference of the retiring or aging leader is taken seriously. And even in more democratic regimes, especially dominant ones such as the Mexican system, the final decision is often made by the incumbent.

A final comment about the functions of the political executive seems in order. In some systems, the functions are concentrated in a single executive. In others, they are allocated to several offices. In either case, an amazingly varied and important set of tasks have been given to a relatively small number of decision makers.

HOW GOVERNMENTS MAKE POLICIES

We will conclude this chapter by describing the policymaking process in three nations: the United States, the United Kingdom, and the Soviet Union. This is a good way to see how differently structured governments make decisions, and how the various executive and legislative institutions interact. Since we cannot examine the government of every nation, three very important ones have been selected. Two are liberal democracies, each with a different governmental structure; the other is the most powerful nondemocratic nation in the world.

A student of the policymaking process can make it as complex as he or she wants, since policies are always the result of a multiplicity of factors. The emphasis in this brief presentation is on the role of major institutions—how policies flow through the government. In Chapters 12 and 13, we will turn our attention to the role of individuals, political parties, and interest groups in this process.

The policy process can be broken down into four stages: *initiation,* when the policy is initially formulated; *consideration,* when the policy is discussed, supported, and opposed; *decision,* when the policy (or its modified version) is approved or rejected by the appropriate political institutions; and *implementation,* when the approved policy is put into effect. The discussion that follows is based on the first three stages; since policy implementation is the main function of bureaucracies, that stage will be the focal point of the next chapter.

Policymaking in the United States

In the United States, policies can be initiated in the executive or legislative branch; but, because of the separation of powers system, they must usually be approved by both branches. In addition, since there are two equal branches of the legislature, each must approve a proposal before it becomes law. Let us trace a typical policy proposal through the government process. Suppose the President decides to support the secretary of education's proposal to begin a massive new college student loan program. Once it is drawn up, the proposal is sent to one of the branches of Congress—for our purposes, let us say it is the House of Representatives. It is sponsored by one or more members of Congress and placed into the legislative process. The next step is to refer it to a committee where, as we have seen, the really important legislative work takes place. The committee will decide whether to consider the bill, whether to change it and, finally, whether to approve or reject it. It is at the committee stage that most of the political activity takes place. Interested groups, members of the executive branch, and even the President himself let the legislators know how they feel and attempt to influence their decisions. The committee holds hearings to gather information but also to provide an opportunity for propagandists to state their point of view.

Many bills have to be considered by several committees. After consideration by the appropriate subject-matter committee (in our case, Education and Labor) the proposed bill, if supported by the committee, will be sent to the Appropriations Committee if government expenditures are involved.

If the bill makes it to the floor of the House, it is debated, amended, and then passed or defeated. If passed, it is sent to the other branch of Congress (in our case, the Senate). The Senate may have already been considering the same or a similar bill. If not, chances are it will make further changes in the House bill. If the Senate approves a bill that is not the same as the House version, a conference committee has to be formed. Made up of members of each branch, the conference committee tries to come up with a bill that both houses can live with. The compromise bill is sent to each house; if both pass it, it is sent to the President. If he signs the bill it becomes law; if he vetoes it, the bill becomes law only if two-thirds of each house vote to override it.

What conclusions can be drawn about the policy process in the United States? First, because of the separation of powers system, there is a need for cooperation between the President and the two branches of Congress. Second, the policy process is complicated and decentralized—out of about 10,000 legislative proposals, only about 10 percent are passed in each session. Third, the President has taken much of the policy initiative, but his proposals are not always approved by Congress. During the 1950s, 1960s, and 1970s, the President's "success rate" was 44 percent.

Policymaking in the United Kingdom

Since the British government is based on the fusion of powers principle, we should expect policymaking to be more efficient and centralized. Let us begin with a few basic features of the British political system. In the general election, each party slates candidates for the nearly 600 seats in the House of Commons. After the election, the party that gains a majority of seats selects its leader as the prime minister. The prime minister then appoints a ministry (the heads of various government departments, numbering about 100) and a cabinet (the most important ministers, numbering about 20 who become the main advisors to the prime minister). The prime minister and the ministry are collectively called *the government.*

The prime minister and the cabinet become the main initiators of legislation. The House of Commons reacts to their proposals; the majority party almost always supports its leader and the minority party can be counted on to question the prime minister's proposals. If the prime minister loses a vote, he or she can resign or ask for a **vote of confidence.** This means exactly what it says. The prime minister asks the legislators if they still have confidence in the government. A "no" vote leads to the prime minister's resignation. Actually, although prime ministers have resigned, only rarely have they done so because of a negative vote (only four times since 1894). The important point is that the prime minister's ability to get proposals passed depends on the support of Parliament. But remember, a prime minister who resigns can also dissolve Parliament. So, members of Parliament, especially those of the prime minister's party, must think twice before voting against the prime minister.

After the bill is proposed to the House of Commons, its general principles are debated. Debate is often heated and the opposition party tries its best to find weak points in the government's proposal. If the house passes the bill, it is sent to a committee whose job it is to review the bill and perhaps propose amendments; the committee cannot itself amend the bill. The bill is then returned to the House of Commons with any proposed amendments. It is debated again and a final vote is taken. If the bill passes, as it usually does, it is sent to the House of Lords. This once-dominant house of Parliament has become almost powerless. It can review, even temporarily delay, an act of Commons; but there is little it can do to change or defeat one. Thus, the House of Lords is not really part of the policy process. The same can be said of the British monarch. All acts of Parliament must be signed by the Queen to become law; but this is a formality, since she always does.

What conclusions can be drawn about the British policy process? First, the only important institution is the House of Commons. Second, parties are stronger and committees weaker than in the American system. Third, the policy process is therefore more centralized and efficient, and the prime minister has more control of the process than the President (during the 1950s and 1960s, Parliament passed 96 percent of the prime minister's proposals).

Policy Making in the Soviet Union

Structurally, the Soviet policymaking process is too complex to compress into a short discussion such as this.[19] In addition, since it is not a democratic process, more goes on behind closed doors—thus the process is more difficult to describe. However, an outline of the network of institutions can be drawn and the process that takes place within can be understood if several basic principles are emphasized.

First, we must appreciate the great significance of the Communist Party and its control of the political system. The government is not unimportant, but it is secondary to the Party when it comes to policymaking. A second point has to do with the hierarchical and centralized nature of the Soviet political system. That is, every organization, whether party or governmental, is based on the model of the pyramid—a few leaders on the top, with more and more followers toward the bottom, and a chain of command going from top to bottom. Most organizations are to some extent hierarchical, but few come close to that of the Soviet system.

All policy proposals come from the Communist Party's **Politburo**, its most important policymaking agency. The Politburo's twenty or so members are the most powerful persons in the party; they also fill the top leadership posts in the Soviet government. They meet, discuss, even debate, policy questions. But after agreement takes place, their public face is one of unanimity.

Policies become official when they are adopted by the Soviet government. Since the Party dominates the system, and since the top government leaders are also Party leaders, the role of the government is to translate the broad policies of the party into workable government programs. The **Supreme Soviet** might be thought of as the Soviet Union's legislature. It is composed of two houses with a total membership of around 1500 members. The main function of the Supreme Soviet is to ratify the decisions made at higher levels. That this is a rubber-stamp activity is clearly indicated by the fact that the Supreme Soviet's votes are always unanimous.

Real government power is possessed by the **Council of Ministers**. It proposes policies to the Supreme Soviet (which, of course, always approves them) and issues binding decrees on its own. Thus, the Council of Ministers and its core group of leaders—the Presidium—are the main source of governmental policies. However, our analysis comes full-circle when we realize that the Presidium always follows the policy proposals of the Politburo. Thus, while there is an elaborate set of political institutions in the Soviet system, it is clear that policy initiatives come from the Party. As we will see in the next chapter, the government, especially the Council of Ministers, is more important at the stage of policy implementation.

SUMMARY

The policymaking and policy administration functions of government are carried out in different ways in different political systems. In some, both executive and legislative branches are involved; in other systems, the executive branch performs both functions.

Liberal democracies tend to follow one of two structural models. In the presidential-congressional system, power is separated between the executive and legislative branches so as to prevent a concentration of political power. In the parliamentary system, power is fused—a single branch performs both legislative and executive functions, with the goal being a more politically responsible government.

Legislatures can be compared according to their functions and main structural features. The variety is great, but there seems to be a relationship between the structure of the legislature and the type of political parties the system has.

There are many kinds of political chief executives, from monarchs to military dictators to democratic presidents and prime ministers. The greatest differences exist between democratic and nondemocratic executives, since the latter are never limited by (separation of powers) or part of (parliamentary) a powerful and popularly elected legislature.

NOTES

1. See Don K. Price and Harold J. Laski, "A Debate on the Parliamentary and Presidential Systems," in Roy C. Macridis and Bernard E. Brown, eds., *Comparative Politics: Notes and Readings* (Homewood, Ill.: The Dorsey Press, 1961), pp. 365–381.
2. See Roy Pierce, *French Politics and Political Institutions* (New York: Harper and Row, 1973), for a discussion of the French presidential system.
3. See Price and Laski, "Parliamentary and Presidential Systems."
4. James Madison, *The Federalist*, Number 47.

5. For a good general discussion of democratic legislatures, see K. C. Wheare, *Legislatures* (New York: Oxford University Press, 1968).
6. Even Charles I, King of England from 1625–1649 and a believer in the divine right of kings and absolute monarchy, found his military ambitions limited by Parliament.
7. For a discussion of presidential-congressional relationships in the foreign policy area, see Thomas E. Cronin, *The State of the Presidency* (Boston: Little, Brown, 1980), chap. 6.
8. For a discussion of the British parliamentary system, see Ivor Jennings, *Cabinet Government* (New York: Cambridge University Press, 1969).
9. For a discussion of the legislative question-and-answer period, see John E. Schwarz and L. Earl Shaw, *The United States Congress in Comparative Perspective* (Hinsdale, Ill.: The Dryden Press, 1976), chap. 7.
10. The Watergate and Vietnam episodes lend support to this contention.
11. For the application of this argument to the American President, see Arthur M. Schlesinger, Jr., *The Imperial Presidency* (Boston: Houghton Mifflin, 1973).
12. Jean Meynaud, "The Executive in the Modern State," in Roy C. Macridis and Bernard E. Brown, eds., *Comparative Politics: Notes and Readings*, p. 342.
13. Lucy Mair, *Primitive Government* (Baltimore: Penguin Books, 1962), p. 64.
14. Monte Palmer and William Thompson, *The Comparative Analysis of Politics* (Itasca, Ill.: F. E. Peacock Publishers, 1978), pp. 137–138.
15. Richard Rose and Ezra N. Suleiman, eds., *Presidents and Prime Ministers* (Washington, D.C.: American Enterprise Institute, 1980).
16. Quoted in Jean Lacoutäe, *De Gaulle* trans. Francis Price (New York: New American Library, 1965), p. 173.
17. See L. V. Padgett, *The Mexican Political System* (Boston: Houghton Mifflin, 1976).
18. Cronin, *The State of the Presidency,* chap. 5.
19. See Frederick A. Barghoom, *Politics in the U.S.S.R.* (Boston: Little, Brown, 1972), for a fuller discussion. Also see Vadim Medich, *The Soviet Union* (Englewood Cliffs, N.J.: Prentice-Hall, 1985).

10

BUREAUCRACIES

One of the most obvious facts of politics is that policies formulated by legislatures and executives mean little unless they are implemented, unless they are actually applied to the society. It is just as obvious that the handful of legislators and executives who are at the heart of the policymaking process cannot be expected to administer their policies to populations numbering in the tens, even hundreds, of millions. Thus, specialized administrative agencies are created to perform this task. Called **bureaucracies,** they are supposed to be efficient and evenhanded in their administration of government policy; many have called them *nonpolitical.*

The last statement is based on the assumption that *politics* and *administration* are very different activities. The former involves the making of policy and all the power moves and wheeling and dealing that policymaking implies; the latter refers to the rational administration of the policies, whatever they are. We are not surprised to find that politicians are working for particular interests (their own, their supporters', or their constituents'); we are supposed to be surprised if bureaucrats do anything except carry out the policies that have been handed to them. After all, bureaucrats are merely agents of a political system; it is their profession to administer its policies.

This clear-cut distinction has been part of political science for a number of years, but more and more political scientists have come to question its precision. Although it is a good way to start our analysis— it emphasizes the policy-implementing function of bureaucracies—the distinction has been recognized as a much too simplified view of political reality because as a matter of fact bureaucracies develop political power of their own and do have an impact on policymaking. Thus, the fundamental purposes of this chapter are threefold: to discuss the role of bureaucracies in the policy implementation process; to consider how they get involved in policymaking itself; and to consider why some political scientists feel bureaucracies are so important that they can be called the "core of modern government."[1]

WHAT IS BUREAUCRACY?

A political scientist who has spent much time studying bureaucracies has defined them as "large, fairly permanent social systems designed to achieve limited objectives through the coordinated activities of their members."[2] This definition gives us the bare bones of bureaucracy; we will flesh it out later in the chapter. But before that, it should be made clear that although many people associate bureaucracy and government—they assume that the only bureaucrats are found in government—as a matter of fact all large organizations are to some extent bureaucratic. General Motors, Exxon, the United Automobile Workers, and the Roman Catholic Church are all bureaucratic in structure. The differences between them and government bureaucracies have to do with the purposes or objectives of each. General Motors and Exxon develop large organizations to increase their ability to make a profit; the UAW to increase its ability to win higher wages and better working conditions for its members; the Roman Catholic Church, to administer its religious policies among its 800 million members. Government bureaucracies, as we have seen, are established to administer government decisions which are by definition, public policies. They are designed for the society as a whole (even if they end up benefiting one segment more than others) and have the backing of government authority.

Students of modern social systems argue that the bureaucracy has become an integral part of technological society. In fact, some claim that bureaucracies are the dominant institutions in modern society: "The decisive reason for the advance of bureaucratic organizations has always been its purely technical superiority over any other form of organization."[3] In short, it is difficult to conceive of modern society without bureaucracies.

However, this should not lead to another misconception: that bureaucracies are purely twentieth-century phenomena. Although an integral part of modern society, they can be found in all historical periods. For example, five thousand years ago the Babylonian and Egyptian civilizations created bureaucratic structures to carry out massive public projects. About two thousand years ago, the Chinese emperors established what has been called the "world's longest-lasting permanent bureaucracy." An analysis of the history of Christianity includes the evolution of what became the most powerful bureaucratic institution of medieval Europe, the Roman Catholic Church.

So, bureaucracies are not unique to political systems. But, given the growth of government, political bureaucracies have become the largest, most important, and most visible examples of their kind. Consider the case of the United States. As of 1983, more than 2,800,000 civilians worked for the executive branch of the federal government, compared with only 50,000 employed by the legislative and judicial branches combined.[4] Thus, about 3 percent of the total work force of the United States was made up of employees of the bureaucratic institutions of the federal government. It should be pointed out that almost 60 percent worked for the two largest bureaucracies, the Department of Defense and the U.S. Postal Service.

Viewed from a historical perspective, the growth of government bureaucracies has been quite remarkable. In 1790, the total number of workers in George Washington's first administration was about 1000, or one bureaucrat for every 4000 citizens. By 1891, the number had grown to 150,000, one for every 463; by the end of the 1970s, 2,800,000 were employed, or about one in 75.[5] What this shows is that the national bureaucracy has grown much faster than the general population. However, it would seem that its growth has peaked; since the mid-1960s when it numbered more than 3 million, there has been a decline in the number of federal government employees. Thus, we might conclude that the American bureaucracy is huge and powerful but not, despite claims to the contrary, growing at an uncontrollable rate. The American experience is instructive, for it seems typical of most Western systems. While the rate of bureaucratic growth has apparently slowed, bureaucratic institutions remain large and powerful; some commentators would say dominant. In the still-developing nations, we would probably find growing bureaucratic systems. Again, we are back to one of the original assumptions: as a society becomes more complex, political bureaucracies become more evident.

The Ideal Model

Why have bureaucracies become so important? Some of the reasons are fairly obvious, but before we attempt a more systematic explanation let us look more closely at the basic nature of bureaucracy. The best way is to examine the first and still most complete model of bureaucracy, the one formulated by the German sociologist Max Weber at the turn of the twentieth century. In his analysis of modern society, Weber was impressed with the apparently indispensable role that bureaucracy plays in the maintenance of industrial society. Thus, he hypothesized a link between the need for rational decision making and the growth of bureaucratic structure.

Weber proposed an *ideal model* of bureaucracy—a set of characteristics that the perfect bureaucracy would have.[6] Of course, there are no perfect bureaucracies in the real world, but the use of an ideal model helps us identify those human organizations that come close to the proposed characteristics; these organizations we can label bureaucratic. Figure 10.1 illustrates the ideal model.

Bureaucracy is based on the assumption that *means* can be developed to achieve any *ends.* In the context of politics, this means that policies can be rationally administered. Weber suggested that in order to do this, an organization should have a particular set of characteristics. They constitute his ideal concept of bureaucracy.

First of all, the structure of a bureaucracy should be based on the principle of *hierarchy;* that is, there must be a system of superior and subordinate positions with ever-increasing power as one goes up the organization and a clear-cut chain of command; everyone in the orga-

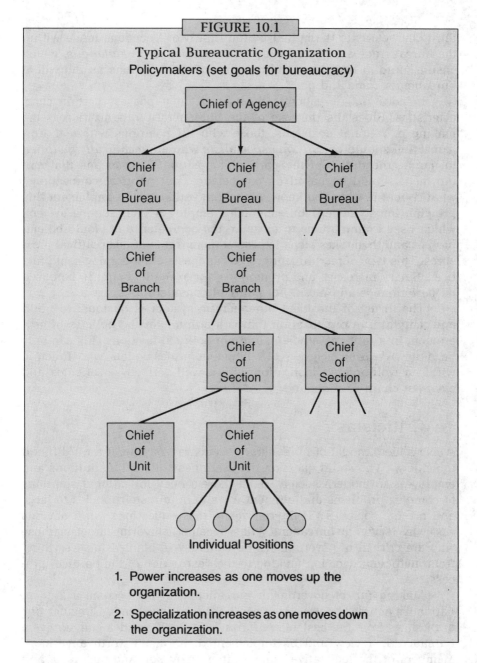

FIGURE 10.1

Typical Bureaucratic Organization
Policymakers (set goals for bureaucracy)

Chief of Agency

Chief of Bureau

Chief of Bureau

Chief of Bureau

Chief of Branch

Chief of Branch

Chief of Section

Chief of Section

Chief of Unit

Chief of Unit

Individual Positions

1. Power increases as one moves up the organization.
2. Specialization increases as one moves down the organization.

nization must be clear about whom he or she is responsible to. This suggests the second characteristic, *fixed areas of specialization and responsibility.* Each position has specific tasks and those who fill these positions are responsible only for the performance of these tasks. A third characteristic is implied by the first two. Decisions made within the bureaucracy are governed by a set of *rules and regulations,* which ensure uniform decisions and a continuity of decisions as individual bureaucrats come and go.

In addition, bureaucrats themselves must possess certain characteristics. Since the purpose of the bureaucratic organization is the making of rational decisions, those who fill positions within the organization should be *full-time specialists* who are *technically qualified* to handle the duties of the particular position. This means that employment should be based on competence, not political connections; what counts is what you know, not whom you know. To implement this principle most modern bureaucracies employ a civil service system, which uses examinations to measure the competence of would-be employees and then takes steps to protect them from outside political pressures. This type of recruitment process suggests other employment practices. Salary increases and promotions, for example, ought to be based on performance and merit, not political considerations.

The thrust of the ideal bureaucratic system is obvious: to build and maintain an organization that can administer the policies of government in a rational, efficient, and nonpolitical fashion. This can only be done by hiring a group of competent professionals who function within a well-ordered institution with a well-defined set of rules and clear-cut chain of command.

Criticisms

Weber's ideal model of bureaucracy seems reasonable, if a bit difficult to achieve. Who could question the usefulness of such institutions and employees in modern society? Isn't there a need for rational solutions to complex problems and efficient ways to administer policies to large and diverse societies? If the answer to these questions is an obvious yes, why is it that bureaucracy has become a favorite target of those who are critical of government? Bureaucracy is blamed for everything from inefficient decision making to the destruction of the political process.

Making fun of government bureaucracies has become a kind of national pastime; books have been based on the theme. Consider one of the laws from the bestseller *Murphy's Law:* "If an idea can survive a bureaucratic review and be implemented, it wasn't worth anything."[7] Members of the legislative branch often enjoy pointing out waste and stupidity in the bureaucracy. Senator William Proxmire of Wisconsin has established himself as a permanent thorn in the side of the bureaucracy by handing out a monthly "Golden Fleece" award for the most wasteful use of taxpayers' money by a government agency.

Drawing by Vietor; ©1981 The New Yorker Magazine, Inc.

"H.U.D. called the F.A.A. The F.A.A. called the S.E.C. The S.E.C. called G.S.A. G.S.A. called O.M.B. O.M.B. called Y-O-U."

Since such attitudes are so widespread, they must be confronted in any analysis of bureaucracy. We cannot make any final judgment except to say that some are no doubt exaggerated, yet others must be recognized as legitimate concerns.

It is interesting to note that almost all of the criticisms of bureaucracy are based on one or another of the defining characteristics of Weber's ideal model. It should also be noted that Weber himself realized some of the potentially negative consequences of a bureaucratic society.

Two broad criticisms of bureaucracy at first appear to be contradictory; but on second analysis, they are seen as two sides of the same coin. The first argues that bureaucracies have become the dominant institution in modern political systems.[8] According to this view, modern politics boils down to government by the experts, the **technocrats**. In the words of one critic, "Power in the government does not reside in gray eminences in black Chryslers . . . it is the great army of middle managers that controls the show."[9]

The second criticism suggests that most bureaucratic systems are decentralized anarchies, that power is divided among a large number of semiautonomous agencies, each with enough power to protect itself from the others, but none with enough power to take over the system.[10] Thus, instead of rationally coordinated policy implementation, the political system finds it difficult to get anything done in an efficient manner.

Both of these criticisms really get at the same basic question. To what extent does the chief executive really have control of the executive branch? As we have seen, presidents and prime ministers are supposed to be the chief adminstrators of their political systems. Officially they direct the implementation of their government's policies. However, in most systems the middle-level managers who staff the bureaucracies are not directly responsible to the chief executive.

Let us return to the first of Weber's principles of bureaucracy, **hierarchy**: the idea is that a rationally organized institution will have a clear-cut chain of command so that each of its members knows who his or her superior is. This establishes a chain of responsibility leading finally to the head of the bureaucracy. An additional assumption of political bureaucracies is that all of the heads are ultimately responsible to the chief executive. They are kept responsible because the chief executive hires and can fire them; this is the ultimate source of executive control. But here we encounter a perplexing situation. In order to create a class of professional administrators who are free from political influence, most bureaucratic positions have been placed under the protection of a civil service system. As a consequence, most bureaucrats are *not* hired and thus *cannot* be fired by the chief executive. It is estimated that in the United States, out of the more than 2,800,000 positions in the executive branch of the federal government, only about 6500 (less than one quarter of one percent) are under the direct control of the President. And, the typical employee of an administrative agency has a much more permanent job than the President and his cabinet. A veteran bureaucrat who began his career in 1942 and is now close to retirement will have served under nine presidents. So, it seems to be the case that in order to make the administration of policies nonpolitical and professional, the political heads of the government must lose some of their ability to govern.

Students of democratic politics find these arguments especially disturbing; if they are valid, it means that the policies of elected officials can be changed or aborted by nonelected officials. Or—and this is a widely accepted variation on the theme—the chief executive and the bureaucracy become rivals; neither is able to control the other and the policy process suffers. It must focus its attention not only on the relationship between executives and legislatures, but also between executives and bureaucracies. One bureaucratic insider has this to say about what he thinks is the most important power struggle in the American national government: "This struggle is the continuous tension between the temporary occupant of the White House and the permanent bureaucracy that he ostensibly leads. This conflict between the President and "his" men and the more than 400 agencies and bureaus of the executive branch, all working in their own interests, dominates both the domestic and foreign policy processes of the federal government."[11] This is why students of the American presidency argue that an effective President must be a good politician. Since a President cannot expect executive decisions to be carried out automatically by the bureaucracy, he or she must be able to use all of the significant sources of power available to persuade administrators that they should do his or her bidding.[12]

Bureaucracies are established to rationally administer the policies and programs of government. Presumably, the policies are designed to accomplish certain social and economic goals: to stimulate the economy, help farmers, or strengthen the national defense. But many critics have argued that once established, a bureaucracy tends to take on a life of its own: it becomes self-perpetuating. After a while, the main concern of bureaucrats becomes protecting their organization and their jobs. This requires larger budgets and staffs—the more money an agency spends and the more workers it employs, the more importannt it must be. Examples such as the following are used to support this argument. In 1920, the Department of Agriculture—one of the agencies of the national government of the United States—employed 19,500 persons to serve a farm population of around 31 million. By 1975, there were 121,000 employees but the farm population had shrunk to less than 9 million.[13] The conclusion is obvious: the Department of Agriculture has increased in size while its clientele has become smaller.

Now, there is little doubt that once established, many bureaucracies become active participants in the game of who gets what. This becomes especially evident during times of retrenchment, when budgets are being cut back. Each administrative agency uses all of its political muscle to head off attempts to cut its share of the budgetary pie. We can assume that the cuts that eventually take place are as likely to reflect the relative power of the agencies as any overall set of policy priorities. When several years ago, Amtrak, the government-operated railway system, was threatened with budget cuts, it announced that a number of routes would have to be cut. (They just happened to include routes through the home states and districts of the eight representatives and senators who chaired committees that dealt with Amtrak.)

However, concentrating on the tendency of bureaucracies to protect themselves produces a lopsided picture. While re-allocations of resources can take place this way, significant increases in budgetary allotments and bureaucratic power usually occur because of the policy choices of executives and legislatures. Of course, bureaucracies can have an impact on these choices but the final decisions are made in the formal policymaking institutions of government. Thus, the Department of Defense has more than 1 million civilian employees and spends almost three hundred billion dollars mainly because American policymakers have given national defense high priority. Likewise, the Department of Agriculture has grown in size largely because Congress and the President have assigned to it a host of new programs to administer, for example, the Food Stamp program. And, even though the farm population has declined, agricultural production has increased significantly in the last sixty years.

We can conclude, then, that the size and power of bureaucracies is the consequence of a combination of (1) the social and economic problems of the society; (2) policymakers' perception of these problems—how important they think they are and what solutions they believe are appropriate and available; and (3) the success that various bureaucracies have in the struggle for resources.

Perhaps the most telling argument about the political significance of bureaucracies is that they have gone beyond policy implementation and have become part of the policymaking process.[14] Most policies are fairly general as they come from the executive-legislative policymakers; they are often mere guidelines. The administrators are usually given room to interpret them and to decide how they should be administered. For instance, the complicated tax laws of the United States are administered by the Internal Revenue Service. In performing its function the IRS must make numerous decisions, including many that take on the status of policy: What criteria should be used in deciding which returns to audit? What is a legitimate business expense deduction? In making these decisions the IRS gets involved in policymaking; deciding who gets audited and what is an applicable deduction are surely components of tax policy.

But bureaucracies do more than interpret policies. Because of their expertise and experience, bureaucrats have become policy advisors, even initiators. Members of the chief executive's staff and the legislature have come to depend on them for policy proposals, since they are the ones who work with policies on a day-to-day basis.

FUNCTIONS AND TYPES OF BUREAUCRACIES

We will now discuss the basic functions of bureaucratic institutions and look at three types of bureaucratic structure that exist in modern political systems.

Bureaucratic Functions and Structures

It can be said at the outset that all administrative agencies are created to perform one or more of several functions. The first, and most extensive, is *administering the basic services* that the government provides. This includes the largest portion of government activities, from the wide variety of social welfare programs to aid to various groups—business, agriculture, college students—to maintaining the national defense.

A second function is *regulation.* Every government formulates policies that limit certain kinds of behavior thought to be detrimental to the "public good"; examples are air pollution, racial discrimination, and unsafe food and drugs. It should be realized, however, that policymakers have different notions of the public interest—what is acceptable in one society may not be in another. The point is that every government establishes administrative agencies to carry out its regulative functions.

A third function of bureaucracies is to *resolve disputes.* As we will see in the next chapter, this is a job usually left to courts. But in most political systems, the resolution of certain kinds of disputes has been turned over to specific administrative agencies. For instance, in the United States, if a labor union believes that a business it deals with has committed an unfair labor practice (the reverse situation is also possible), it can appeal to the National Labor Relations Board, an agency of the federal government, for a ruling. The NLRB has the power to hold hearings and make a legally binding decision (it can be appealed to the courts, but usually it isn't). In Great Britain, the National Coal Board performs the same kind of function for the coal industry.

With these functions in mind, let us examine several types of bureaucratic structure. We will use the United States as our model since it is roughly typical of the bureaucratic structures of other Western liberal democracies.

Cabinet Department. The first type of bureaucratic institution is the **cabinet department, executive department,** or **ministry**. Although they have different labels in different nations, they all have one thing in common: each is led by an executive official who is appointed by the chief executive (president or prime minister). Thus, the cabinet secretaries or ministers are the highest-ranking executives next to the chief executive and they are always directly responsible to him. Cabinet departments are organized according to subject-matter areas—foreign affairs, labor, agriculture, and so on. The names and numbers may vary—there are thirteen departments in the United States, twenty in Great Britain—but the basic areas of government activity will all be covered since it is through the cabinet department that the policies of government are carried out. Cabinet or executive departments are subdivided into agencies or bureaus that carry out more specific tasks. Thus, the Department of the Interior includes the Bureau of Land Management, the Bureau of Mines, and the National Park Service.

The administrative system of many nations includes other agencies that are not part of the major executive departments. They are usually created to perform special functions, often of a political or highly technical nature. In the American system an example of the former is the International Communications Agency. Its function is to inform the world about the United States using the mass media; its most famous operation is the Voice of America. An example of a technical agency is the National Aeronautics and Space Administration, whose function is to manage the American space program. Like cabinet departments, such agencies are headed by an administrator who is appointed, and can be fired, by the chief executive.

One of the most important questions to ask about any executive department is, How far into the bureaucracy does the control of the chief executive reach? That is, How many of the top administrators are hired and can be fired by the president or prime minister and how many are career civil servants? The typical situation in most executive departments is to have political appointees at the head and career civil servants under them running the day-to-day affairs of the department.

But this leads to a related question. How are the career administrators recruited and trained? As we have seen, in all political systems, an attempt is made to create a corps of professional administrators to staff the government bureaucracies. In some nations this has led to the development of an **administrative elite**, a group of administrators who tend to be drawn from the same social class and the same educational institutions. In France, almost all top civil servants are recruited from one of three professional schools, the Ecole Polytechnique (engineering), the Ecole Libre des Science Poliques (political science), and the Ecole Nationale d'Administration (public administration). And, given the fact that entrance to the schools is based on very competitive examinations, only those who have already received an excellent education have a chance. This means that few working- and lower-class students will be found among the enrollment. And so, the very powerful French bureaucracy is staffed almost exclusively by members of the middle and upper-middle classes. The situation in Great Britain is somewhat similar. More than half of its civil service is made up of graduates of Cambridge or Oxford.

Independent Regulatory Commission. Some governments establish agencies to regulate particular industries or particular segments of the society for the good of the society and make them somewhat independent of the executive and legislative branches. In the United States they are called **independent regulatory commissions**. Instead of being directed by an executive who is directly responsible to the chief executive, they are led by boards of commissioners who function outside executive supervision. A justification of this independence takes us back to the ideal of the nonpolitical bureaucracy. If the Interstate Commerce Commission, the oldest independent regulatory commission in the United States, is to regulate interstate commerce in an equitable fashion, it must not be subject to political pressure from the White House. However, many political scientists have pointed out that as time goes by, independent agencies tend to become the captives of the very industries they are supposed to regulate; thus they become more interested in protecting the industry than in achieving the public good. This is accomplished, so the critics argue, by having representatives of the industry appointed to the commission. To cite an example, of the top fifteen administrators appointed in 1981 to the Environmental Protection Agency, eleven came directly from the industries (steel, oil, coal, paper, and chemicals) that the EPA spends most of its time regulating. Defenders of this practice say that such individuals are logical choices because they are familiar with the industries in question. But critics see the situation somewhat differently. It is a clear attempt, by the industries, they say to blunt the agency's regulatory effectiveness. Thus, in being made independent of the other branches of government, the regulatory commissions become more vulnerable to influence from the private sector.

Public Corporation. A third kind of bureaucratic structure is the **government**, or **public corporation**. This relatively recent development in administrative organization is found in just about every type of political system. Its basic purpose is easy to identify: to accomplish a specific purpose, usually economic, by creating a government-owned corporation. One would expect to find such organizations in socialist systems; after an industry such as steel is nationalized, its private corporations become public and are, in effect, run by the government. Public corporations are also found in capitalist systems such as the United States. Examples include the Tennessee Valley Authority, a huge public utility; the Federal Deposit Insurance Corporation, an insurance company for bank depositors; and perhaps the ultimate service corporation, the United States Postal Service.

The public corporation is not totally independent; its board of directors is usually appointed by the chief executive and there is some legislative overseeing, but for all intents and purposes, it runs itself. The justification for public corporations is that they can do things, such as build massive dams and irrigation systems and ensure the bank deposits of millions of savers that no private corporation could afford to do.

In more socialist systems, the creation of public corporations is also justified on the grounds that some industries are too important to the public to be left in private hands. Thus, the leading broadcaster in Great Britain is the British Broadcasting Corporation, a public corporation renowned for its quality programming and political independence.

Bureaucracies in Marxist-Leninist Systems

So far we have concentrated on bureaucracies in democratic systems. Although the administrative apparatus of the Soviet Union and other communist systems have much in common with democratic nations, several important differences ought to be mentioned.[15] First, there is no bureaucratic system as complicated as the Soviet system. And, it is a huge system, not surprising when we realize that the state controls every aspect of the society—there are no private concerns to speak of—and everything is a public agency or corporation.

At the top of the Soviet administrative hierachy is the **Council of Ministers**, which is roughly equivalent to the cabinet in Western political systems. The Council of Ministers is in charge of administering the policies of the government; however—and here is the crucial variance from Western systems—the Communist Party maintains control of the administrative process by placing party members in all bureaucratic agencies from the top (the Council of Ministers is staffed by the highest ranking Party officials) to bottom (where they monitor the actions of bureaucrats to make sure that their actions conform to party policy). Top-level Soviet bureaucrats constitute an elite similar in certain ways to Western bureaucratic elites. The recruitment process emphasizes technical training but even more important is Communist Party membership. This is not surprising when we think back to Lenin's theory of party elite and its essential role in the development of the communist society.

In China, the other great Marxist-Leninist society, an interesting situation exists. Earlier in the chapter, we mentioned that China has what is probably the oldest continuing bureaucracy in the world. But when the Communist Party gained control of the government in 1949, its leader Mao Tse-tung identified the bureaucratic system with the newly defeated regime. Thus, during his leadership, there were many attempts to weaken the bureaucracy. Some observers praised him, some condemned him; but it is interesting to note that since Mao's death in

1976, the new, more moderate Chinese leaders have attempted to restore the bureaucracy to its previous level of importance.

SUMMARY

Policies mean very little if they are not effectively administered—this is the function of bureaucracies. Bureaucracies exist everywhere and are an important—some would say essential—part of every political system in the world. In fact, some students of politics believe that a new "bureaucratic culture" has developed with its own values and behavior patterns. Let us quote one such student: "As the globe contracts and office space expands, bureaucracy is fast becoming the dominant culture in the world. It flourishes under communism and capitalism and seems quite able to control and outlast both."[16]

The ideal model of bureaucracy visualizes a rational process of decision making, carried out by well-trained, responsible specialists. But critics of bureaucracy argue that such specialists too easily become concerned with their own security rather than the performance of their designated social functions.

There is no doubt that bureaucracies have not only grown in size but also in power. Thus, although the original and still primary function of bureaucracies is the implementation of policies made by executives and legislatures, bureaucracies have gotten more involved in the policymaking process. There are several reasons for this tendency; one is that it is the bureaucrats who must work on a regular basis with the policies that are presented to them. This often requires them to interpret broad policy guidelines. Another source of bureaucratic power is their relative independence from executive control.

The growth of bureaucracy is a good barometer of political development. As a society becomes more complex, its bureaucracies become larger and more important. This suggests that although they sometimes abuse their power, bureaucracies perform absolutely essential functions. It has even been suggested that a strong bureaucracy can see a government through periods of turmoil and upheaval. When political leaders and parties are changing, peacefully or violently, the bureaucracy often maintains continuity of government.

NOTES

1. Carl J. Friedrich, *Man and His Government* (New York: McGraw-Hill, 1963), p. 464.
2. Robert Prethus, *The Organizational Society* (New York: St. Martin's Press, 1978), p. 1.

3. Max Weber, "Bureaucracy," in Hans Gerth and C. Wright Mills, eds. *From Max Weber* (New York: Oxford University Press, 1946), p. 214.

4. *Statistical Abstract of the United States,* 14th ed. (Washington, D.C.: Bureau of the Census), 1984, p. 277.

5. Bruce D. Porter, "Parkinson's Law Revisited: War and the Growth of American Government," in Bruce Stinebrickner, ed., *American Government 82/83* (Guilford, Conn.: The Dushkin Publishing Group, 1982), p. 118.

6. Max Weber, "Bureaucracy." For an analysis of Weber's ideas, see Reinhard Bendix, *Max Weber: An Intellectual Portrait* (Garden City, N.Y.: Doubleday, 1960).

7. Arthur Bloch, *Murphy's Law: Book Two* (Los Angeles: Price, Stern, Sloan, 1980), p. 27.

8. For an early warning about the power of bureaucracies, see Guy S. Claire, *Adminitocracy* (New York: Crowell-Collier, 1934).

9. Matthew P. Dumont, "Down the Bureaucracy," in Walter Dean Burnham, ed., *Politics-America* (New York: Van Nostrand, 1973), p. 166.

10. For an in-depth application of this idea to a particular decision, see Graham Allison, *The Essence of Decision: Explaining the Cuban Missile Crisis* (Boston: Little, Brown, 1971).

11. Morton H. Halperin, "The Presidency and its Interaction with the Culture of Bureaucracy," in Charles Peters and James Fallows, eds., *The System* (New York: Praeger Publishers, 1976), p. 2.

12. See Richard Neustadt, *Presidential Power* (New York: John Wiley, 1979).

13. Porter, "Parkinson's Law Revisited," p. 119.

14. For a specific example, see A. Lee Fritschler, *Smoking and Politics: Policymaking and the Federal Bureaucracy* (New York: Appleton-Century-Crofts, 1969).

15. For a discussion of the Soviet bureaucracy, see John A. Armstrong, *The Soviet Bureaucratic Elite* (New York: Praeger, 1959).

16. Charles Peters, *Inside the System* (New York: Praeger, 1973), p. 137.

11

COURTS AND JUDICIAL POLITICS

In this chapter we turn our attention to the third of the great institutions of government, the judiciary. Our discussion begins with an interesting problem. It is often assumed that courts are not part of the political process. Many people think that judges are independent of the forces that influence members of legislative and executive branches of government. According to this view, judges make impartial decisions, motivated by a sense of justice rather than a consideration of who stands to gain or lose. In our earlier discussion of the "game" of politics, it was suggested that one of the things that characterizes politics is the fact that the players of the game are also the formulators of the rules that govern the game. In this sense, there are no neutral players; everyone has something to win or lose. The notion of unbiased judges adds a new type of player to the game; a player whose job it is to apply rules without benefiting from them. We do not have to question the motives of judges to see that this view is much too naive to fit the real world. As a matter of fact, whatever the motivations of judges, their decisions often result in the distribution of benefits and costs. Astute political actors, being aware of this fact of political life, view the courts as part of the political system as they plan their strategies.[1]

There are some significant differences between courts and the more visibly political branches of government. For one thing, judges seem more insulated from political pressures and in most systems they carry out what some might consider nonpolitical functions—deciding a dispute between two private citizens over who owns a piece of property, for instance. But, this relative isolation and apparent nonpolitical decision making should not cause us to take an overly restrictive view of judicial activity. Our main concern is the significant role that courts play in the policy process—how they are involved in decisions which decide who gets what.

Courts probably develop because every society must find peaceful ways to settle disputes that occur among individuals, groups, and institutions.[2] That is not, of course, to say that all disputes are settled by judges operating within formal judicial institutions. Primitive cultures depend less on institutional mechanisms for resolving disputes than do more developed ones, and there is less likelihood that primitive cultures have specialized judicial officials called judges; disputes are more often settled by chiefs, tribal elders, or clergy. Of course, all such conflict-resolving mechanisms are designed as substitutes for violent techniques of conflict resolution. The fact that violence occurs indicates that nonviolent techniques don't always satisfy those who are involved in disputes. Chapter 14 will discuss political violence in greater detail.

In most societies that have moved beyond the regular use of violence, disputes are resolved within a system of law. Furthermore, courts typically become the main users and interpreters of law. Thus, in most minds, law and the judicial system are inseparable. There are, then, two interrelated tasks before us; in addition to discussing the nature and political functions of courts, we must consider the nature and function of law.

THE LAW

In the broadest sense, laws are designed to regulate the interactions of the individuals, groups, and institutions of a society. Or, returning to our analogy of politics as a game, laws are the rules according to which the game is supposed to be played. They indicate what the players may and may not do and what happens to those who violate the rules. This suggests a distinction between two traditional ways of thinking about law.

Sources of Law

There are two basic levels of law—**natural** and **positive**. According to this view, there are moral principles which are universally true. To some advocates of natural law, these principles have been handed down by God (the Ten Commandments are an obvious example); to others, they are the basic foundations of nature and self-evidently true for all rational beings. In either case, natural law is thought to be independent of human whim, beyond human control. We do not create natural law; at best, we discover it. The second level of law is positive, or human, law, law that is formulated by humans to regulate their day-to-day lives. To those who believe in natural law, it is obvious that human law should be based on the universal principles of natural law. Thus it is possible to distinguish between good and bad human law—the criterion used is whether or not it is consistent with natural law. This describes the natural law tradition of legal philosophy, a tradition which believes that there are universal principles of right and wrong and that all law should be based on them.

On the other side is the positive law tradition, which argues that since there is no way to know what is ultimately right or wrong (there is no such thing as natural law), all law must be thought of as positive. This tradition views law as a human creation, with each society formulating rules according to its own particular values and needs. Thus, it is worthwhile to describe the content of various legal systems and to examine their origins (What are the sources of law?). But there can be no answer to the question, Is this particular law ultimately right? since the very existence of natural law is in question. To translate positive law into political terms, it can be designed to regulate human behavior that is backed by the power and authority of government. Thus, the laws of the United States are those rules that are made and enforced by the government of the United States; the laws of France, those rules made by and backed up by the government of France; and so on.

Since this book deals with politics and not the nature of ultimate truth, we need not get involved in the debate between proponents and opponents of natural law. However, it does make sense to examine the question of where positive human laws come from; that is, Upon what do human societies base their laws? After what we have just said about natural law, it may seem strange to mention it as a significant basis for positive law. But, whether or not we accept natural law as valid, we must recognize that many people and societies do. This becomes most obvious in societies where a particular religion has become dominant. It is likely that the laws formulated by the government of such a society will reflect the moral principles found in the religion. A prime example is the Islamic republic instituted in Iran by the Ayotollah Khomeini and his followers. We should not assume, however, that religion is a source of positive law only in self-proclaimed theocracies. The legal systems of the West are to a large extent based on the moral doctrines that have filtered down through the centuries from the Judeo-Christian religious tradition.

Another source of law is custom and tradition. According to our notion of law, customs and traditions do not gain the force of law until they have received the legitimizing sanction of the political system. A good example of this process is the development of the **common law** systems that evolved in a number of societies, most notably Great Britain. In the twelfth century, several British kings began the practice of sending judges from one area to another to hear cases and settle disputes. Since there were few written laws to use as a basis for their decisions, they had to rely on their common sense, the customs of the community, and precedent (the decisions that judges had previously made in similar cases). The result was a body of law that synthesized the customary values of the society and the authority of the judge. Common law still serves as a foundation for the British legal system and has had a significant impact on nations that have been British colonies. But, the central point for this chapter on the function of courts is that common law is judge-made law, derived not from formal legislative statutes but from the judge's interpretation of customary standards.

Given an earlier discussion of the law-making functions of legislatures, it might seem obvious that the major source of law is the legislature. In all modern liberal democracies, the legislature is the main producer of laws; but, as we have just seen and will continue to see in more detail later in the chapter, courts also make law as they legitimize custom and establish precedent. The main point is that whether the result of legislative or judicial action or a combination of both, law is a consequence of the political process.

Types of Law

Given the complexity of modern legal systems, it is not surprising that laws can be classified in many different ways. We will mention only two classification schemes that are especially useful for our analysis. One broad distinction divides law into its private and public varieties and a second distinguishes between civil, criminal, and constitutional law. Let us examine each one in turn.

Private law includes all those rules designed to handle disputes between private—that is, nongovernmental—individuals and institutions (a disagreement over who owns a piece of property, for instance). **Public law**, on the other hand, covers situations in which the government is a party to a dispute; the government claims that an individual or institution has violated a rule or policy or the reverse, an individual charges that the government has violated a rule. According to our view of courts, both private and public law can be considered political since even in the case of private law the political system is there to back up the resolution of the conflict.

A more refined classification distinguishes among civil, criminal, and constitutional law. **Civil law** overlaps to a large extent with private law. It is designed to handle disputes among individuals. The three basic categories are the **law of torts** (actions of one individual that may harm another, such as slander and negligence); **property law** (disputes over property rights and obligations); and **contract law** (which deals with agreements, including those between institutions and those between individuals). The same principles underlie each area of civil law: individuals and institutions can be held responsible for their actions and those who are negatively affected by them can seek redress. Civil law does not seek to punish but to hold the members of society responsible for their actions. Courts become part of this process since they make the final determination of liability and redress.

Criminal law comes into play when a crime is committed. A crime is any act defined as harmful to society. Actually, most crimes are one-on-one actions. However, the underlying assumption is that since they disturb the order of the society, society—through its government—has the right and obligation to punish those who commit such acts.

A third kind of law, and in a political sense the most important of all, is **constitutional law**. Since the constitution of any political system provides the system with its basic outline and structure, constitutional law deals with questions that arise about the relationship among the various parts of the government and its citizens.

Constitutional law is the most obviously political kind of law, since the government or one of its institutions is usually a party to the dispute and the typical constitutional question is one of fundamental political relationships. We should not lose sight of the fact, however, that civil law exists only because there are institutions such as courts that can resolve disputes between individuals and enforce their resolutions; criminal law exists only because there are official ways to punish those who have committed a crime.

In most societies, especially the liberal democracies, a serious attempt is made to keep "politics" out of civil and criminal law. This suggests that the finding in a civil case, or the determination of guilt or innocence in a criminal case, is to be based on truth and justice, not the political interests and power of the parties involved. This is perfectly realized only rarely, but it is always a desirable goal. In this sense, civil and criminal law are nonpolitical. However, because they are formulated and administered by government, they must be considered political in a broader sense—after all, all decisions allocate benefits and costs.

In many societies, the distinction between political and nonpolitical law is even fuzzier than it is in liberal democracies. It might be argued that in totalitarian systems the distinction is pretty much nonexistent. Thus, in a society structured around a particular ideology or religion, it is considered criminal to commit an act that violates the principles of the ideology or religion. It must be admitted that all political systems have prohibitions against treasonous acts, acts that threaten the very existence of the state—selling military secrets to an enemy, for instance.

Where this all seems to lead is to the realization that while we can map out some meaningful distinctions between political and nonpolitical law, all law is in a sense political since it is either formulated or enforced by the political system. And, to repeat the critical point, in most societies it is the function of the courts to apply civil, criminal, and constitutional law as they go about settling disputes. However, public and constitutional law are the most significantly political kinds of law since they deal directly with the powers and responsibilities of and limitations on the institutions of government.

COURT SYSTEMS IN THE POLITICAL PROCESS

As we have seen, courts have probably evolved out of the need to find peaceful ways to settle disputes. It is also clear that a parallel occurrence is the development of a system of laws designed to handle the disputes. Once these facts are realized, it becomes clear that courts and laws intersect because judges became the main users of law—they take on the function of applying the law to the day-to-day lives of the members of society. In this sense, their function is comparable to that of bureaucrats. More people are likely to come into contact with bureaucrats and judges than with presidents, prime ministers, and senators, since the former apply the policies devised by the latter.

However, just as we saw that bureaucrats exercise more discretion in their administrative decision making than is often realized, so it is with courts and judges. Every time a judge makes a decision in either a civil or criminal case, someone wins and someone is likely to lose—an allocation of benefits and costs takes place. It is even more important to realize that courts not only allocate values and benefits to the parties in the case, but at the same time make decisions whose consequences go beyond the specifics of the particular case. What this means is that judges not only *apply* the law, they *make* it. Whenever a court establishes a precedent, it is making law; whenever a court legitimizes a custom, it is making law. And, whenever a court *interprets* a law, which it must do quite often, it is making law.[3]

Let us pursue the question of interpretation, for it lies at the heart of the political function of courts. Even the most elaborate and highly structured legal systems have ambiguous laws and social, economic, and political disputes that are not neatly covered by the law. There will be changes in the society that are not accompanied by corresponding adjustments in its legal codes. In each situation there is a need for an interpretation of the law—a decision about what the law means. When we recognize that judges must interpret law, we have given up the notion that they simply apply the law handed down to them. And to admit that judges interpret the law is to recognize that they do more than settle specific disputes: they make policy.

It is, of course, a basic characteristic of just about every judicial system that courts consider only real disputes between real parties. For a court to state any general principle of justice, it must wait for the case to come before it. Some cases are so important, however, and deal with such fundamental questions that the decision goes beyond the specific interests of the parties to the dispute. These are, in the words of one observer, ". . . the big cases—big in the sense that many people are interested in the outcome, whose economic or other interests are directly affected, or whose emotions are engaged by the contending principles involved."[4] This is the stuff of politics in the larger sense.

Some critics of judicial power have argued that judges should not be involved in policymaking. This is an unrealistic view of the political system. An examination of the constitution and legal system of any society indicates that interpretation will always be necessary. Take, for instance, the Constitution of the United States. This tremendously significant document, which has provided a framework for the American system for almost two hundred years, fills only about eight pages of a modern-day textbook. Given the social, political, economic, and cultural changes that have taken place, it seems unrealistic to expect this rather brief set of rules to cover all contingencies. Thus, over the years, the courts—especially the Supreme Court—have taken on the job of interpreting the Constitution. This doubtless represents policymaking of the highest order.

Judicial Review

The ultimate kind of political power that a court can possess is the authority to declare the actions of other political actors and institutions, including laws that they have passed, illegal or unconstitutional. This power is called **judicial review**. It can exist only if two conditions are met: first, if there is a constitution viewed by the members of the political system as the basic law of the land, and second, if the judicial branch is recognized as the legitimate interpreter of the constitution. Because it is so difficult to meet both conditions, few court systems have been able to assume the power of judicial review.

No court in the world has more authority than the Supreme Court of the United States and the most important manifestation of its authority is its use of judicial review.[5] A court with the power of judicial review has the opportunity to make decisions of the most basic nature—decisions dealing with individual rights and governmental prerogatives, and the proper relationships among the various institutions of government and between the government and the private sectors. Ultimately, through judicial review, a court can help determine the basic goals of the political system and the role its government will play in achieving them.

The best way to see how judicial review works is to examine its development within the political system that has seen its maximization, the American system. What we see is the growth of a political institution, the Supreme Court, with power equal to the executive and legislative institutions. Several other important points can be noted:

The United States Supreme Court. Back row from left: Sandra O'Connor, Lewis Powell, John Paul Stevens, and Antonin Scalia. Front row from left: Thurgood Marshall, William Brennan, William Rehnquist, Byron White, and Harry Blackmun.

1. Judicial review and the ability to interpret the constitution are significant sources of power for the Supreme Court.
2. In using these sources of power, the Supreme Court ends up supporting certain broad interests and helps establish or reinforce the interests of some segments of the society.
3. As a society changes over time, so do the Supreme Court's interpretations.

The Constitution of the United States establishes a Supreme Court but says nothing about the power of judicial review. The Supreme Court assumed this power as it refereed conflicts between the various parts of the American political system. The first thing the Court did was to establish its authority, in 1801 in the famous case of **Marbury v. Madison.** In this case, the Supreme Court, led by a politically astute Chief Justice John Marshall, declared unconstitutional a part of an act that Congress had passed in 1789. Interestingly, it was an act that added to the Court's own jurisdiction, but in doing so it led to the establishment of the much more significant principle that the Supreme Court has the right to declare an act of Congress unconstitutional. In short, Marshall and his colleagues made the Supreme Court an equal partner in the new American government.

Although the power of judicial review was seldom used during the early years, the Supreme Court made a series of decisions over the next three decades that laid the foundation for a national economy regulated by a strong central government. They included the striking down in 1819 of a tax levied by the state of Maryland on the Bank of the United States (*McCulloch* v. *Maryland*). In another decision, *Gibbons* v. *Ogden* (1824), the Court interpreted a clause in the Constitution that gave Congress broad powers to regulate interstate commerce so as to give the federal government control over almost all types of commerce and trade within the nation. In effect, the Supreme Court had accomplished several tremendously important political goals in its first years. First, it successfully claimed the right to interpret the Constitution and to exercise judicial review. It became the custodian of the Constitution, so to speak. Second, the Supreme Court made decisions that favored the commercial interests of those who wanted the protection of a strong national government over those whose interests, largely agricultural, pointed in the direction of more power to the individual states. A corollary of this theme was the establishment of the national government as the dominant partner in the federal system. These developments helped lay the foundation for the American Civil War.

We will not trace the remainder of the history of the U.S. Supreme Court, except to say that it has continued to make decisions which have provided the ground rules of politics, economics, and social relations ever since. It has "changed its mind" on some issues from time to time, but it has steadfastly remained the custodian of the Constitution.

This takes us back to the initial point of this chapter: courts are part of the political process because they make political (who gets what) decisions. An important question emerges from this analysis. Does the Supreme Court of the United States—or any court for that matter—follow the lead of other components of the political system, or does it take the lead in its interpretation of the Constitution? For instance, in *Brown* v. *Board of Education* (1954), when the Supreme Court ruled that the "separate but equal" doctrine of racial segregation is unconstitutional, was it simply confirming a national policy that had already been unofficially established or establishing a new policy? We can make sense out of this question only if we consider another. How are courts related to other governmental institutions?

The Structure of Court Systems

Every society has courts to resolve the conflicts that result from the day-to-day interactions of its citizens. Even totalitarian systems such as the Soviet Union have civil and criminal courts which, by all accounts, function with some efficiency and fairness.[6] But, when it comes to the more broadly political functions of courts, we find a different story. As we have seen, some courts, such as those in the United States, play a crucial role in the policymaking process. Courts in totalitarian systems, on the other hand, play no real role.

The political power of courts is largely the result of the degree of independence they have from other governmental institutions. The greater the independence—that is, the less they are controlled by the executive and legislative branches—the greater will be their role in the political process. An examination of court systems around the world indicates that there is wide variation in their independence.[7] At one extreme is a government such as that found in the United States which, because it is based on the principle of separation of powers, has given significant independence to its court system. Not only do the legislative and executive branches check each other, but the judicial branch has become a check on the other two. As we have seen, a separation of powers system can make policy only if all institutions support the policy.

There is evidence that the framers of the Constitution did visualize a significant role for the Supreme Court in the new nation. In the words of George Washington, it was "the chief pillar upon which our national government must rest." However, few could anticipate just how powerful the courts would become. Even the judges themselves were only partially aware of what they were doing.

In other governments that have strong and politically independent court systems, the process has been more direct and intentional. West Germany, which, next to the United States, has the most independent and politically powerful courts in the world, wrote its new post-World War II constitution in 1949. It was to a large extent a reaction against the totalitarian excesses of the Nazi regime. It contains an elaborate bill of rights designed to protect individuals from state power, and creates a federal system to prevent the centralization of power that was so obviously a part of the Nazi system. It also establishes a high court, the Federal Constitutional Council, with the power to rule on the constitutionality of laws passed by the legislature, and the responsibility to resolve disputes between the central government and the Bundesländer (states). But its most important function, in the eyes of many Germans, is to protect individual liberties and minority rights. The point is that the Federal Constitutional Council could do none of these things if it were not for the fact that the 1949 constitution established the principle of judicial independence and despite some conflict, the other parts of the political system have come to accept the role of the court as legitimate.

A number of political systems have established courts designed to exercise judicial review without the independence necessary to have a real impact on the political process. For instance, France's highest court, the Constitutional Court, can pass on the constitutionality of legislative bills, but only at the request of the French president or premier. Thus, while it has some power of judicial review, its power is limited because of its lack of independence from other political institutions.

In some political systems, judicial review has even less significance. Some are liberal democracies, such as Great Britain, where the tradition of parliamentary supremacy is strong. British constitutional law makes it clear that an act of Parliament cannot be contested by any court. In a far different type of system, the Soviet Union, courts have no real political independence either. They are, like all other Soviet political institutions, instruments of the ruling Communist Party. We have already mentioned that all societies, including the Soviet Union, must have methods for resolving disputes that occur among their citizens. Thus, the Soviet Union has a court system that handles criminal and civil law. But, when political questions come up—that is, when the Soviet government or Communist Party is involved—the courts lose their significance. Given the dominant position of the Communist Party, it would be surprising if it were otherwise.

It is interesting to note that the absence of judicial independence is justified in Great Britain and the Soviet Union with opposite arguments. To the British, judicial review implies an undercutting of liberal democracy and parliamentary supremacy. If the objective of a liberal democracy is to make the policymaker responsible to the people through the electoral process, their argument goes, the will of the people, working through elected representatives, must take precedence over any court. In the case of totalitarian one-party systems, the rejection of a powerful judiciary is based on the assumption that nothing must thwart the will of the party.

In those liberal democracies that do have independent courts, the justifying argument is that there must be a powerful institution whose job it is to protect the rights of individuals even if it means overruling a decision of the more popularly based branch of government. We have really come back to a defense of the principle of limited majority rule. The Supreme Court has played the role of defender of individual and minority rights in the United States. And, in West Germany, the government that was formed after World War II gave this function to the highest court. This is not to say that an independent and powerful judicial system is absolutely necessary for a liberal democracy, only that it sometimes plays a crucial role.

One way to get a clearer fix on the power and independence of courts is to consider how judges are recruited or how they take office. In most judicial systems, judges are appointed by the executive branch, usually by the chief executive. And in many cases, the appointment must be confirmed by the legislative branch. In almost all cases, judges serve "for life or good behavior," which means that realistically, unless they commit some horrendous act, they can expect to hold their judicial position until they resign or die. In most nations, a judge can be removed from office only by a special, and usually difficult, action of the legislature. In Great Britain, this is called an "address of Parliament"; in the United States, "impeachment."

The fact that judges are usually appointed and can be removed from office by the other branches of government implies that the executive and legislative branches will always have the upper hand. This is not necessarily the case. For one thing, the difficulty of most judicial removal procedures means that few judges have actually been removed from office. And, there are other factors—the jurisdiction of the courts, the political culture within which they have evolved—which are equally important determinants of their power.

Some supporters of liberal democracy argue that the best way to establish a judicial system that is independent of the other branches of government is to have judges elected by the people. In this way, they will be directly responsible to the people and will not have to depend on the executive for their gaining of power, nor on the legislature for their remaining in power.

More judges are elected in Switzerland and the United States than other liberal democracies. It is important to realize that some federal systems, including the Swiss and American, have two fairly distinct court systems: one at the federal level and the other at the state (United States) or canton (Switzerland) level. Judges at the state or canton level are popularly elected. Most American states elect all or some of their judges. And in many, appointed judges can be recalled. That is, if enough citizens sign a petition, indicating their displeasure with a judge's performance, an election is held to see if he should continue.

In Switzerland, a number of judges are popularly elected at the canton level. At the national level the Federal Tribunal, the equivalent in some ways of the U.S. Supreme Court, is elected in more indirect fashion. Its members are selected by a vote of the Swiss legislature, the Federal Assembly. One of the other significant aspects of the election of judges is that unlike most of those who are appointed, those who are elected serve fixed terms and then must stand for reelection.

In Japan, members of the Supreme Court are selected by a complicated system that combines executive appointment and popular election. Supreme Court judges are initially appointed by the Japanese cabinet, but then they must be confirmed by the voters in an election and must be reconfirmed every ten years. Thus, even a veteran judge can be removed by the voters if he offends their sense of justice.

There seems to be consensus among political scientists and constitutional lawyers that a responsible and independent judiciary is best achieved through executive appointments with some kind of legislative confirmation and "good behavior" term. This method gives the more directly elected branches of government the initial power of deciding who sits on the court, but limits their ability to exert undue pressure once the judge takes office.

Those who defend the popular election of judges argue that democracy is best served by judges who are directly responsible to the people. The defenders of executive appointment reply that while individual courts such as the Supreme Court of the United States are surely an integral part of the political process, they must retain their independence not only from the pressures of executives and legislators but from the transient demands of the public.

Courts in the Liberal-Democratic Process

We began this chapter by saying that courts are part of the political process. We can now clarify and modify that claim; it is true if we take the broad view that the resolution of any conflict is a political decision. However, if politics is defined as policymaking, making the broad kinds of decisions that determine who gets what throughout the society, then many fewer court systems around the world are involved in politics.

Courts are an important part of the policy process in only a relatively small number of governments, and all of these are liberal democracies. The best example is, of course, the United States. Other systems that give some authority to their courts include West Germany, France, Japan, and Italy. We would not expect courts to play a role in the policymaking process of totalitarian systems. In the non-West world of developing nations few courts have any policymaking functions. When they do, it is usually to legitimize policies already made elsewhere in the system.

Thus, the crucial question about the policymaking function of courts comes down to their proper place in the political process of liberal democracies. We find two different positions, each reflecting a particular democratic emphasis. One emphasizes the absolute sovereignty of elected representatives. This tradition is most evident in Great Britain and a number of other parliamentary systems. It is no accident that the courts of such systems have little policymaking power. On the other hand, in political systems such as the United States and West Germany the courts have become major factors in policymaking, especially in the protection of individual and group rights. Using the Supreme Court of the United States as their prime example, supporters of a less expansive role for courts argue that independent courts have often gone too far in limiting the power of the majority. Thus we have once again returned to an earlier issue: the never-ending "juggling act" between majority rule and minority rights. All we can conclude at this point is that courts will continue to be at the heart of this controversy. Thus, the court system has been brought into the policy process and plays an integral role in legitimizing policies and even originating them.

SUMMARY

Every society must have a process for resolving disputes. Typically, this function is performed by courts through the application of a system of law. Thus it can be said that laws are the rules that courts use to maintain justice and order in societies.

There are many types and sources of law. The most basic classification distinguishes among civil, criminal, and constitutional law. Constitutional law is the most obviously political, but the need to apply and interpret all kinds of law makes any judicial system political to some extent. Thus it is not easy to keep separate political and nonpolitical court activities. This separation is most likely to be accomplished in liberal democracies.

Another reason for viewing the decisions of courts as political is the fact that every judicial decision results in the allocation of benefits and costs; sometimes, the allocation applies only to the direct parties to the case. But often, in more wide-ranging cases, groups and broad interests are affected.

The ultimate kind of political power that a court can have is judicial review, since this power gives a court the authority to interpret and limit the power of other government institutions. Only a few courts in the world are independent enough to have this power.

There are a number of ways to structure court systems and to select judges. The most important feature is the degree to which a court system is independent of the other institutions of government. This leads back to the questions of political power and judicial review. It is no accident that the most powerful and most independent court in the world is the Supreme Court of the United States.

NOTES

1. For a discussion of courts as political institutions, see Jack W. Peltason, *Federal Courts in the Political Process* (New York: Random House, 1955).
2. For an interesting analysis of medieval courts, see Helen Cain, *Law-makers and Law-finders in Medieval England* (New York: Barnes and Noble, 1963), pp. 85–94.
3. Glendon Schubert, *Judicial Policy-Making* (New York: Scott, Foresman, 1974).
4. David F. Maxwell, "The Supreme Court in the American Constitutional System," in John M. Swarthout, ed., *Materials on American National Government* (New York: Oxford University Press, 1962).

5. For a comparison of the American judicial process with that of other democratic nations, see Henry J. Abraham, *The Judicial Process* (New York: Oxford University Press, 1980).

6. Harold J. Berman, *Justice in the USSR: An Interpretation of Soviet Law* (Cambridge, Mass.: Harvard University Press, 1963).

7. Theodore L. Becker, *Comparative Judicial Politics: The Political Functioning of Courts* (Chicago: Rand McNally, 1970).

POLITICS FROM GROUND UP: PARTICIPATION

12

PUBLIC OPINION AND VOTING BEHAVIOR

We have examined the cultural, economic, ideological, and institutional contexts of politics. Let us now turn our attention to the ways that political actors, both individual and group, operate within this environment, how they play the game of politics. In the next three chapters, we examine the ways that people participate in politics, from voting to violently overthrowing governments. This will also require us to consider the major political agencies for organizing poeple and channeling their demands into government: political parties and interest groups. Most of our attention will be focused on participation in liberal democracies, which are based on the principle of popular control. But we will not ignore authoritarian and totalitarian systems, where participation takes different forms and performs different functions than it does in liberal democracies.

Our analysis of political participation begins in this chapter with public opinion and voting. It is fair to assume that public opinion is found in every political system. It is very difficult for people not to have feelings about the world around them and about the performance and policies of their governments. The questions are, To what extent are these feelings translated into politically significant opinions? and To what extent can opinions have an impact on political policies? The second section of the chapter deals with voting. Before we get involved in the details of public opinion and voting, however, it might help to lay out the full range of political activities available.

POLITICAL PARTICIPATION

Participation is a term that needs little explanation. We are all participants in a number of activities—religion, sports, education. What is it that constitutes political participation?[1] At this point in our discussion, the natural answer would seem to be, "any type of activity that might have an impact on decisions about who gets what." This is a good definition as far as it goes, but it applies more to the political process of liberal democracies. It is mainly in liberal democracies that people participate in order to influence policy decisions. In nondemocratic systems, participation usually means being on the receiving end of government decisions. One way to straighten this out is to go back to the systems model and make a distinction between input and output participation. The former refers to political activities that send something into the political system—a demand, a vote, an act of support, or withdrawal of support. The latter refers to the receiving of an output—a benefit or a cost. In liberal democracies, citizens participate at both ends of the political system; in authoritarian systems, they are almost exclusively receivers, not senders. In totalitarian systems, citizens are mainly participants on the output side, but are, as we have seen, often asked to demonstrate their support for the system.

Cultural Styles

We can shed more light on the styles of political participation by referring back to our discussion of political culture. Remember the distinction among participant, subject, and parochial cultures.[2] This important classification scheme is really based on the way that people typically participate in their political systems. The participant culture is characterized by citizens who are active in expressing their demands and making choices among candidates and policies. The typical citizen of a subject culture participates by passively accepting the decisions of the political system—obeying laws, paying taxes, and being a loyal subject. Remember that those living in a parochial culture might not even consider themselves members of the political system. This can lead to apathy (not voting when you have a chance to) or its opposite: intense radical attempts to overthrow the system that one does not feel a part of.

Ways to Participate

There are many ways to participate in politics. Some require relatively small amounts of time and energy, while others require a real commitment. This distinction gives us a useful framework for systematically classifying the types of political participation, ranging from the easiest to the most difficult. As political activities become more energy- and time-consuming, we find many fewer people participating in them.

Because it requires little time or effort, the least costly political activity for most people is *expressing an opinion* about a leader or issue. It may involve nothing more than answering a question: "How do you feel about President Reagan's tax proposal?" or "Do you agree with Israel's handling of the PLO problem?" This has led one political scientist to define an opinion as "an answer a person gives in response to a situation in which some general question is asked."[3]

It takes more effort to attempt to *persuade someone else* that your opinion is correct. Only those who feel more strongly about issues and candidates and who are willing to invest some time in talking about them will attempt to persuade others. There is, then, a difference between responding to someone else's question and volunteering your ideas and actually trying to bring someone around to your position. It is safe to conclude that it is the latter, less numerous but more vocal group that politicians are aware of; but perceptive politicians recognize

that the more passive types can be activated, either positively or negatively, if the right issue comes along.

Persuasion takes some effort, but it can be accomplished in the
backyard or on the golf course. It takes more effort to travel to a voting
booth to cast a vote. In those political systems that allow voting, there
is always some portion of the eligible voting public that does not take
advantage of the opportunity. In the United States, this sometimes constitutes more than half the eligible voting population. Since voting is
such an important part of liberal democratic systems, we will devote
an entire section of this chapter to its analysis.

Some people, especially those in liberal democracies, do more than
vote. In their attempt to influence the policies of government they *contact decision makers;* in the United States this includes sending letters
and telegrams to congressmen, senators, and even presidents. In some
political systems this type of activity is unthinkable, but it is not un-
heard of to find mechanisms for citizen input in authoritarian systems.
A fine example is the way that the classic authoritarian monarchy of
Saudi Arabia schedules regular meetings between the king and the people, during which the people can discuss their problems and make requests of the king. (Tradition requires that he take such comments and
requests seriously.)

For a smaller proportion of the population of liberal democracies,
voting and contacting public officials is not enough, so they get involved
in other political activities such as *joining political interest groups.* An
interest group is made up of people who, because of a common interest
(economic, social, or religious), organize and make demands on government. While interest groups are quite common (some political scientists might even say essential) in liberal democracies, most people
are not active members.

Another way to participate in politics is to *join a political party.*
As we will see in the next chapter, the parties of various nations have
different membership requirements; some are wide open while others
are very restrictive. Examples of the former are the parties found in the
United States, where all those who think of themselves as Democrats
are Democrats; likewise for the Republicans. An example of a restrictive
party is the Communist Party of the Soviet Union; it is very selective
and those who become members are expected to demonstrate their loyalty on a regular basis.

While most Americans call themselves Democrats or Republicans,
few actually get involved in party activities. For instance, even though
in 1980 about 70 percent of the American public identified with one
party or the other, only about 7 percent worked in a political campaign.
We see an even lower level of participation when we examine other more
time-consuming political activities. The activity that attracts the small-

est number of participants is, not surprisingly, competing for political office. Even in liberal democracies, where the political culture would seem to suggest that all citizens should enter into the decision-making process, only a tiny proportion of the total population ever runs for political office.

The picture that emerges, then, is one of a hierarchy of political activities arranged in order from the least expensive in time and energy (having an opinion) to the most expensive (running for office). Several of these activities will be examined in more detail in this chapter (having an opinion and voting) and several in the next chapter (political party and interest group membership). Another political activity will be the subject of Chapter 14: unconventional participation, or political activity that takes place outside the political system because it is designed to make fundamental changes in the system. The best known examples of unconventional participation are revolution and terrorism.

PUBLIC OPINION

Public opinion exists in every society; even though it is more easily articulated in liberal democracies, every government—democratic, authoritarian, or totalitarian—must sooner or later pay attention to the opinions of its citizens. In liberal democracies, public opinions will have a direct impact on some policies. They will have a smaller impact in nondemocratic regimes. But, even in the latter, public opinion may set the limits for government policies since every regime needs the support of a substantial portion of its citizens if it is to survive for any length of time.[4]

What, then, is **public opinion**? An earlier definition of *opinion* was "an answer a person gives in response to a situation in which some general question is asked." This is a bit technical. A more down-to-earth definition would be that opinions are the expressed feelings that we have about social, political, and economic issues. With our opinions we evaluate issues and policies—that is, we decide whether we approve or disapprove of them.

Simply put, a public opinion is an opinion that is made public; that is, one that others besides its holder know about. This is nothing new since we already know that an opinion is an expressed feeling. However, it is not just any expressed feeling that captures the interest of politicians and political scientists, but those that are held by fairly large numbers of people—by *publics*. Thus, public opinion can be defined as "the complex of beliefs expressed by a significant number of persons on an issue of public importance."[5] Finally, it can be said that the public opinions that especially interest political scientists are those that might have an impact on the political process. In the words of one of the first serious students of public opinion, "Public opinion consists of those opinions held by private persons, which governments find it prudent to heed."[6]

One of the most misleading notions that enters into discussions of public opinion is what might be called the **personification of the public**. We must not think of the public as some "great being" that speaks as one voice on all issues. This mistake leads to many misconceptions about the impact of public opinion on political policymaking. When you hear that "the nation was opposed to the Vietnam War" or that "the public favors prayers in the public schools," be wary, for the implication is that there is an opinion that reflects the feelings of all the people. In fact, at any given time there are a number of publics in any society, each one concerned about a particular issue. Since most issues directly affect only a part of society, sometimes only a small part, the bulk of the population is usually not involved. For example, even though nearly everyone is eventually affected by the government's milk price support policies, only dairy farmers and consumer advocates have opinions about them. They are the publics that the President and Congress must consider as they formulate their policies.

Every now and then, an issue becomes so important, or touches so many people that almost everyone becomes a member of the public. It is difficult to imagine very many Americans during the 1930s not having an opinion about President Roosevelt's New Deal, or many citizens of Great Britain being unconcerned about the activities of Adolf Hitler as World War II got underway. But it takes a big issue to turn the entire population into a public. Even then, some people will still have no opinion. There will always be at least a few who are not even aware of the issues. Neither a World Series nor a presidential election, for example, is sufficiently dramatic to become known to all Americans. And remember that the United States has as farreaching and efficient a communications system as any in the world.

The Impact of Public Opinion on Political Decision Making

The central question lies before us. What kind of impact does public opinion have on political decision making? In order to answer this question, we must distinguish between the making of broad policies and the day-to-day application of these policies. Most political decisions are influenced by public opinion. But, as we have seen, publics vary from issue to issue. In most cases, only those who are directly concerned will express themselves. These concerned publics then might have an impact on decisions. Of course, the decision maker will probably have to sort through several different opinions and decide which one, if any, should be listened to—the concerned public rarely speaks as one voice.

On the big issues, a large proportion of the population becomes concerned. Thus, decision makers will probably have to spend more time trying to gauge their feelings. But the problem is really no different in kind, just in scope. Instead of small numbers of concerned people, the executive or legislator must now consider hundreds of thousands, even millions, of people. And once again, since there are usually divergent opinions on any issue, the decision maker must exercise some judgment.

Many political scientists would argue that the most important function of public opinion comes into play when the government or one of its representatives seems about to violate a cherished belief or long-standing policy. Consider, for instance, the reaction to official hints that the Reagan administration was considering some changes in the Social Security system. Since its creation about fifty years ago, the Social Security system has become such a basic part of American society that it is almost untouchable. Any policymaker who suggests that benefits may have to be reduced in order to put the system on a sound financial basis should be prepared for massive opposition from a significant segment of the public. This presents thoughtful policymakers with a real dilemma; they might be convinced that, given present revenue and benefit levels, the Social Security system faces almost certain bankruptcy. But both logical solutions—higher taxes or lower benefits—go against the grain of public opinion. Many would say that it is at this point that a courageous decision maker must assume the role of trustee and risk the negative repercussions.

A vivid example of what can happen to a leader when he violates the accepted norms of political culture was Richard Nixon's fall resulting from the Watergate scandal. The original break-in at the Democratic Party headquarters could have been considered a minor political indiscretion, but the ensuing legacy of deceit, cover-up, and general disregard for the basic "rules of the game" proved too much for a significant portion of the American public. Unfair as it may have seemed to Nixon and his supporters, the issue was not so much a question of his guilt or innocence, but that he was perceived to have violated a code of conduct that Americans ascribe to their elected officials, particularly to American presidents.

Another example involves the Israeli army's movement into Lebanon in 1980, ostensibly to remove their archenemy, the PLO. As the military operations escalated, Israel came under fire [first from the world at large, and then from a significant segment of its own populàtion] for going too far. This was especially significant for a nation such as Israel which, in the eyes of the world, gains much of its legitimacy from certain moral principles. Many defenders of Israel suggested that the world has a double standard—the military actions of other nations are never scrutinized as thoroughly as those of Israel. This may be true, but it overlooks a crucial point: perhaps Israel has always been grounded in a set of moral principles that applies to few other nations. These principles, stemming from the terrible holocaust during World War II, are what give Israel its special status; to see them ignored or violated is a blow to the very heart of Israeli national identity.

The Impact of Decision Makers on Public Opinion

So far our discussion of public opinion seems to be based on what might appear to be a questionable assumption; that public opinion is a one-way process with decision makers simply sitting and waiting to find out what publics want. Although this assumption describes the ideal situation in liberal democracies, it is much too simple and thus needs further clarification.

The assumption must be amended to point out that political leaders are not only influenced by public opinion, they can themselves shape the opinions in the first place. The public opinion process is really a two-way relationship between publics and leaders. Every astute politician attempts to keep track of the opinions of concerned publics and tries to figure out how the silent public might react to various policies. But effective politicians also know how to lead and shape public opinion.

There are several opinion situations that political leaders can find themselves in. One is the **opinion vacuum**; in this situation, few citizens know and/or care enough about an issue or its impact on them to have an opinion about it. There may be a concerned public, but its size is small and its members fixed in their opinions; thus, it is not a major factor as political leaders map their strategies. It is the more numerous, uncommitted citizens whom the leaders will try to influence, manipulate, and persuade. We see this quite often in the foreign policy area, where most citizens know little about the issues. A popular, persuasive, and respected leader can often sway opinion in his or her favor. Key sources of power in this type of situation are personal popularity and charisma, a reputation for honesty and integrity, and the authority of office. In other words, the central question is, Will the people believe their president, prime minister, or monarch when they are asked to make a particular value judgment about a policy? In 1986, President Reagan went to the American people and asked them to support his request for more military aid for a group of rebels opposing the Marxist government of Nicaragua. Surveys seemed to indicate that most Americans were not overly concerned about this issue; thus, Reagan's appeal did not initially lead to great popular pressure on Congress to support his request.

Another opinion situation that leaders often find themselves in is one in which many people already have opinions. Obviously, the most difficult situation of this sort is one in which many of the opinions oppose the leader's. What this calls for is changing minds. Again, the leader must rely on an ability to persuade, on his or her professional reputation, and public prestige. A leader in this situation has the greatest chance of changing the minds of those who think highly of him or her or respect the office. He or she will probably not be able to influence those who disagree with his or her policies and/or have little respect for either the leader or the office. This automatically limits what even the most persuasive leader can do.

Someone who respects a leader but disagrees with one of his or her policies is in a **dissonant situation**. That is, the opinions conflict with each other. Psychological evidence shows that most of us feel anxious in such dissonant situations and we attempt to reduce the anxiety by making our opinions more consistent.[7] Suppose you are a long-standing admirer of Ronald Reagan; you have for many years viewed him with great respect as a man of integrity and a supporter of the right policies. You are excited when he becomes President because now he can use the authority of that prestigious office to implement these policies. But, let us also suppose that you are a bitter opponent of tax increases—in fact, this is one of the reasons that you voted for Reagan. What do you do, then, when Reagan advocates a $100 billion tax increase? How do you react when he works overtime trying to win approval of the tax increase? What is your response when he appears on national television, putting his reputation on the line by asking Americans to support his proposal by placing pressure on their representatives in Congress?

There are several possible reactions. You might turn away from the President out of a sense of betrayal. Or, you could support his proposal by convincing yourself that since he is worthy of your respect, his apparent shift in position must be justified. Your decision will be influenced by the strength of your desire to get out of the dissonant situation and Reagan's ability to convince you that support for him is more important than opposition to tax increases.

But the President runs a risk if he makes this attempt. Every wise political leader knows that trying to change minds can be costly. They may end up losing more than they gain; they may win enough support to pass a particular proposal but drive so many supporters away that future success is jeopardized. This is the risk that Reagan took when he supported the tax reform bill of 1982. He won the battle but may have lost the war because many of his strongest conservative supporters refused to go along with his proposed tax increase. The question is, was this a temporary disagreement or a more permanent rejection of Reagan as a betrayer of conservative causes? If the latter is true, the political costs of the President's proposal may be greater than the benefits.

So, we can say that public opinion is an important part of every political system, both democratic and nondemocratic. Democratic leaders may have to pay more attention to it on a day-to-day basis, but in the long run, even authoritarian and totalitarian leaders cannot ignore public opinion, for without general support for their regimes, even the most powerful dictators and kings will find that their authority rests on a crumbling foundation. It must also be realized, however, that the public opinion process is a two-way street—leaders can have an impact on what publics believe and value.

ELECTIONS AND VOTING

Voting is the most visible and important kind of political participation in liberal democracies, but it also occurs in a number of nondemocratic systems. What we will do in this section is look at two aspects of voting: first, the *functions* it performs; and second, the *structural framework* of voting; that is, the rules of the game in different political systems within which voting takes place. In the next section, we will look at *voting behavior*—why people vote and how they decide which candidates and issues they will vote for.

The Functions of Elections

We have already seen that in liberal democracies, elections serve two main purposes. First, elections are used to make choices among candidates and issues; and second, because of the desire for reelection, elections keep officials responsible between elections. But, we also saw that elections are not peculiar to liberal democracies—they also take place in nondemocratic systems. The question is, why are elections held in nations where no popular choices are allowed? The answer is that holding an election is a good way to create a psychological link between people and their government. People feel closer to something with which they have interacted. Thus, even when they are not used to make choices, elections can end up reinforcing the legitimacy of the government. And, speaking of legitimacy, having large numbers of people vote is a fine way to demonstrate to the rest of the world that your regime is based on widespread popular support.

The Structure of Electoral Systems

In order to understand how various electoral systems function, we must understand how they are structured.[8] It is safe to assume that the rules according to which elections are held reflect political culture and the distribution of power. Thus, in liberal democracies such as the United States, elections are the major way that people can exercise control. In nondemocratic systems such as the Soviet Union, the main purpose of elections is to solidify the control that political leaders have over the people.

Every political system that allows voting must have rules indicating who has the right to vote. Although one of the defining character-istics of liberal democracies is that every adult citizen must have the right to vote, as a matter of fact most have from time to time excluded one group or another, usually on the basis of economic class, race, eth-nic background, or sex. For instance, in the early years of the United States, only white adult males who owned property could vote. One by one the restrictive qualifications were removed so that in 1920, universal suffrage became a basic rule of American politics. This is true in a constitutional sense, but it should be realized that some states still set up roadblocks to universal suffrage. This is what prompted introduction and passage of the Voting Rights Act of 1965.

The extension of the right to vote is part of the history of liberal democracies. But some political systems still limit voting to certain groups. The best-known example is South Africa, where blacks, who constitute more than two thirds of the population, have not yet received the right to vote and only recently has it been proposed that other racial groups, the colored (racially mixed) and Asians, be given the right to vote.

Although universal suffrage is the rule in liberal democracies, four reasonable conditions must still be met to become an eligible voter. They are reasonable in that they do not undercut the democratic pro-cess. First, every democratic system requires that its voters be citizens since it is only citizens who should have the right to make decisions affecting their nation. A second requirement is that only citizens who have been residents of the nation or part of it—county, state—for a minimal period of time (thirty days, for instance) should be able to vote. This rule is designed to prevent multiple voting; democracy is undercut if citizens can travel around, voting in many areas.

A third, and closely related, requirement is that citizens be reg-istered before they vote, so that at any given time, there exists a complete list of eligible voters. In the United States it is a citizen's responsibility to register. It is a well-known fact that many Americans never get around to registering and so never become eligible to vote. In Great Britain and most other European liberal democracies, government officials are responsible for keeping the registration list up to date. This involves going to potential voters to make sure that they are registered. As might be expected, a much higher proportion of otherwise eligible voters are registered in the British system than in the American system, where the citizen must take the initiative.

The fourth requirement is that voters be adults. Although the principle is reasonable, there is some disagreement over the definition of "adult." There is no definitive answer as to when a person reaches the age that allows him to cast a meaningful vote; some observers would argue that many voters never reach that stage. Be that as it may, every liberal democracy establishes an official definition of adulthood for purposes of voting. That this age can change is clearly demonstrated by the lowering of the voting age from 21 to 18 in the United States.

It is obvious that there is a difference between having the right to vote and actually voting. The basic formal requirement of liberal democracy is the former—there is no guarantee that everyone will avail themselves of the opportunity although some democratic theorists, including Thomas Jefferson, have felt that once given the chance, citizens will want to vote. We will discuss the social and psychological motivations of voter turnout later in the chapter. At this point, let us simply make note of the fact that some democratic nations require voting—that is, they levy fines against eligible voters who fail to vote. The most thoroughgoing compulsory voting system in the world is found in Australia, which also happens to have the highest turnout rate, an impressive 95 percent. The relationship is probably not a coincidence.

Another set of rules specifies what voters are voting for. The possibilities are initially obvious: voters make a choice either between policies or candidates. The former is *direct* democracy, the latter *indirect* democracy. Since all liberal democracies are primarily indirect, most elections are used to select representatives. It would seem that the greater the number of political offices that are filled through popular elections, the more democratic the system is. In most liberal democracies we can trace a gradual expansion of the role of the people in selecting public officials. Let us use the United States as an example. Under its original constitution, only members of the House of Representatives were elected directly by the people. Members of the Senate were selected by the state legislatures. The President was selected by an electoral college, made up of electors who were selected by the state legislatures. Over the years, the people took over the election of the President, even though the electoral college lingers on. And, in 1913, the Constitution was changed to provide for popular election of senators.

Even though all liberal democracies are primarily indirect, most give their people the opportunity to make direct policy decisions from time to time. Such an election is called a **referendum**. It should be realized that referenda are also held in nondemocratic political systems; naturally, they are not designed to give voters a chance to choose among policies, but to demonstrate popular approval of decisions supported by or already made by the government.

Take, for instance, the referendum held in 1982 to ratify the new Turkish constitution. Turnout was over 90 percent. Voters were presented with the choice of voting for or against a new constitution which had the following features: it automatically gave the president, General Evien, an additional seven years in office, added to the powers of the presidency, and restricted the activities of opposition parties. While the high acceptance rate seems to indicate wide support for the constitution, it must be realized that the rules of the referendum specified that (1) no one could campaign against the constitution, (2) any registered voter who did not vote would lose voting rights for five years, and (3) voting involved selecting either a white ballot (signifying acceptance) or a blue ballot (signifying rejection), placing the ballot in a transparent envelope, and then depositing the envelope in the ballot box in view of government officials. To say that the cards were stacked in favor of ratifying the constitution seems an understatement. Thus, this kind of vote cannot really be viewed as an example of direct democracy, since its function is not to make popular choices, but to allow a ruling elite to claim legitimacy for its policies.

In liberal democracies, referenda are usually popularly initiated; that is, most liberal democracies give citizens the right to put proposals on the ballot if they can get enough other citizens to sign a petition supporting such a move. In addition, some referenda are placed on the ballot by legislatures, often as a result of public pressure. The most extensive use of referenda at the national level has taken place in Switzerland. In 1971, a successful referendum gave women the right to vote. In the United States there has never been a national referendum (one that makes policy for the entire nation). But, within the federal system, referenda are not unusual at the state level. Perhaps the best-known recent example was California's famous Proposition Thirteen, a 1978 proposal to cut property taxes.

The controversy that this proposal stimulated, not only in California but throughout the nation, brings into focus the basic arguments for and against the use of referenda in liberal democracies. Supporters argue that it is the ultimate form of popular control—what could be more democratic than policymaking by a direct vote of the people?

Those who oppose the use of referenda point out that Proposition Thirteen was a typical (and thus inadequate) proposal because it asked voters to say yes or no to what is a very complicated issue: tax policies involve many technical questions which the average citizen has neither the time nor the inclination to become familiar with. In addition, the many possible consequences of such direct policymaking (in California, the drastic cuts in government services that eventually resulted from the cut in tax revenue) are usually not considered by voters.

Despite the occasional use of referenda, all modern liberal democracies are primarily indirect in nature. Thus, the most important kind of electoral rules are those that regulate the election of representatives. One of the first things that must be established is whom the representative is to represent. The initial answer is obvious—the representative represents people called **constituents**. But, the question remains, Which constituents does each representative represent? The solution is found in the creation of geographical districts, each one with one or more representatives. Some liberal democracies, including the United States and Great Britain, use **single-member districts**. Other liberal democracies have **multiple-member districts**. Israel has a unique system in that each of the 120 members of its legislature, the Knesset, represents the entire nation—they are elected at large.

In addition to the choice between single- and multiple-member districts, each democratic political system must decide what it takes to win a legislative seat. Most single-member district systems operate according to the **winner-take-all principle**. This means, simply, that whoever wins the most votes becomes the representative. This clearly allows for **plurality elections**, elections involving three or more candidates, in which no one receives a majority of the vote. If there are three candidates, A, B, and C, and A receives 40 percent, B 35 percent, and C 25 percent, A would be elected even though 60 percent of the electorate voted for someone else. This is the system used in the United States, Great Britain, and most other English-speaking liberal democracies. France adds run-off elections when no candidate receives a majority. In such cases, the two candidates who have received the greatest number of votes (A and B in the above example) would run against each other in a second election, thus ensuring that someone ends up with a majority.

There are persuasive arguments both in favor of and against the single-member district system. On the one hand, it can be a source of political stability because different factions are likely to come together and support a single candidate. The person who emerges as the district's representative has to support policies that reflect the wide variety of views that probably exist in the district; the policies are thus made more moderate. On the other hand, it can be argued that the single-member district system so homogenizes opinions and interests that many citizens will not be represented. And, with only one representative, voters will not have the kind of choice that a liberal democracy ought to provide. A party that receives a steady but relatively small portion of the vote, say, 20 percent, will never get one of its candidates elected. Thus, smaller parties tend to drop out of the system.

An alternate system of representation is used quite extensively in such European nations as West Germany, Sweden, and the Netherlands, and it is based on assumptions different from those that support the single-member district, winner-take-all system. This alternative is called **proportional representation** (PR). Its underlying assumption is that the elected branches of government should reflect fairly accurately the various interests of the voting public. This assumption can be realized only if the representation that various parties have in government is proportional to the vote they receive in the election. Thus, if a party receives 20 percent of the popular vote, it should receive about 20 percent of the seats in the legislature. If, for instance, a legislature has 100 members and ten equal districts, each district would have ten representatives. Let us assume that one district has three parties participating in the election. If Party A receives 40 percent, Party B 40 percent, and Party C 20 percent, then A and B would each send four, and C two representatives from the district to the legislature. In other words, no party that receives an appreciable amount of support is shut out.

There are several variations on the PR theme. The most typical system presents the voter with a list of candidates from each party. In the above example, each of the three parties would formulate a list of ten candidates in each district. Voters vote for the party of their choice. Then, each party receives representation equal to its proportion of the popular vote. If Party A gets 40 percent of the vote in a district that has ten representatives, then the top four names on its list would be elected. In some nations that use PR, voters can rearrange the list of candidates. In Israel, with its "nation as a single district" system, each party presents a list of 120 candidates and voters vote for a single party. The 120 seats are then handed out according to each party's portion of the national vote.

Whatever its details, each PR system is based on the assumption that democracy is best realized when the range of interests represented is maximized. The supporters of the winner-take-all system reply that PR leads to political instability since the division of governmental power and responsibility is likely to be carried to an extreme.

VOTING BEHAVIOR

We can now turn our attention from the formal structure of voting systems to the way that citizens behave (or don't behave) within these systems. There are two dimensions of voting behavior because the act of voting requires two decisions. First, citizens must decide whether to vote or not; then, those who choose to vote must decide *how* they are going to vote. The first dimension is called **voter turnout**, the second, **voter preference**. In the real world, these two decisions are often made at the same time. The typical citizen probably does not say, "Today I'll decide whether or not to vote; tomorrow, I'll decide whom to vote for." As a matter of fact, some of the factors that influence one decision often have an impact on the other. We know, for instance, that those who closely identify themselves with a political party not only usually vote for the candidates of that party, but also tend to vote more regularly than those with no party identification.

However, in order to make sense of the way people vote, we will examine voter turnout and voter preference separately. We will see that while there is some overlap, each dimension has its own set of causal factors.[9]

Voter Turnout

The question of why people vote (or don't vote) gets to the heart of the democratic political process. While 100 percent turnout cannot be expected (and to some defenders is not even desirable), one wonders if a nation that can get no more than 5 percent of its eligible voters to the polls can remain a democracy very long. After all, widespread voter participation demonstrates support for the democratic process. We can't say what level of turnout is necessary to keep a democracy going, but it is possible to identify too-low rates.

A quick look at Table 12.1 shows that the turnout rate for liberal democracies ranges from a low of about 53 to a high of 93. Table 12.2 demonstrates that even within a single nation, voter turnout can vary significantly from region to region and from election to election.

What explains these variations? There are several ways to attack this question. One way is to attempt to discover the relationship between various social and economic factors and voter turnout. A second method looks for the psychological factors that underlie voting or nonvoting. We will use both approaches since they are closely interrelated.

Socioeconomic Factors. Socioeconomic factors such as income and education seem related to voting turnout for the same reasons that eco-

TABLE 12.1

VOTING TURNOUT RATE OF TEN LIBERAL DEMOCRACIES, 1960–1978

NATION	AVERAGE TURNOUT OF ELIGIBLE VOTERS	NATION	AVERAGE TURNOUT OF ELIGIBLE VOTERS
Italy	93%	Canada	71%
Sweden ·	86	Japan	71
Australia	86	France	70
West Germany	84	United States	59
United Kingdom	74	Switzerland	53

From *Electoral Participation: A Comparative Analysis* edited by Richard Rose. Copyright © 1980 by Sage Publications Ltd. Reprinted by permission of Sage Publications, Inc.

TABLE 12.2

VOTING TURNOUT RATE IN SELECTED STATES IN 1980 AMERICAN PRESIDENTIAL ELECTION

STATE	TURNOUT OF ELIGIBLE VOTERS (in percent)	STATE	TURNOUT OF ELIGIBLE VOTERS (in percent)
Minnesota	70%	Maryland	50%
Wisconsin	67	Kentucky	50
Maine	64	California	49
Utah	64	New York	48
Iowa	63	Florida	48
Oregon	61	Texas	45
Michigan	60	Arizona	44
Massachusetts	59	South Carolina	40

Source: U.S. Department of Commerce, *Statistical Abstract of the United States: 1985* (Washington, D.C.: Government Printing Office, 1985), p. 254.

economic development and literacy are necessary for the maintenance of democracy. In an earlier chapter, we stated that democracy cannot survive where people still worry about the source of their next meal. This explains why regular mass voting is an unreasonable expectation in most of the less-developed parts of the world. It is interesting to note that even in the more developed nations, where voting is accepted as a basic mechanism for making public choices, there are similar relationships. Most of them can be reduced to the following statement: people with *higher social status* tend to vote more often than those with lower social status.

There are a number of ways to measure social status. One of the more obvious indicators is *income.* Generally, those with higher incomes tend to vote more often than those with lower incomes. The same is true of *occupational status.* Higher-status occupations (the professions) are related to higher turnout; lower-status occupations (unskilled and semiskilled labor), to lower turnout. That income and occupation are both significant determinants of voting is not surprising when one realizes that they are closely related to each other. High-status jobs usually, but not always, pay the best.

Another fact that seems to be related to voting turnout is *education.* There is a steady increase in voting turnout as one moves up the educational ladder. Thus, those who have received little or no formal education tend to vote less than those who have gone to school; those who have graduated from high school tend to vote more than those who haven't and those who have gone to college tend to vote more than those who haven't. Once again, we can take one step back to the previous two factors to see that education is related to them. People who have high income and high-status jobs also tend to have higher levels of education.

Many studies of voting behavior seem to show that race is related to voting turnout. In the United States, for instance, research indicates that blacks and other nonwhites vote less than whites. But one must look beyond the raw statistics to discover the more meaningful relationship. The nonwhite population has a lower rate of participation mainly because it also ranks lower on the socioeconomic scale. However, when whites and blacks of the same social and economic background are compared, it becomes clear that they have comparable turnout rates.

All voting studies suggest a strong relationship between age and voting turnout. What emerges is the fact that middle-aged people (35–64) vote at higher rates than younger and older age groups. The youngest have the lowest rates of all. The usual explanation is that middle-aged people have had more political experience and have formed more lasting attachments to the political system. Younger people, especially those who have just become voters, are less likely to have developed these attitudes, while those in the higher age categories find them weakening as they grow older.

There is one more relationship that must be examined in any discussion of voter turnout. Voting studies indicate that women have traditionally voted at lower rates than men. This is not surprising given the fact that until the twentieth century women did not have the right to vote in most liberal democracies. This, of course, was a reflection of male-dominated cultures. The point is that gaining the right to vote is not the same as feeling comfortable with the voting process. Thus, politics was still a man's game and women tended to participate less. In recent years this has changed. Until about the mid-1970s, the turnout rate for women in the United States was typically 10 to 20 percentage points less than that for men; in the 1976 and 1980 elections, the rate for women caught up to that of men. This same tendency is evident in most other liberal democracies. Thus, what was once a very striking difference is now all but nonexistent.

If we combine the socioeconomic factors related to voting and nonvoting, we can construct profiles of typical voters and nonvoters: a high-income, high-status, highly educated, middle-aged citizen is more likely to vote on a regular basis than someone with the opposite set of characteristics. Table 12.3 provides some data to support this assertion.

Psychological Factors. The socioeconomic factors that we have just discussed are useful in predicting voter turnout. Why do these relationships exist? In order to answer this question, political scientists and social psychologists have identified a number of psychological dimensions that explain why some types of people vote more regularly than others.

The first and probably most important psychological factor is **efficacy**. The authors of the most famous voting study defined it in the following way: "the feeling that individual political action does have, or can have an impact on the political process. . . ."[10] This is really a common-sense idea, but it is an extremely powerful explainer of voter turnout. If you think your vote could make a difference, that it could have an impact on the policies of government, you are more likely to take the time to vote. If you see voting as a waste of time because "People like me don't have any say about what the government does," you are much less likely to vote. The relationship between the level of efficacy and voting turnout is very clear. Study after study shows that those with a great deal of political self-confidence (high efficacy) exhibit high levels of turnout; those who have doubts about their political importance (low efficacy) vote less often, if at all.

What makes efficacy especially useful is that it seems to underlie most of the social and economic explanations of turnout. We would expect high-income, high-status, and highly educated people to have

TABLE 12.3

VOTING TURNOUT IN AMERICAN NATIONAL ELECTIONS, BY SOCIOECONOMIC FACTORS, 1972 AND 1980

Percentage That Claimed to Have Voted

FACTOR	1972	1980
Male	64.1%	59.1%
Female	62.0	59.4
White	64.5	60.9
Black	52.1	50.5
AGE		
18–20	48.3	35.7
21–24	50.7	43.1
25–34	59.7	54.6
35–44	66.3	64.4
45–64	70.8	69.3
65+	63.5	65.1
EDUCATION		
Less than 8 years	47.4	42.6
9–11 years	52.0	45.6
12 years	65.4	58.9
More than 12 years	78.8	73.2

Source: *Statistical Abstract of the United States 1980* (Washington, D.C.: Government Printing Office, 1980), p. 500.

higher levels of political efficacy. As a matter of fact, their experiences seem to reinforce the belief that the world is not beyond the control of individuals like themselves—wealth, status, and knowledge are producers of confidence. Likewise, middle-aged people are more likely to feel that their vote makes a difference than do younger or older citizens. And, until recently, the typical man had a higher sense of efficacy than most women.

So, with the concept of efficacy, we can show that those in the low turnout socioeconomic categories often have a common psychological motivation for not voting. But there are other psychological factors that add to our understanding of voting turnout. **Alienation** describes the feeling that one is cut off from the political system. Alienation can be of the *input* or *output* variety; for most alienated people it is a combination of both. The former refers to the belief that one is totally cut off from the political decision-making process—it is a more extreme form of low efficacy. Output alienation describes the feeling that the decisions of government have nothing to do with one's own needs and wants. The response of a Mexican woman to the questions of a researcher catches the essence of both types of alienation: "Its (government) activities have no effect on me as I have nothing to do with government." Alienation thus boils down to a "them and me" feeling. Government is perceived as something distant and foreign. It is not surprising that highly alienated people have low rates of turnout.

Another psychological factor that, in a sense, appears to be a mild form of alienation is **cynicism**. Cynical citizens might not feel cut off from the political system, but they have little faith in its ability to make just, efficient, and responsible decisions. Thus, cynical citizens tend to vote less than those who have a more optimistic attitude toward government.

In the next section we will see that **partisan identification** (the degree to which one feels part of a political party) has a powerful impact on how people vote in liberal democracies. However, the strength of this partisan identification is also a factor in determining whether or not one votes in the first place. Thus, in the American political system, those who are strong Democrats or strong Republicans tend to post higher turnout rates than those who identify with no party. When one realizes the functions that political parties perform for citizens, the relationship is no mystery. In large and complicated democratic political systems, the one thing that seems to be constant, the one thing that gives a sense of direction, is the political party. Issues and candidates come and go, but the political parties seem to stay around forever. Therefore, those who have learned to identify with one of these parties have a permanent link to the political system. This is not to say, of course, that all independents (those who identify with no party) feel politically impotent, only that they are more likely to than strong identifiers.

One more psychological factor must be included in our discussion of voting turnout; it is important because it explains why some citizens who have the characteristics of regular voters—high income, status, education, efficacy, and partisanship—don't vote. There is a good chance that such people are **cross-pressured**, that is, pulled in opposite directions by the factors that affect one's voting choice. For many voters, these factors pull in the same direction. But for the cross-pressured, they may not. When, for example, a person who comes from a long line of Democrats gets a job in a very Republican corporation, what does he do? His past pulls him toward the Democratic candidates, but his present pulls him toward Republicans. Or, consider Catholic Republicans who were confronted with a Catholic Democratic candidate in the 1960 presidential election. These might be the words of a woman who found herself in this situation: "I'm so confused this election year . . . I'm a Republican and a Catholic, and religion and politics are important to me." Her choices were clear: vote on the basis of party identification, vote her religion, or don't vote at all. The latter is the choice of many cross-pressured citizens, and so we can conclude that as the degree of cross-pressures increases, the turnout rate decreases. The easiest resolution to this psychologically uncomfortable situation is to escape from it.

A 1976 survey of nonvoters in the United States substantiates what we have just said about the reasons for nonvoting. Although it is based on a sample of only about 500 people, it does provide us with a vivid portrait of nonvoters in one election, which can probably be generalized to others.

The first category of nonvoters is straightforward enough. It includes those who were legally ineligible (they did not meet residency requirements) and those who were physically unable to vote. Together, these groups constituted about 19 percent of the nonvoting sample.

A less obvious—but, for political scientists, more interesting—category of nonvoters is comprised of those who failed to vote because of one or more of the psychological factors just discussed. About 22 percent is made up of those called *politically impotent* because they felt that their vote made no difference. In other words, they had very low efficacy. Another group of nonvoters felt alienated from the system and were called the *bypassed.* They made up about 13 percent of nonvoters.

A smaller, but very interesting, segment of nonvoter was the *naysayers,* people who were so cynical of government and politics that they found it impossible to vote. So strong was their belief in the unresponsiveness of government that they became active nonvoters, proud of their nonparticipation. Naysayers were characterized by a high level of information about the system; thus, even though it might be said that they are in a sense alienated from the system, they are not passive. It is probably reasonable to assume that finding a large number of naysayers in any political system indicates that the system is in trouble—in more unstable systems, naysayers can become revolutionaries. In this sample, only about 6 percent of the nonvoters fell into this category.

Another relatively small (5 percent) portion of nonvoters were *cross-pressured.* They all had the basic characteristics of the cross-pressured citizen: different partisan forces pulling in opposite directions.

The largest category, about 35 percent of nonvoters, are *positive apathetics.* They failed to vote because they had not developed close ties to the system (they had low partisan identification) and were satisfied with the performance of the system. Evidence for the second point is found in the fact that the positive apathetic's social status was not low, as was the case with many other nonvoters. So, the existence of this category reinforces the important role that learning a party identification has in bringing people into the political system and giving them a sense of belonging. On the other hand, among those who do not develop a strong party identification, there are many who, being satisfied with their social and economic situation, see little reason to participate.

Voter Preference

Having decided whether or not to vote, the citizen must decide how to vote. Political scientists have spent much time trying to explain this choice. In the process, they have identified a large number of factors that seem to be important, but they can all be reduced to three attitudes that the voter takes into the voting booth: party identification, feelings about the candidates, and feelings about the issues.[11] The main question is, What is the relative importance of these three factors? An initial answer would probably be, "It depends on the election—sometimes one factor is more important, and sometimes another." This is true if we take elections one at a time, but a more systematic examination of many elections suggests that the single most important factor in most of them is party identification. That is, most people most of the time vote for candidates who belong to the same party as the voter does. Let us make this point clear: not everyone identifies with one party or another, but more do than don't. And, party identifiers don't always vote for the candidates of their party, but they usually do.

Party identification is a very powerful factor in determining voting preference; this is, to a large extent, because party identification tends to be passed on from generation to generation, from parents to children. Thus, if both of your parents are Democrats, odds are that you will be also. The inheriting of party identification is common in the United States, Canada, Great Britain, and in many other liberal democracies. In others, such as France, a more volatile party system leads to a more fluctuating set of party attitudes.

In the previous section, we saw that a major reason for the positive relationship between strength of partisan identification and voting turnout is the sense of being part of the political system that party membership gives to a citizen. Likewise, when it comes time to making the voting decision, identifying with a party gives one a sense of direction, even if the issues of the campaign are confusing; if there are no other clear-cut guides, as is often the case, the party provides order.

At this point, we should distinguish between party label and party ideology. Many people identify with a party's name and symbols without understanding what the party stands for. This is often because the party stands for very little. As we will see in the next chapter, some parties are more ideological than others—those of the United States are among the least ideological: "The parties (of the United States) do not represent themselves as spokesmen of special social classes and do not develop strong ideologies to express special class interests. In their appeal to the electorate, they tend to emphasize broad party virtues, the righteousness of party heroes, past and present, and the general ineptitude, if not wickedness, of the opposition. As the electorate's major source of political education, they create a public image of politics as a competition between parties per se rather than a choice between alternative policies."

Evidence in recent years shows that parties have become less important in liberal democracies. This is borne out by the fact that there are now fewer party identifiers and more independents. If this is true, it seems reasonable to conclude that party identification will play a less significant role in influencing voting preference. However, another conclusion is possible: if partisan identification is a determinant of voting turnout then having fewer identifiers should lead to fewer voters. As a matter of fact, turnout in American elections has declined in recent years.

Many political scientists argue that as party identification becomes less important as a guide to voting, the *candidates* themselves become more important. In other words, the personal characteristics of the candidates become central in the minds of the voters. Candidates have never been unimportant in the electoral process of liberal democracies; this is most evident in the case of charismatic individuals such as Franklin Roosevelt, Winston Churchill, and Charles de Gaulle. It has even been possible for the candidate of the minority party (the party that fails to win the greatest number of identifiers) to win the election if he or she is popular enough. Such was the case in the United States during the 1950s, when General Dwight Eisenhower won two clear-cut victories as a Republican, even though there were far more Democratic identifiers among the voting public. Apparently, the same can be said of the Reagan victories of the 1980s.

While common, such elections are the exception. Most elections are decided primarily by party identification. The typical voter votes for candidate X not because of candidate X's personal characteristics, but because he or she is supported by Party Z. However, because there are

Even though he represented the minority party, in this case the Republican Party, General Dwight Eisenhower was popular enough to win two clear-cut victories in the 1950s.

so many exceptions, and because party identification seems not to affect as many people as it once did, we should consider how candidates do play a role in the voting decision.

We must first make clear what we are talking about. By "candidate" we mean the person running for office, independent of his or her party and independent of the issues that he or she is campaigning for or against. We are really talking about the candidate's personality—does the candidate appear to be friendly or hostile? accessible or aloof? articulate or incomprehensible? Will the candidate be a strong leader or an easily manipulated figurehead? The characteristics go on and on, and their significance varies from voter to voter. However, one thing seems clear: under some circumstances, enough voters are persuaded one way or another to elect or defeat a candidate because of his or her personality. Referring back to the case of President Eisenhower, it is widely agreed that he had the ideal personality for his time: a friendly, grandfatherly war hero who had such a distaste for politics that he promised to be a nonpolitical President—just what people wanted after more than a decade of war and conflict.

Some students of democratic politics suggest that the candidate's personality is less important than the image that he or she projects. That is, what counts is not what the candidate is really like, but what the public thinks he or she is like: what image the public relations experts can create during the electoral campaign. This argument usually emphasizes the role of the mass media, especially television, in creating a positive image. There is not enough evidence to prove this contention one way or another. But it could be argued that while a candidate's attractive characteristics can be reinforced and negative features de-emphasized, a complete repackaging of a personality is virtually impossible, even with the most effective television advertising campaign. John Kennedy was portrayed as witty and charming—but he really was; Ronald Reagan is portrayed as personable and optimistic—but he really is.[12]

This raises some important questions about the role of the *campaign* itself as a determiner of voting choice. Much is said and written about campaigns and campaign strategy. Much is spent on election campaigns: more than $300 million was spent in the United States in the 1982 election, a nonpresidential year. Election costs have been on the rise in just about every liberal democracy.[13] All of this tells us that candidates and their campaign managers think campaigns are important. But, some are skeptical. There is general agreement that campaigns can perform several important functions. For candidates who are not widely known, they may provide name recognition. For a candidate who has some negative image problems, a campaign may be able to build a more favorable image. But there are limits to what a campaign can accomplish. Most experienced campaign managers admit that even the best campaign strategy has only a small impact on the outcome of the election, but if the election is a close one this can make all the difference.

One of the main reasons for the relatively small impact of the campaign takes us back to the significance of party identification; as long as party identification is the main factor, most voters will have made up their minds before the campaign is in high gear. This is especially true of those who are the most likely to vote. However, the campaign can serve the purpose of activating those who, because of their party identification are predisposed to vote for a particular candidate but for one reason or another might not make it to the voting booth.

Campaigns are usually less important than many people think they are because of the often inflated reputation of *issues* as determinants of voting preference. Let us consider the role of issues in a bit more detail. According to the classic model of liberal democracy, issues should be the main determinant of voting preference. The function of electors is, after all, to elect public officials who will truly represent the people at home; this assumes that the voters will select candidates who agree with them.

While this model sometimes describes political reality, more often it is an exaggeration. The reasons boil down to the basic fact that most voting is not the result of a consideration of the issues. In order for an issue to affect a voter's behavior, several conditions must be met. First, the voter must be aware of the issue and must consider it important; in short, the issue must be *salient* to the voter. But even if it is salient, the voter will not be able to use it as a guide to voting if he cannot figure out how the candidates feel about the issues, or if no policy differences between the candidates are detectable. When one or both conditions are not met, other guides, such as party identification or the candidates' personalities, must be used. The evidence seems to indicate that in the United States and many other liberal democracies, this is usually the case. In short, because either no issue seems important enough, or no candidate has taken a clear enough position, most citizens are not issue voters.

This is not to say that issues are never important. There will always be some issue-oriented voters. The question is, are there enough of them to make a difference in the election? When the answer is yes, it means that we are looking at an issue so significant that it affects most of the population; world wars and great economic crises are the most obvious examples. When such events occur, large numbers of voters may change not only their voting preference but their party identification, thus bringing about a realignment of party strength.

Thus, the issue-oriented election is the rarest, but most significant, type of election because it can affect the political decisions of the next several generations. The last **realigning** election in the United States was that of Franklin Roosevelt in 1932. The Democrats have been the dominant (but not always victorious) party ever since, although there is some evidence that the great popularity of President Reagan has brought a resurgence of Republican identification during the 1980s.

SUMMARY

This chapter begins our analysis of the ways that people participate in the political process. There are many types of political participation, ranging from those that require small amounts of energy (expressing an opinion) to those that require much greater amounts of energy (running for political office). The styles of political participation that are typical of a particular political system will reflect, to some extent, the political culture of the system.

Public opinion exists in every society. And, while public opinion is most easily communicated in liberal democracies, it is a factor that even authoritarian leaders can't totally ignore. But, one must not lose sight of the fact that decision makers can also have an impact on the formation of public opinion.

Voting is the most visible and significant kind of political participation in liberal democracies. Since all liberal democracies are primarily indirect, the most important functions of elections are to elect representatives and to keep the representatives responsive between elections.

The analysis of voting behavior involves two basic questions: Why do people vote? (turnout) and Why do people make the voting choices that they do? (preference). A number of factors can be used to answer each question. Voting turnout is related to several socioeconomic factors, such as age, education, and income; and to several psychological factors, such as efficacy, sense of citizen duty, and cross-pressures. Voting preference can best be explained with the use of three factors: party identification, the candidates, and the issues.

NOTES

1. See Sidney Verba and Norman Nie, *Participation in America: Political Democracy and Social Equality* (New York: Harper and Row, 1972) and Sidney Verba *et al.*, *Participation and Political Equality* (Cambridge: Cambridge University Press, 1978).
2. Gabriel A. Almond and Sidney Verba, *The Civic Culture* (Princeton, N.J.: Princeton University Press, 1963).
3. Carl I. Hovland, Irving L. Janis, and Harold H. Kelley, *Communication and Persuasion* (New Haven, Conn.: Yale University Press, 1953), p. 6.
4. See Bernard Hennessy, *Public Opinion* (Belmont, Calif.: Brooks-Cole, 1981).
5. *Ibid.*, p. 24.
6. V. O. Key, *Public Opinion and American Democracy* (New York: Alfred A. Knopf, 1961), p. 3.
7. See Stephen E. Bennett, "Modes of Resolution of a Belief Dilemma in the Ideology of the John Birch Society," *The Journal of Politics,* 33 (1971), pp. 735–772.
8. See Vernon Bogdanor and David Butler, eds., *Democracy and Elections: Electoral Systems and Their Political Consequences* (New York: Cambridge University Press, 1983). Also see Douglas Rae, *The Political Consequences of Electoral Laws* (New Haven, Conn.: Yale University Press, 1967).
9. There are many important studies of voting behavior. The most famous American study is Angus Campbell *et al.*, *The American Voter* (New York: John Wiley, 1964). A comparative examination of several political systems is found in David Butler *et al.*, eds. *Democracy at the Polls: A Comparative Study of Competitive National Elections* (Washington D.C.: The American Enterprise Institute, 1981).
10. Campbell *et al.*, *The American Voter,* p. 516.
11. This is the basic approach taken in *The American Voter.*
12. For a case study in the selling of a political candidate, see Joe McGinnis, *The Selling of the President 1968* (New York: Simon and Schuster, 1970).
13. The United States still has the most expensive campaigns. In the British general elections of 1983, each candidate for the House of Commons was limited to spending $6,633.72. In the United States, the average amount spent by a candidate for the House of Representatives was over $200,000.

13

POLITICAL PARTIES AND INTEREST GROUPS

This chapter continues our discussion of political participation. However, attention shifts from the participation of individuals to the activities of such organizations as political parties and interest groups. An examination of modern politics suggests that just as governmental activities have become more institutionalized, political participation has become more organizational; that is, it is carried on, more often than not, by organizations. Individuals by themselves have little direct power in large and complex political systems. It is when individuals organize that they are likely to gain access to the decision-making process. This in no way diminishes the significance of elections in liberal democracies, but it should reinforce what has been made clear in the last chapter: the main function of elections in contemporary liberal democracies is to select governmental officials. Citizens thus have an important but indirect role in the policymaking process. What we are about to consider in this chapter are those organizations that attempt to influence and even take control of the policy process; the most important ones are political parties and interest groups.

Our discussion will show that in some political systems the two overlap; in a few, they overlap to such an extent that it is difficult to tell them apart. But in most systems there are clear differences between the nature and functions of parties and interest groups; thus, there is reason to examine them separately. The most important difference is that parties attempt to gain control of government, while interest groups usually try to influence government decisions without actually taking control of government. However, each in its own way performs the crucial function of linking the political system to the larger society.

POLITICAL PARTIES

One recent study concluded that there are more than 500 political parties in the world.[1] Few political systems function without them. One would expect, given the wide variety of political systems, that there would be an equally wide variety of political parties. On the surface this is true—it is not surprising to find that the Democratic and Republican parties of the United States are in many ways different from the Communist Party of the Soviet Union or that the parties of a highly industrialized nation differ from those of a newly developing nation.

Functions of Parties

However, it is just as important to realize that all parties have something in common: their basic reason for being, which is to gain control of government. This is true of both liberal democracies (where taking control means getting members of the party elected to governmental office) and nondemocratic systems (where party control is the result of other, less democratic techniques, including violence). What we are talking about, then, is the variety of methods used by political parties in different situations and political systems to take the reins of government. This implies a number of differences including the extent to which the party, once in control, allows opposition parties to compete. Only in a liberal democracy would we expect all parties to accept the principle that the opposition has the right to campaign freely for office.

The common objective of parties is evident when we consider their origins. Political historians seem to agree that the first political parties developed within early legislatures from groups of legislators who discovered that they had common interests and objectives.[2] After awhile, they were organized enough to begin thinking about trying to get more of their members into the legislature. It didn't take long for other groups, not yet part of the government, to organize and attempt to become part of the action; thus opposition parties were born. This all began to happen in the early 1800s, in the first liberal democracies. Later, parties developed in authoritarian and totalitarian systems. They, of course, did not rely on elections to gain power, but they can still be considered parties since their main objective was to take control of the government. During the twentieth century, parties have become an important part of most political systems, democratic and nondemocratic, developed and developing. They have been born in a number of ways, some as an act of power consolidation by a ruling elite, others as the result of a revolutionary movement; but they all have one thing in common, an attempt to take control of government.

We are now ready to make a first attempt at a definition of **political party**. It can be said that a party is a group of individuals that seeks to provide the personnel and direct the policies of the political system. This definition says several things about parties:

1. They are made up of people.
2. They are organized.
3. Their objective is to control government, first by getting their members into office and then by making the policies of government.

In this chapter, we will see that some parties are much better at the first job than the second. In the United States, the Democratic and Republican parties are very good at getting candidates elected to office, but much less efficient once they win. This is a result of several factors, some having to do with the structure of the American political system, others with the nature of the parties themselves. In Great Britain, political parties are much better at actually making government policy. And, of course, in a totalitarian system such as the Soviet Union, the main policymaker is the Communist Party, and no one doubts that it controls the government.

In addition to placing its members in government and formulating the policies of government, political parties perform several other broader functions for the society. Most parties provide a framework for organizing the attitudes of large groups of people. In unstable societies, it is often a party ideology that brings people together and gives them a common purpose. In stable democracies, party identification provides most people with a sense of direction and an indication of how to vote. In the most general sense, political parties link the society at large to the government. In liberal democracies this linkage exists at both the input and output sides of the political system. Parties help organize attitudes and interests of people and direct them into the decision-making process; they also mobilize support for political candidates and regimes. On the output side, parties in liberal democracies have an impact on the decisions that in turn affect individuals and groups in the society. In nondemocratic systems, the emphasis is more on the output functions of parties. In the Soviet Union, for instance, the main function of the Communist Party is to make policies and to see that they are implemented.

Classifying Political Parties

How do political parties differ? A way of analyzing this is to examine four dimensions, each describing a particular characteristic of parties or party systems.[3] The dimensions are as follows:

1. Who can belong to the party? What is the basis for membership?
2. How disciplined is the party? To what extent can party leaders inspire other members to follow them?
3. To what extent is the party based on an ideology?
4. How many parties are there in the political system?

It should be made clear that we are discussing both individual parties and party systems. For instance, in the United States, the Democratic and Republican parties exist as independent political organizations and can be studied accordingly. But, together, they constitute a political system, not only because they interact with each other, but because they are part of a larger political system. It is the second fact that explains why the parties of any political system, despite substantive differences, are usually similar in *structure*.

Party Membership. As is the case with all other political games, party politics has rules indicating who can play. The rules indicate both how many parties are allowed to compete in a particular political system, and what it takes to become a party member. We will take up the first issue later in this section; our main concern now is with rules that define party membership. In order to talk about political party membership, a distinction must be made between leaders and rank-and-file members. A closer examination of the typical party shows a more complicated set of levels; these include active participants, active supporters, and passive followers. Many studies of party structure have concluded that political parties, like other types of human organizations, tend to become elitist in nature. That is, even the most democratically oriented party will probably have a small group of leaders that sets the agenda and creates a disproportionate impact on party policy. However, even if this elitist tendency is evident in all parties, there are many variations in terms of who can become a party member, who has a chance of becoming a party leader, and the relationship between leaders and nonleaders.

Some parties—the American Democratic and Republican are good examples—have such liberal membership rules that anyone who *thinks* of himself as a Democrat or Republican *is* one. At least 70 percent of the adult population in the United States consider themselves either a Democrat or a Republican. We are, of course, talking here about mass party membership, not party leadership; but the point is still significant. As we will see, American parties are notoriously undisciplined; that is, leaders find it difficult to control the actions of followers. This is related to the fact that just about anybody can join an American political party. Both the Democratic and Republican parties are considered **cadre** parties because they are headed by small groups of leaders meeting in caucuses on an irregular basis, mainly to nominate candidates and sometimes to map out strategies and formulate general policies. However, they have no control over who becomes a member of the party since with such loose organization, membership is primarily a state of mind.

In other democratic parties—the social democratic parties of Europe, for instance—membership is more than a state of mind. Being a party member involves paying dues, attending meetings, carrying a membership card, and perhaps most importantly, following the official party line. Thus, while such parties are more tightly organized, and therefore one would think less democratic than the wide-open parties of the United States, their leaders are usually more in touch with the rank-and-file members.

A third type of membership exists in the one-party systems that are typically found in totalitarian nations. The parties in these systems are **mass-based** (everyone in the society is expected to be an active supporter), yet actual membership is very restrictive. It is often the case that membership in the party is by invitation only; one must apply and meet certain qualifications before being admitted as a card-carrying member. The Communist Party of the Soviet Union (CPSU) is probably the best example of the restrictive membership party.[4] Following Lenin's concept of the small, tightly organized, elitist party, the present CPSU includes as members only about six percent of the nation's population. An examination of the route a Soviet citizen must follow to enter the party explains this small percentage. A would-be member must be sponsored by three party members and, if accepted by the Party, must prove his or her loyalty during a probationary period. Even after being formally admitted into the Party, the member can be expelled for such indiscretions as failing to pay dues, insufficient Party activity, and deviation from official Party policy. Over the last thirty years, from 50,000 to 100,000 members have been expelled annually. So, even though all political parties have members, the nature of membership varies greatly from party to party.

Party Discipline. Let us now look more closely at the relationship between party leaders and rank-and-file members. The most important aspect of this relationship is the degree to which leaders can motivate party followers. The greater the control, the more disciplined the party is said to be. As might be expected, there is a relationship between the way that people become members of the party and the degree of discipline. Parties that have more restrictive membership rules are better able to control those who are brought into the party. Parties that are more open, naturally find it more difficult to control those who have decided to come into the party. But there is more to it than that. The leaders of some parties have powerful tools available to them for keeping members in line, especially those who are, or would like to become, part of the government.

British political parties are among the most disciplined in the world, largely because anyone who has any intention of moving up through the party knows that his career is in the hands of party leaders.[5] The leaders have much to say about who will be allowed to run for Parliament, and they can deny a member of Parliament a reelection bid. Although this veto power is seldom used, the fact that it is available tends to keep the MP's in line. Another reason for the high level of party discipline in British parties involves the basic nature of British government. As we saw in a previous chapter, the policymaking process in Great Britain depends on the ability of the prime minister and the cabinet to keep their party behind them. When the parliamentary leaders lose this support, they can no longer govern and new elections must be held. This would seem to give the MP's great power over their legislative leaders—the latter's leadership depends upon the continued support of the former. The political truth actually moves in the opposite direction, for new elections require that the old Parliament be dissolved. A member of the majority party, for example, will probably think twice about voting against the prime minister, since this action could lead to the loss of his own job. And, it must be remembered that the prime minister has the power to dissolve Parliament and call for elections at almost any time. The operation of the British government and party system, when it is working, has all of the characteristics of a positive nonzero-sum game—members of the majority party keep their jobs as long as they support their leaders, who thus keep theirs. When the system doesn't work, the result is a negative game, in which all members of the majority party lose their jobs.

American party leaders, from the President on down, have fewer and less effective tools to enforce party discipline. This is to a large extent a consequence of the fact that the United States has a federal and separation of powers system.[6] Because of federalism, state parties are fairly autonomous. That is, each state has in effect its own party system, dependent in only a minimal way on the national party. This means that senators and congressmen are more responsible to their state parties than to the national parties. Then, when they go to Washington, they find themselves members of a legislative body which, because of the separation of powers system, is independent of the President—Congress has its own significant role to play in the political process.

Thus, Republican senators can often vote against the proposals of a Republican President without worrying much about political repercussions. The President does have some sources of power, and an effective President knows how to use them; but in no way can he command the attention and control the behavior of legislative members of his party the way the British prime minister can.

Differences in party disciplines are not so much the result of differences in the political skills of British and American party leaders, as in the institutional structures of the two systems. The concept of party discipline can be used to explain the fact that British parties do a better job of running the government than do their American counterparts.

Party Ideology. Another important characteristic to look for in the analysis of any political party is the extent to which it is based on an ideology. In an earlier chapter, ideology was defined as a coherent set of political, social, and economic values that guide political action. One might assume that every political party has a set of policies that it plans to implement if it gains control of the government. In democratic systems these policies are supposed to guide the party's electoral strategy—they should be used to appeal to voters who, it is presumed, sort out the issues, and then link them with policy positions of the parties. Likewise, it might be expected that in nondemocratic systems, the ruling elite takes power with a particular set of ideological goals in mind.

The catch is that this analysis applies only to some parties; these are the ones that are considered *ideological.* They exist for the purpose of implementing a particular ideology. Now, in the real world, there are no perfectly ideological parties; among those that come the closest are socialist and communist parties. Despite many substantive differences, such parties have a common strategic goal: using the party to achieve social, political, and economic goals.

At the opposite end of the spectrum are those parties that have little or no ideological foundation. Their main purpose is to gain control of the government rather than to implement a particular set of social, economic, and political goals. One such nonideological-type party is the **broker** party. Its policies remain very flexible so that its appeal extends as far as possible. The label "broker" describes its primary strategy: be general, even vague, so that a coalition of many different groups can be put together (brokered). The more groups the party is able to attract, the greater its chance for electoral success, but the harder it will be to adopt any clear-cut policy position. This is the heart of the matter; it explains the nonideological nature of such broker parties as the Democratic and Republican parties in the United States.

It is true that Republicans are commonly viewed as more conservative and pro-business, while Democrats are more liberal and pro-labor. But the limits of these impressions are clear when one realizes that both parties contain liberals and conservatives, and both are supported by business and labor groups. If there are differences, they are probably less important than the pluralistic nature of both parties and the resulting nonideological nature of their approach to governmental strategy.

Although we tend to associate broker parties with industrialized liberal democracies, they are also found in developing countries. A good example is the National Front Party of Malaysia. Malaysia is one of the world's more culturally pluralistic nations. The population is multiracial, with about 44 percent Malay, 36 percent Chinese, and 10 percent Indian. Despite episodes of racial and ethnic conflict, Malaysia has managed to build a fairly stable political system, largely because of the ability of leaders of the main ethnic groups to work together in a coalition party, the National Front. Although it is dominated by the Malay faction—the United Malays National Organization—the National Front

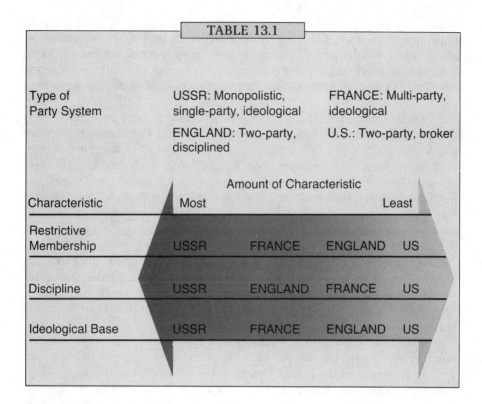

TABLE 13.1			

Type of Party System	USSR: Monopolistic, single-party, ideological	FRANCE: Multi-party, ideological
	ENGLAND: Two-party, disciplined	U.S.: Two-party, broker

	Amount of Characteristic			
Characteristic	Most			Least
Restrictive Membership	USSR	FRANCE	ENGLAND	US
Discipline	USSR	ENGLAND	FRANCE	US
Ideological Base	USSR	FRANCE	ENGLAND	US

has remained in control by steering clear of any hard-and-fast ideological line.

As we classify political parties by characteristics, several patterns begin to emerge. Table 13.1 attempts to illustrate some of these patterns. Parties that are less ideological also tend to be less disciplined. At the same time, nonideological parties tend to have more open membership rules. Once again, the American party system provides us with the best examples. Both the Democratic and Republican parties are nonideological, low-discipline parties with open membership rules. On the other hand, parties that are more ideological tend to be more disciplined, with more restrictive membership rules. These characteristics describe many of the socialist and communist parties of the world. These relationships are by no means perfect (France has parties that are very ideological but relatively undisciplined), but are strong enough to warrant explanation.

It would appear that if a party exists to articulate and implement a particular ideology, it will be much more concerned about maintaining party discipline. One of the ways it does this is by keeping a watchful eye on who is admitted to the party. If, on the other hand, a party's main objective is to gain control of government by placing its leader in office, then it will tend to be much less concerned about a pure ideological line; it will do what it has to do to gain support. This also means more wide-open membership rules and probably a less disciplined party.

These relationships ultimately help determine the way that different parties perform the functions identified earlier in the chapter. Broker parties (and other nonideological types) are better at gaining office than at implementing a consistent set of policies; the reasons are clear enough. Parties that are more ideologically inclined and disciplined are less effective at gaining office (at appealing to a wide range of groups); but if they do gain office, they are more likely to pursue a consistent set of policies.

Number of Parties. To the casual political observer, the most obvious characteristic of party systems is the number of parties that compete for power. Theoretically, a political system can have any number of parties. Realistically, we can identify three categories: one-party systems, two-party systems, and multi-party systems.

The purest **one-party systems** are found in totalitarian nations such as the Soviet Union. As we have seen, the Communist Party monopolizes power in the Soviet Union; no other party is allowed to exist, since it is claimed that only the Communist Party represents the true interests of the people. Germany acquired a **monopolistic one-party system** with the Nazi rise to power in 1933. Even though Adolf Hitler gained power in an electoral struggle with other parties, he soon made his party the only legal one. Totalitarianism and one-party systems seem to go hand in hand—the party becomes the most effective instrument of control.

Some of the developing nations also have monopolistic one-party systems. They tend to be more authoritarian than totalitarian, in that the party is used more to keep a particular elite in power than to gain total control of the people's lives. But, they are no less monopolistic since other parties are declared illegal and unnecessary. A good example is the Arab Socialist Union of Libya, led by Moammar Khadafy. Typically, such parties are used to mobilize the masses in support of the leader's vision of his nation's destiny.

Another variety of one-party politics is found in some of the nations that might be labeled quasidemocratic. The label **dominant party system** describes the situation farily well; what we find in nations such as Mexico, India, and Malaysia is a constitutionally competitive party system (many parties are allowed to compete) that is actually dominated by a single party. The dominant party retains control by building a broad-based coalition and often gains legitimacy through its links to a great event in the nation's past—a revolution or struggle for independence.

In India, the Congress Party never receives an absolute majority of the popular vote but because the opposition parties are small and fragmented, it almost always receives a majority of the seats in Parliament.[7] The Congress Party's stranglehold on governmental power was broken when a coalition of opposition parties and dissident factions of the Congress Party won a majority of seats in 1977. The victory was short-lived, however, for the Congress Party was back in power by 1979. This, of course, indicates that there are fundamental differences between dominant party systems and monopolistic one-party systems.

The Institutional Revolutionary Party (PRI) of Mexico has been an even more dominant party. Since its formation in 1946 as the most recent in a string of parties and movements that developed out of the revolution of 1910, the PRI has never lost a presidential election. Its success is the result of several factors, including its ability to bask in the glory of the great revolution, still so close to the hearts of Mexican citizens. Like the National Front in Malaysia and the Congress Party in India, the PRI is dominant not because other parties are legally suppressed, but because it has adapted the strategy of the broker party to the special circumstances of a developing nation.

One last note about dominant party systems: every democratic nation has pockets of single-party dominance. In the United States, some areas of the South almost never elect a Republican and some areas of New England almost never elect a Democrat. Likewise, Great Britain has its traditionally Labour and Conservative districts. This is really not so surprising; it is just a way of saying that party strength is not distributed equally throughout a political system. Great variations can be observed even within small areas. Many large American industrial cities—Chicago, Detroit, and Cleveland, for instance—are overwhelmingly Democratic, yet many of the immediately adjacent suburbs are strongly Republican. So, when we call a nation a two-party system, we are referring to the level of competition at the national level.

Two-party systems are found in most of the Anglo-American nations—the United States, Great Britain, Canada, Australia, and New Zealand. The basic nature of such systems is fairly obvious. The political process revolves around the competition between two major parties; only members of these parties fill important government posts. There may be other smaller parties, but they rarely gain representation in the policymaking process.

Several factors have been cited to explain the existence of two-party systems. They all try to answer the question, why are there no more than two major parties in pluralistic liberal democracies? The answer has something to do with the tradition of always having two parties and something to do with the structure and rules of the political system. As we saw in a previous chapter, the *winner-take-all, plurality* electoral system tends to make survival very difficult for minor parties. There have been a number of minor parties in American history (one recent study identified more than 1100), but only 10 have received as much as 5 percent of the vote. All have either gone out of existence or been swallowed up by one of the major parties.[8]

Great Britain has what must be considered a two-party system, but it is not as pure an example as the American system. The two major parties, Conservative and Labour, control most of the seats in the House of Commons and thus alternate control of the government. But nine other parties regularly place members in Parliament. They include the Liberal Party (the largest of the minor parties) and eight much smaller parties representing particular regional interests; examples are the Welsh National and Scottish Labour parties. In 1981, a new and potentially significant development took place. Several members left the Labour Party, claiming that it had moved too far to the left. As a consequence, they formed their own more moderate Social Democratic Party and began making overtures to the Liberal Party. Despite this development, British politics is still pretty much a contest betwen the two major parties—only once since World War II has a coalition government been necessary.

Canada's parliamentary system works much like Great Britain's. There are two major parties, the Liberals and the Conservatives, and several minor parties. The most important of these, the New Democratic Party, consistently receives from 15 to 20 percent of the popular vote, but a much smaller proportion of parliamentary seats. The two major parties have traded power during Canada's life as a nation; but occasionally, when neither is able to win a majority in Parliament, the New Democratic Party takes on added significance.

The continued dominance of two major parties in the parliamentary systems of Great Britain and Canada is largely the result of a single-member district system much like the one in the United States. Estimates are that if the British system employed proportional representation, minor parties, especially the Liberal Party, would receive more representation in Parliament. In the 1979 election, minor parties won about 19 percent of the popular vote but only 4 percent of the seats in the House of Commons. Canada also had elections that year and the same bias toward the major parties was evident; minor parties were able to translate 22 percent of the popular vote into only 11 percent of the legislative seats.

Most democratic political systems, including a majority of those on the continent of Europe, use **proportional representation** to allocate legislative seats. (Details of the PR system were discussed in the last chapter.) There is a relationship between an elective system that allocates legislative seats in proportion to the popular vote, and the existence of more than two viable parties. In short, it is no accident that most **multi-party systems** use proportional representation; parties can continue to play a significant role in the political process even though they receive only a small portion of the popular vote.

Another factor that is often cited to help explain the continued existence of multi-party systems is the more ideological nature of most of their parties. The political parties of continental Europe tend to have more clearly identifiable ideological bases than the Anglo-American major parties. There are, of course, exceptions, such as the socialist-oriented Labour Party of Great Britain. But the many parties of France and Italy divide themselves much more obviously along ideological lines, and they tend to attract voters on that basis. Thus, the electoral system allows many parties to survive and their ideological leanings keep them going as separate parties.

INTEREST GROUPS

In some political systems it is not easy to tell the difference between political parties and interest groups. However, in most there are important differences. Both are organizations designed to accomplish political goals, and each provides links between the society and the political system. Still, in most political systems, parties attempt to gain control of the political system by filling government offices, while interest groups spend their time trying to influence the decisions of those who already hold office. Although this is an oversimplified distinction, it gets us started in our analysis of the role of interest groups in modern political systems.

An **interest group** can be thought of as a group of people, with a common interest, who make claims on society. Thus, when workers organize and demand higher wages from their employer, they have become an interest group. The workers have united because of a common interest (the desire for higher wages) and have made demands on the institution in society that has the authority to satisfy their demands (their employer). But, suppose that the union decides that the company is not bargaining fairly. It might decide that the only way to satisfy its demands is by appealing to government—by asking a court to force the employer to bargain, or requesting that the legislature strengthen the laws that regulate collective bargaining. The interest group has now become a **political interest group**.[9]

Interest groups become political interest groups when the government intervenes to try to meet the group's demands. Here, striking United Airlines pilots react to news of a settlement at an A.F.L.–C.I.O. convention in Philadelphia.

Three basic elements come together to form a political interest group: There must be people with a *common interest,* who *organize,* and then attempt to satisfy their interest by *making demands* on political institutions and decision makers. This says several things about interest groups. First, they are based on a common interest, or set of interests, ranging from the most narrow and concrete—more economic benefits from a particular group—to the most philosophical and universal—justice for all mankind. The point is that even though many people associate *interest group* with *selfish interest,* some groups do work for what they conceive of as the good of all.

A second point is that interest groups are organized; they structure themselves to better achieve their goals. There are, without a doubt, many interests in every society that are unorganized, even latent. (These we have already discussed in the section on public opinion.) The opinions and attitudes of the public may or may not be translated into an organized interest group. Thus, even though public opinion can have an impact on political decisions, an interest group can have an even greater impact because it is organized and thus able to focus its political power on key points in the political process. But, many opinions remain unorganized and many interests remain unarticulated.

Every society has a variety of interests—economic, military, racial, ethnic, religious, ideological—the list goes on and on. Even government institutions have their own interests. The various agencies of the American federal government employ hundreds of people whose job it is to make sure that their agencies get a fair shake in the legislative process. If every society has interests, then it follows that just about every society will have interest groups. And, given the central role of the political system, many will become political interest groups. The question then is not so much, Do interest groups exist in a particular society? but What form do they take? and How much power do they have in the making of political decisions? Power varies from group to group, depending on the nature of the social, economic, and political systems and the political resourcefulness of the group.

The Place of Interest Groups in Politics

There are several theories about interest groups and their proper place in the political process. On one hand is the theory of **pluralism**.[10] Its basic assumption is that democracy requires a pluralistic society, which in turn implies a society made up of a large number of groups representing the various interests of the society. Democratic politics then involves groups making claims on each other and ultimately on government. According to pluralist theory, liberal democracy could not exist without a variety of groups; only they can provide the competition that is the source of energy in any democratic system. It is through interest groups that the demands of the society are channeled into the political system.

Defenders of pluralism point out that it is the weakness of independent interest groups that provides the foundation for authoritarian and totalitarian governments. In fact, one of the first things that a totalitarian regime tries to do is either infiltrate and take over or eliminate existing interest groups. The reason is obvious: no ruling elite can gain or retain control as long as interest groups are allowed their own power and the freedom to make demands on government.

Many political observers have a different, and less positive, view of interest groups; they prefer the label **pressure group**. More recently, it has become fashionable to speak out against **special interests**, those groups that put their own, selfish demands ahead of those of the public.[11] The labels *pressure* and *special* summarize the negative feelings that many people have toward interest groups. *Special* suggests that all such groups represent only a narrow and selfish range of interests. *Pressure* describes the tactics that they use to get their way in the political process.

One would have to be very naive to deny that interest groups usually do represent a particular segment of the society and that they use power to gain their objectives. Because of this, most governments that allow interest groups, have established rules to regulate their behavior; requiring them to register with the government is one fairly ineffective rule. But to emphasize the negative is to miss the centrality of interest groups to all political systems, especially pluralistic liberal democracies.

The point is that no society is totally monolithic and no culture perfectly homogeneous. Thus, every society has a number of social, economic, and political interests. If the political system is to function in a stable manner, the various interests must be able to make demands on government (or at least feel that they can make demands). To the extent that interest groups are not given this opportunity, political leaders will have to use various types of power to convince the people that it would be wise not to make demands. A case in point is the development of the Polish labor union Solidarity. Despite formal and informal obstacles created by the Polish government, this significant group of workers refuses to cease its attempts to change government policy.

Those who defend the role of interest groups go on by analyzing the concept of "special interest." They ask if there are any interests that are not special. Are there any interests that represent the entire society? Is there an overriding "public good" that should supersede any particular special interest? The more one pursues this matter, the more philosophical it becomes. We do not have to answer the philosophical issue to reach a reasonable middle ground between those who claim that all interests are special and those who insist that there are some that represent everyone.

The middle-ground position states that it is not an "either-or" so much as a "matter of degree" question. Some interests are very narrow, others are much broader. Many government policies satisfy broad and narrow interests at the same time. A strong national defense is usually viewed as good for the entire society but the defense spending needed to maintain it is especially good for a select number of defense contractors. Furthermore, if it is true that all benefits are costly, then even those policies that seem to be in the public interest—cleaning up the air, for instance—will have costs that must be assigned to someone. Thus, when we talk about the differences between the public interest and special interests, we are getting at a significant distinction, but one that is more a matter of degree than kind. One of the most interesting developments in recent years has been the formation and increased visability of **public interest groups** such as Common Cause.[12] Such groups claim to represent broader interests than typical interest groups; all consumers, for instance.

Another way to analyze the question of special and public interests is to introduce the concept of power. Even if one believes that all interests are to some extent selfish, a question remains: Do all interest groups have equal access to the political process? What if we discover that the narrowest interests have gained the most power? In a pluralist society, every interest is supposed to have the right to be heard, and it seems to undercut the systems if a few groups have disproportionate power.

It seems to follow that the way to achieve the public interest is not to impose a single notion of the public good, but to attempt to make sure that as many interests as possible can gain access to the policy-making process. This clearly brings us back to the question of power and how it is distributed.

Interest Groups and Government

For an interest group, success means having an impact on government policy; and having an impact means wielding power. Thus, we must consider the techniques used by interest groups to influence decision makers.[13] Actually, two questions must be considered simultaneously. First, in entering the political arena, where does the interest group focus its attention? This leads to a discussion of the *access points* of government—those individuals and institutions that make decisions and are open to the influence of interest groups. The second question is, What techniques does it use to influence decision makers? This naturally leads to a discussion of the types and sources of power available to various interest groups. Actually, the two questions are related; some techniques are appropriate only when dealing with certain access points.

Access to Government. The number and types of **access points** depend on the structure of government. In the United States, with its federal separation-of-powers system, interest groups can and do operate at many levels and decision-making points: in Congress, the committees and individual senators and congressmen; in the executive branch, from the President and his White House staff down to numerous bureaucrats; and in the judicial system, all the way to the Supreme Court. And, because so many decision makers are dependent on electoral support for their political lives, interest groups often attempt to activate constituent pressure.

In Great Britain, because decision-making authority tends to be concentrated in the prime minister and cabinet, the individual members of Parliament are much less-important targets of interest group activity. In short, there are fewer access points in the British political system. In addition, reflecting the more centralized and unitary political system within which they work, British interest groups tend to be more centralized and concentrated. That is, each tends to represent a greater proportion of its public than do interest groups in the United States. The National Farmer's Union includes about 90 percent of all British farmers and is the only powerful interest group representing this crucial segment of the society. In the United States, only about one third of all farmers are organized, and they are divided among three groups. About two thirds of all American labor unions are affiliated with the AFL-CIO, but not much more than 20 percent of all workers are unionized. In Great Britain, the Trades Union Council speaks for almost all of the more than 50 percent of unionized British workers. The Federation of British Industries represents at least 85 percent of all British manufacturing firms. Its American counterpart, the National Association of Manufacturers, has probably never represented more than 10 percent of all American manufacturers. Thus, in Great Britain, we find a situation where a small number of large interest groups are focusing their demands on a fairly small number of political access points.

Interest-Group Techniques. The techniques of interest groups can be discussed in a logical sequence. Since the first objective of an interest group is to gain access to the government, it will often attempt to influence the selection of government officials. The best kind of access point is a legislator or administrator who is already tuned in to your interest. Some groups have what seems to be built-in access. In American politics, for instance, one finds more lawyers in government than in any other profession. Thus, the legal profession has to worry much less about having its demands considered than, let us say, taxi drivers.

In a liberal democracy, many interest groups devote much time and money to the *campaigns* of candidates who they think will work for their interests. Some observers see a danger in this activity. They fear that because electoral compaigning has become so expensive, the wealthiest interest groups will gain an unfair advantage. This is why some governments have passed laws regulating campaign spending. In the United States, presidential campaigns are funded by a public fund, supported by taxpayers. The idea is that if candidates receive public money to pay their campaign expenses, it is less likely that they will become obligated to particular interest groups.

In all political systems, interest groups like to see friendly people in important administrative positions. Thus, whenever possible, they attempt to influence the selection of bureaucrats. If, for instance, an agency is created to regulate the trucking industry, interest groups representing the industry will work to get friends appointed to the agency. This is why so many of the regulatory agencies in American government (FCC, ICC, FTC) are staffed by people who have been recruited from the industry that the agency is supposed to regulate.

The second, and probably the best-known, interest-group technique is **lobbying**. Lobbying can be defined as the attempt by an agent of an interest group to influence the decisions of a political decision maker. This practice is so pervasive that in some minds it is almost equivalent to politics.

Lobbying is often associated with political corruption. Some people, aware of periodic scandals such as ABSCAM, assume that the major lobbying technique is bribery. It is probably true that when political corruption does take place, it is likely to occur between lobbyists and political decision makers, but it is a mistake to assume that this is the primary technique of most lobbyists. It can be argued that a typical relationship between lobbyist and decision maker is one of power, especially coercive ("We will withdraw our support if you don't vote for our bill") or utilitarian ("We promise to support you if you do"). But, the main source of control available to a lobbyist is *information.* Most decision makers, especially members of legislatures, find it impossible to keep up with all the issues that come before them. Thus enter the agents of interest groups with their specialized knowledge of particular policy areas. The agent can use the information in a number of ways— from supplying hard-to-get statistics to writing speeches for the legislator.

This suggests something else about lobbying; lobbyists spend most of their time helping decision makers who are already likely to support their interests and some of their time trying to persuade those who haven't yet made up their minds. This means that a major function of lobbying is reinforcement: making sure that those who are going to defend your interests inside the government, have all the ammunition they can possibly use. It also means that most successful lobbyists spend little of their time trying to change the minds of those who already oppose them; trying to change minds is not a very cost-effective use of time and money.

Since public opinion can have an impact on decision makers— more so, of course, in liberal democracies—interest groups sometimes attempt to *mobilize and even shape the opinions of constituents.* The strategy is fairly obvious: get the relevant public or publics to contact their representatives to voice their opinions about decisions that have, or might be made. Often this involves nothing more than informing a concerned public of a proposed policy change and then mobilizing them. At other times, when the public is not already in support of the interest group position, propaganda might be in order. There are many times when mobilizing and channeling constituent pressure is the most effective way to persuade a legislator that it is in his best interests to support the interest group's demands.

A discussion of interest-group techniques is not complete without a mention of the available resources that enable the groups to use various techniques. This takes us back to the sources of power and, as we have said several times, the sources of power vary from group to group. Among those that are especially significant for interest groups are the following:

1. Numbers—interest groups with many members, such as labor unions, can more convincingly promise to give or threaten to withdraw support.

2. Wealth—money is perhaps the most important ingredient in today's expensive political process and it gives wealthy groups such as big corporations and banks some significant advantages.

3. Status or prestige—a smaller group can often gain significant power because its members belong to a prestigious profession—the American Medical Association is an example.

4. Organization—some groups rely mainly on their tight organization and concentration on a narrow range of issues to achieve significant power—the National Rifle Association's ability to influence proposed gun control legislation comes readily to mind.

5. Quality of leadership—quality of organization and political effectiveness is often the result of having highly skilled leaders; such leaders can even compensate for a relative lack of some of the other resources, since political skill really boils down to knowing how to use the sources of power that are at your disposal.

RELATIONSHIPS BETWEEN INTEREST GROUPS AND POLITICAL PARTIES

As we have already mentioned, it is commonly assumed that the objectives and tactics of political parties differ from those of interest groups. Political parties work to get their leaders into government office, while interest groups spend most of their time trying to influence those who already hold government office. This is a valid distinction up to a point, but there are exceptions and variations.

In Anglo-American systems, where interest groups probably have the greatest significance, the two types of political organizations are quite distinct. This is especially true in the United States. Parties tend to be broad coalitions seeking the support of many interest groups.

Interest groups keep their independence in order to gain as much influence as they possibly can.

In France and Italy (and, to some extent, in West Germany and the Scandinavian nations), it is harder to tell interest groups and political parties apart, mainly because interest groups tend to be less autonomous. Parties tend to be linked closely to particular interests: Socialist parties and labor unions, Christian Democrats and the Catholic Church. Thus, parties are less coalition-oriented; instead, they usually represent a more narrow range of interests, much like interest groups in the United States. Thus, almost all of the multi-party systems of continental Europe have at least one labor party, one business party, one farmer's party, one Catholic party, etc. (This also helps explain why they are multi-party systems in the first place.)

In some developing nations, neither political parties nor interest groups are important. Traditional groupings—class, caste, tribe, family—take their place. This is simply a reflection of the less specialized nature of political institutions in such societies; highly structured groups, with the particular functions of organizing the demands of society and articulating them to political decision makers, have not yet developed.

In several of the more advanced developing nations we find a somewhat different situation. In these nations, there exists a single dominant political party, which remains dominant because of its ability to continually amalgamate the main interests of the society. A good example is the PRI of Mexico. This party's membership includes the major labor, agricultural, and business organizations of society plus representatives of various government bureaucracies. Thus, when a political system is dominated by a single party, as it is in Mexico, interest groups cannot afford to remain autonomous organizations. Instead, any interest group that wants to impact government policy must find its place in the dominant party (since it is, after all, the only game in town).

We must conclude, then, that the distinction between political parties and interest groups is a valid one; but it takes various forms in different political systems, ranging from real autonomy for interest groups to their subordination in a dominant political party.

SUMMARY

Politics has become more institutionalized—large institutions and organizations have in many ways become more important than individuals in the political process. Thus, a discussion of political participation must include the analysis of political parties and interest groups: those organizations that play such a central role in the participation of citizens.

Although they overlap to a certain extent, there is an important functional difference between political parties and interest groups. The former attempt to gain control of government while the latter spend their time trying to influence government policies. It must be recognized, however, that in some systems this distinction is blurred.

In addition to performing the primary function of gaining control of government, parties perform several other functions. These include organizing attitudes and providing people with a sense of political direction.

The variety of parties and party systems is great. Among the most important distinguishing characteristics are the rules that define party membership (who can play the game of party politics); the degree of discipline (the ability of party leaders to control the members of the party); the ideological nature of parties (the extent to which parties are based on a particular set of beliefs and values); and the number of parties in a society. Several patterns emerge as we examine the various characteristics of political parties. These help explain how well various parties perform their political functions.

Every society has a variety of interests and in most societies, groups organize around these interests. Political interest groups develop when a group of people with a common interest organize and make demands on government. In pluralistic systems, interest groups play a crucial role in influencing government policy, but they are often criticized for pursuing their own special interests instead of the public interest.

Interest groups use a variety of techniques to gain access to and influence the decisions of government. They include affecting the selection of government officials, lobbying government officials, and mobilizing and shaping the opinions of the constituents of public officials.

NOTES

1. Kay Lawson, *The Comparative Study of Political Parties* (New York: St. Martin's Press, 1976), p. 1.
2. See Leon D. Epstein, *Political Parties in Western Democracies* (New Brunswick, N.J.: Transaction Books, 1980).
3. The most influential classification of parties is found in Maurice Duverger, *Political Parties* (London: Meuthen, 1954).
4. Alfred G. Meyer, *The Soviet Political System* (New York: Random House, 1965).
5. See Samuel H. Beer, *Modern British Politics: Parties and Pressure Groups in the Collectivist Age* (New York: W.W. Norton, 1982).
6. See Frank J. Sorauf, *Party Politics in America* (Boston: Little, Brown, 1984).
7. See Myron Weiner, *Party Politics in India* (Princeton, N.J.: Princeton University Press, 1957).

8. See William N. Chambers, "Party Development and the American Mainstream," in William N. Chambers, ed., *The American Party Systems* (New York: Oxford University Press, 1967), pp. 3–32.

9. Among the best analyses of interest groups are David B. Truman, *The Governmental Process* (New York: Knopf, 1961); Allan Cigler and Burdett A. Loomis, eds., *Interest Group Politics* (Washington, D.C.: Congressional Quarterly, 1983).

10. See Robert Dahl, *Pluralist Democracy in the United States* (Chicago: Rand McNally, 1968).

11. See, for instance, Everett C. Ladd, "How to Tame Special Interest Groups," in Bruce Stinebrickner, ed., *American Government 84–85* (Sluice Dock, Conn.: Dushkin, 1983).

12. Andrew S. McFarland, *Common Cause: Lobbying for the Public Interest* (Chatham, N.J.: Chatham House, 1984).

13. See Carol S. Greenwald, *Group Power: Lobbying and Public Policy* (New York: Praeger, 1977).

14

UNCONVENTIONAL POLITICS: POLITICAL VIOLENCE AND REVOLUTIONS

It must be recognized that the political process goes on in less than stable situations, in situations that do not encourage the peaceful activity of parties and interest groups. In Chapter 13 we considered the functions of parties and interest groups. While these organizations do exist in political systems that would have to be considered less than stable, they function best when the government is stable enough to allow them to compete peacefully.

Those of us who have grown up in relatively stable political systems tend to take peaceful competition for granted. It must be realized, however, that in any system—in some much more than others—there are individuals and groups who feel it is necessary to resort to more radical and even violent means to make their demands. Often this is a result of a perceived failure of the political system to provide satisfaction; at other times, because of the desire of one elite to seize power from another elite. In any case, we must recognize that politics is at times a violent process, far removed from the competitive but peaceful give-and-take activity that the citizens of liberal democracies accept as the norm. Even Americans have had their political idealism shattered from time to time, occasionally with lasting affects. Many historians would argue that political life in America has not been the same since the assassinations of President John Kennedy, Senator Robert Kennedy, and Dr. Martin Luther King, Jr. Americans were awakened to the fact that political and social leaders, even presidents, are vulnerable to the less rational forces of politics. More recently, that least violent of liberal democracies, Sweden, had its views of politics at least temporarily changed with the assassination of its Prime Minister, Olaf Palme.

This chapter is devoted to the analysis of unconventional forms of political participation, including violence. By "unconventional," we mean "outside the normal political process and different from the acceptable political practices of the system." It should be realized that unconventional politics is to a certain extent a relative concept, since what is considered normal or conventional in one system might not be in another. How, for instance, should we analyze the continued violence in Lebanon? Is a ten-year-old civil war taking place among a variety of political factions unconventional, or conventional for Lebanon? Most people would probably answer that continued internal violence can never be considered conventional when it takes place on such a wide scale and leads to the disruption of so much of the rest of society.

POLITICAL CHANGE

Unconventional political participation usually results from demands from one segment of the society or another for change. Thus, it makes sense to spend a few moments considering the nature of political

	TABLE 14.1		
	TYPES OF CHANGE		
	Degree of Change	**Methods of Change**	**Typical Results**
Conservative	Resist planned change—can accept evolutionary change	Wide variety methods to resist planned change	System changes very gradually
Liberal	Moderate	Within system through government institutions	Incremental change
Reformer	More drastic change of one institution or process	Within system (can use more direct methods)	Major change of a part of system
Radical	Basic change in entire system	Outside system	Major overhaul of system
Revolutionary	Basic change in entire system	Outside system—violence	Major overhaul with violent consequences

change.[1] We start with the realization that every society is changing. The questions that must be asked are, How much change? Why is it happening? Who does or does not benefit from it? In attempting to answer these questions a basic distinction must be made between change that occurs because of the development of the political, economic, and social systems that is largely beyond the control of human actors (evolutionary change) and demands for change from groups and individuals within the society. The latter type is what mainly concerns us, since it is a form of political participation.

In almost all societies, assorted groups demand different kinds and degrees of change. Table 14.1 illustrates this reality. In one way or another, the groups are all asking for more change than the society's conservatives think is appropriate. A **conservative** wants to maintain the status quo, to keep things pretty much as they are. While most real-world conservatives are not opposed to all change, they do prefer as little as possible. The basic point of most conservatives is that human beings should refrain from attempting to change the political, social, and economic systems that have naturally evolved. (Politically, it is interesting to note that those who make such arguments tend to be those who are benefiting the most from the existing arrangements.)

Those who advocate change disagree about how much is necessary. They range from liberals (who support gradual change) to revolutionaries (who work for a total overhaul of the political system). In addition to the amount of change, there is a question about the methods for bringing it about. The primary choice is between working for change within the established political system or going outside the system. This often leads one to consider the need for violence. We can take these two dimensions—degree of change and methods for bringing it about—to develop a classification of the most typical approaches to change in the real world of politics.

Liberals accept the necessity of change, but only if it is gradual and incremental; that is, only if it is carried out in a step-by-step, trial-and-error manner, with room for correction. This suggests that the liberal is supportive of the basic system; the needed changes are viewed as adjustments in what has worked up to that point. It can be seen that the liberal believes in working within the system. In this sense, the conservative and liberal are often not far apart. They both accept the basic system; they disagree when it comes to the degree of change needed to make the system work. This can lead to some significant disagreements, but rarely ones that are not subject to compromise. It is probably accurate to say, then, that the leadership corps of the most stable systems is composed of conservatives and liberals.

There are, at any given time, political actors who, while they accept the basic structure of the existing system, see the need for more drastic changes than the liberal is willing to support. A **reformer** believes that a particular institution, process, or policy is in need of a major overhaul. Thus, while a liberal probably accepts the need for gradual adjustments in the income tax system, a tax reformer might advocate a much more basic restructuring of tax policy. While not asking for an overhaul of the entire system, a reformer sees the need for some significant changes in particular parts of it. It is not at all unusual to find someone who is a liberal most of the time, becoming a reformer on a particular issue.

We are now ready for a significant step from inside to outside the system. A **radical** takes this step because of the perception that reforming certain parts of the system will not provide the needed change. For example, to a radical, it is not just the tax laws that are unfair and inadequate; the problem is the system that produced them. Thus, more extensive and wide-ranging change is called for. It also follows that if the system as a whole needs basic change, then one must move outside the normal political process to accomplish the change. This means doing more than the reformer, who lobbies decision makers to change existing laws, supports candidates who will support desired reform, and

Demonstrators against the building of a nuclear power plant in Diablo Canyon in California. Techniques used by such groups are often direct and sometimes have drastic results; however, they are more reformist than radical since they attempt to change only one often important aspect of the system.

works to increase public awareness of the needed reform. If more drastic change is needed, more drastic methods must be used, methods such as demonstrations, strikes, and general attempts to embarrass and even disrupt the normal decision-making process.

The line between militant reformism and radicalism is often fuzzy. How, for instance, should we label the civil rights movement in the United States during the 1950s and 1960s? Was Martin Luther King, Jr., a reformer or a radical? Many of the techniques used by civil rights groups, the nuclear freeze movement, or pro-life or pro-choice groups are direct and drastic. Yet, even though they often bypass the conventional legislative, executive, and judicial processes they are still in a sense more reformist than radical since they are attempting to change only one aspect (often a very important one) of the system.

Just as the line between the militant reformer and radical is a fuzzy one, the distinction between the radical and the **revolutionary** is not always easy to draw. The distinction must be linked to the relative willingness of each to use violence; the revolutionary is the radical who accepts the need for violent techniques of change. In the end, the distinction between radical and revolutionary activity turns on one's definition of violence; the broader the definition, the less distinct the line.

POLITICAL VIOLENCE

Since so much depends on the definition of *violence,* let us look more closely at the meaning of the word. Violence can be defined as "a threat or exertion of physical force that causes bodily injury." This definition emphasizes the physical nature of violence, but makes clear that the threat of physical force can itself be considered an act of violence; thus, it is clearly linked to coercive power.

If we are to discuss the role of violence in politics, we must attempt to identify the special characteristics of political violence. According to some views, just about all violence must be considered political. Marxists, for instance, tend to see violent crime as the result of the economic exploitation that results from a class-based society. Thus, in a sense, violent criminals are striking out against their society and its government. Other observers say that it adds little to our understanding of politics to say that all violence is political. Most of us view violent crimes such as rape, murder, and robbery as acts committed by one individual against other individuals. The government gets involved because it is responsible for the apprehension and punishment of those who commit the crimes. But there is a difference between these acts of private violence and actions that might be defined as political violence.

The distinction is based on the motivations for and targets of violence. Violence is political when it is designed to change or support the political system. Thus, a revolutionary who uses physical force to overthrow the existing system is engaged in political violence. But, we should also recognize that when a government orders the army to resist such revolutionary acts, it too is engaged in political violence.

Legitimate Versus Nonlegitimate

What we must do, then, is make a distinction between **legitimate** and **nonlegitimate political violence.** The former refers to acts of political violence carried out by the established government to maintain order and to keep itself in control. Nonlegitimate or unconventional violence is designed to change the legitimate government. In stable political systems with highly legitimate governments, this distinction is a fairly clear-cut one. We accept the government's right to maintain the capacity to use violence to protect the nation; thus, the need for a national defense force. We also realize the need for police forces to maintain internal order and security, and in liberal democracies, to prevent some individuals and groups from violating the rights of others. But, under less stable and ordered conditions, when there are widespread doubts about the legitimacy of the government, the distinction between legitimate and nonlegitimate violence begins to blur.

How, for instance, do we analyze a society in which there is a general uprising against a small elite, an elite that has very little support from the masses? We must still view the government as having some legitimate authority, but we do so with some hesitation. Or, consider a nation racked by civil war, with equally balanced groups, each using violence to gain control of the government. Can we say that there is any legitimate authority? Can we say that there is any legitimate violence? We must conclude, then, that while the distinction between legitimate and nonlegitimate political violence is essential to an understanding of the political process, it is not always easy to apply the concepts to the real world of politics.

Reasons for Political Violence

Revolutionary violence has the greatest potential significance for any political system. If successful, it leads to massive changes in the society; even if unsuccessful, great instability and turmoil can result. This is why we will devote most of the remainder of this chapter to the nature and causes of revolution. But first, it must be made clear that not all political violence is revolutionary; there are motivations for political violence other than a desire for complete change.[2]

Some political violence is the result of accumulated frustration. Long periods of economic deprivation or political injustice can lead to spontaneous and extremely violent uprisings; examples include the riots in Detroit, Cleveland, Los Angeles, Newark, and a number of other American cities in the 1960s. The participants in such uprisings are not revolutionaries; they have no plans to destroy the existing system and create a new one. This is why an experienced student of social and political violence has called this form of violent behavior the "issueless riot:" "Such riots are issueless in the sense that a critique of the social order and the belief that violence will help bring about needed social change are relatively unimportant as motivating factors."[3] An issueless riot can be a spectacular and destructive event as long as it lasts, but it may have little effect on the government and its policies. However, what begins as a spontaneous, issueless riot can become the opening shot of a revolution.

Other more intentional forms of political violence still fall far short of a full-fledged revolution. For instance, some groups commit violent acts—bombings, assassinations, kidnappings—to call attention to their demands. The members of such terrorist groups apparently feel that the normal channels of political communication are not open to them. Their purpose then is not to bring about systemwide change, but to focus attention on a particular area of perceived injustice. Some terrorist acts are viewed by their perpetrators as revolutionary; they are designed to begin the process of undercutting the existing government. But often, the terrorist group is so small that its activities have a significant impact on neither the government nor the society at large.

THE NATURE AND CAUSES OF REVOLUTION

We have said that a revolution involves the use of violence to bring about basic social, economic, and political change. Since this is a very broad definition it includes many historical events. One survey of political violence concluded that since 1945, there have been more attempted revolutions than elections in the world.[4] The last four decades are not unique in this regard; we sometimes forget that a number of contemporary political systems—most notably, the United States, the Soviet Union, and Mexico—came into being as a result of revolutions.

To understand these great events we must look more closely at their inner workings and ultimately at their possible causes. One of the major problems in accomplishing these goals is the apparent uniqueness of each revolution. Given the wide diversity of political, social, and economic systems, what could the American, Russian, and Mexican revolutions have in common, other than the fact that violence was used to achieve change? The answer is that despite historical differences—no two revolutions are exactly alike—we can sort them out into several categories. And while there are many possible explanations of revolution—one political scientist has identified 21—there are a few that political scientists have found especially useful.

Disequilibrium Theory

Aristotle made the main point 2500 years ago. Based on his examination of many political systems, Aristotle concluded that the main cause of revolution is the feeling by a major portion of the society that they are being treated unjustly, that they are not receiving benefits in proportion to their contributions. Because of his positive view of politics, Aristotle felt that the right to participate in politics was the ultimate reward. Thus, an economic class that has accumulated wealth and thus economic power will, if denied political power, seek to change the system. Likewise, those with political power will expect their share of the economic rewards.

Several general points emerge from Aristotle's analysis. Revolutions are most likely to occur when the various parts of the society are out of balance, when the political, economic, and cultural-value systems are moving in different directions.

This theory has been adapted by contemporary political scientists to explain modern revolutions.[5] They usually begin with two assumptions. The first one is that every stable society needs a set of values (ideology, religion, moral philosophy) that explains its political, economic, and social institutions. A second assumption proposes that change is natural and inevitable; change sometimes begins with a shift in values (the acceptance of a new religion), sometimes with a new development in the society (the growth of a new technology). Whatever the source of change, the basic parts of the society no longer correspond to each other; the society is in a state of **disequilibrium**. It is up to the political leaders to restore the equilibrium. If they don't, a revolution may occur as groups in the society attempt to do it on their own. This action may be initiated by those who advocate new values to fit the new society, by those who want to restructure the society to fit a new set of values, or by those who would like to go back to the old values even if it means going back to the old institutions. Most historical revolutions seem to fit one or several of these models. If the political leaders make the necessary adjustments, the revolution may be headed off; if they don't, they will have to rely more and more on force and coercive power to maintain control. It is likely, of course, that their reliance on force will only push the society further in the direction of revolution.

The Iranian Revolution of 1979 fits the basic theory fairly well.[6] The government under the Shah was an oppressive, authoritarian system, with tremendous inequalities in wealth and power and several developments that threatened its internal stability. It should be noted that instability had become a way of life: since 1890, until the regime of the Ayatollah Khomeini, five of six Iranian rulers had been forcibly removed from office. Several of the more important sources of instability resulted directly from the Shah's own policies. One, the use of violence and oppression, was certain to stimulate some opposition, so widespread was its use. But, several other decisions led to equally significant reactions.

First, the Shah instituted a program of economic modernization; its official label was the "White Revolution." In emphasizing land reform, industrial development, and the importation of Western technology, the economy was given a boost, but so was a potential source of dissension: the middle class, which doubled between the mid-1950s and the 1970s. The expectations of the new middle class and of many workers began to outstrip the economy's capacity to satisfy them, and they began to ask for more political rights than the government was willing to give. At the same time, the Shah stepped up his campaign against the very powerful Shiite Muslim religious community. As we now know, this proved to be a mistake for it reinforced the religious leaders' opposition to the increasingly secular regime of the Shah.

The actual revolution of 1979 involved most segments of Iranian society. Workers, students, bankers, businessmen, soldiers, communists, and Muslims all rose up against the Shah and his government, for many different reasons: bankers and businessmen because the Shah had not modernized enough; Shiite leaders because he had modernized too much and had thus moved the system away from traditional Muslim values; communists because of the continued oppression of workers; the list goes on and on. The point is that a classic case of extreme social disequilibrium could not be resolved by the Shah's army and police force and so he was finally forced out of power and out of his country.

What happened after the downfall of the Shah adds to our understanding of revolutions and their consequences. A power struggle ensued, as each group tried to gain the upper hand. The religious faction gained control, and under Khomeini's direction, has attempted to create a society based on its strict interpretation of Muslim values. The resulting level of oppression suggests that the outcome of a revolution does not necessarily improve the life of the average citizen.[7]

Relative Deprivation Theory

There are those political scientists who argue that the systems model just discussed does not say enough about the role of attitudes in the development of revolution. After all, revolutions don't just happen—they are the result of human decisions. So, some students of revolution have based their theories on the attitudinal antecedents to a revolution.

The simplest such approach emphasizes *deprivation*—people who are economically and socially deprived will be the first to revolt.[8] But, some of the poorest nations have had the least revolutionary activity; so even though great deprivation and the resulting dissatisfaction can be a major source of revolutionary fervor, there must be additional factors. The one that has been identified the most often is **relative depri-**

vation. It is not just being deprived—having a low standard of living, few political rights, or no religious freedom—but recognizing that others are receiving more, or that one is being treated unjustly, that sows the seeds of revolution. It is interesting to note that we are moving back to Aristotle.

People will tend to accept—but not necessarily enjoy—poor living conditions until they begin to recognize that they should and can receive more. This is what social scientists have labeled **rising expectations**. As long as people's expectations remain fairly constant, they will not expect more from society and government. But, once their expectations are raised, they will expect more, as did the middle class of Iran.

As people expect more, the government will probably try to satisfy some of their demands. As the demands are satisfied, people's expectations rise again and so the cycle of rising expectations takes off. Somewhere along the line, the government will probably decide it either cannot or should not further increase its level of performance. At that point, the possibility of revolution increases. Revolutionary activity begins when the level of expectations and the ability or willingness of the government to satisfy them have moved so far apart that only a major change, often accompanied by violence, can bring them back into equilibrium.

Our discussion has now come full circle. A discussion of revolution makes us realize that not all political activity takes place within political systems. The stable, ordered distribution of benefits and costs is not something to be taken for granted. When groups within a society feel that the system is not working for them, they may attempt more direct, unconventional, and or violent methods of reordering the distribution of benefits and costs. Thus, distasteful as it is, violence must be considered as one form of political participation.

SUMMARY

Political participation is not always peaceful and does not always take place within the political system. Thus, unconventional political participation must be included in any analysis of politics.

Unconventional political participation is usually the result of demands for change. Several degrees of change can be demanded, ranging from the moderate change of the liberal to the more basic changes of the reformer and radical to the violent change of the revolutionary.

Political violence takes place for a number of reasons. Sometimes it is caused by accumulated frustrations; sometimes it is designed to bring about major, systemwide change, known as revolution.

Several theories have been used to explain revolution. One of the most popular views revolution as the result of certain disequilibriums in a society; that is, revolution occurs when the parts of a society are out of balance. Another type of explanation emphasizes the attitudes of people in the development of revolutionary situations. The most widely used attitude of this sort is relative deprivation, the feeling that one is being treated unjustly in comparison with others.

NOTES

1. For a discussion of the broad issues of social and political change, see Samuel P. Huntington, *Political Order in a Changing Society* (New Haven, Conn.: Yale University Press, 1968).
2. Fred von der Mehden, *Comparative Political Violence* (Englewood Cliffs, N.J.: Prentice-Hall, 1973), chap. 1.
3. Gary T. Mark, "Issueless Riots," in James T. Short and Marvin E. Wolfgang, eds., *Collective Violence* (Chicago: Aldine, 1970), p. 50.
4. Ted R. Gurr, *Why Men Rebel* (Princeton, N.J.: Princeton University Press, 1970), p. 3.
5. The most elaborate explanation of this sort is found in Chalmers Johnson, *Revolutionary Change* (Boston: Little, Brown, 1966).
6. For a brief analysis of the Iranian Revolution, see Richard Cottam, "Revolutionary Iran," *Current History,* January 1980.
7. Mansour Farhang, "Revolution and Repression in Iran," *Harvard International Review,* May/June 1984.
8. James Davies, "Toward a Theory of Revolution," *American Sociological Review,* 27 (1962), pp. 5–19; and Ted R. Gurr, *Why Men Rebel,* pp. 46–56.

WRAPPING IT UP: A COMPARISON OF POLITICAL SYSTEMS

15

INTERNATIONAL POLITICS

The first fourteen chapters of this book examined various aspects of politics within nation states. But no introduction to politics can be complete without an analysis of politics between them. It is obvious to any citizen that governments spend much of their time interacting with foreign governments. This perception results to some extent from the extensive coverage that the news media give to the often dramatic events that take place in the international arena: wars, terrorist bombings, summit meetings, threats of nuclear war, and debates over exotic new outer-space weapons.

THE BASIC NATURE OF INTERNATIONAL POLITICS

However, the importance of international politics is not primarily the result of the decisions of journalists. The world is really made up of a number of interdependent parts, primarily nation states, which affect each other's behavior in many profound ways. Thus, whether we like it or not, national governments must spend much of their time, and significant portions of their societies' resources, dealing with other governments.

A World of Sovereign but Interdependent Nation States

The nature of international politics directly reflects the fact that the world is divided into nation states. Let us pause for a moment and consider what a nation state is. A **nation state** has three elements: a people, a territory, and a government. The first element constitutes a nation, that is, a group of people with a common culture, history, and often language. The Palestinian people can be thought of as a nation in this sense, but they are not a nation state since they have neither a territory to call their own nor a government able to make authoritative decisions for the people. When all three elements are present, a sovereign nation state exists. Sovereignty is the crucial element that structures contemporary international politics. It means that the government of a nation state has control of its people and territory, and is not subject to the control of other nation states and international organizations, such as the United Nations.

However, despite their sovereignty, in almost every area of human activity the nation states of the world have become interdependent. This is most obvious in economics; there is truly a world economy. A recession in one nation can have an impact on the economy of other nations. The discovery of a new reserve of an important source of energy such as oil can have serious repercussions throughout the world. Or, the decision by one significant oil producer to increase its output of oil will have both positive and negative consequences in other nations. Rapid developments in communications and transportation have brought the regions and nations of the world closer together. They have also, of course, played a role in the creation of a global economic system.

Another reason for the interdependence of nations is, on its face, much more negative. Although war has been a universal phenomenon observable during every period of human history, the development of nuclear weaponry has altered the basic nature of the international system. With the introduction of nuclear weapons, the rules of the game change, because once they are introduced, they seem to take on a life of their own. The nations of the world now struggle with the problem of how to protect themselves from this ultimate weapon that they created.

On one hand, it has become more and more evident to both political leaders and nonleaders, that in terms of nuclear strategy, what one nation or bloc of nations does has a direct impact on the survival of all nations. Thus, another source of international interdependence has been born from the universal desire to survive. The relevance of Thomas Hobbes' theories of how people emerge from the state of nature because of their desire for security, should not be overlooked. But, as we will see in this chapter, the question remains, can the international political system develop ways to handle this new problem?

There is a complicating factor. These trends toward greater international interdependence have come at a time when the world is undergoing many fundamental changes. Some societies are emerging from centuries of economic and social stagnation into the modern world of high technology. There are colonial societies demanding more respect and independence. And, because of the higher stakes of international politics, competition and conflict seem to take place at a higher level of intensity.

Perceptions of International Politics

How do we come to grips with a world of increasingly interdependent nations, but growing potential for destructive conflict? One way is to see if the concepts and theories that explain the internal political process of nations also work when we apply them to international politics. Because of our use of the systems model, we ask if there really is an international political system. There certainly is a set of interdependent elements—nation states. But, do nation states operate in the same way as individuals, interest groups, and political parties in national political systems? Do they make demands on an international policymaking body that in turn makes decisions about who gets what? And, what provides the framework for determining who gets what, a basic set of binding rules recognized by nation states or the amount of power that each has?

Most students and practitioners of international relations have emphasized the distribution of power. They tend to see international relations as a struggle for power between sovereign nation states.[1] The emphasis on power rather than rules or laws is based on several perceptions. First, if we stand back and examine the international political system at a distance, it appears to be similar to the fragmented cultures discussed in an earlier chapter. What we call the global society is really a fairly large number of smaller societies, each with its own identity and claim to sovereignty. In addition, there are built-in economic differences between the Western world, Communist world, and the Third World. Add to this numerous cultural, religious, and ideological conflicts, and one becomes very pessimistic about the chances of any kind of stable international political system.

A second perception is that unlike the political systems of sovereign nation states, the international system has no authoritative decision makers—it has no institutions that can allocate benefits and costs and make the allocations stick. Once again, we seem to be back in Hobbes' somewhat anarchic state of nature, where everyone is theoretically free (because they are sovereign) but insecure (because there are no enforceable rules).

Another way to get at this question is through the game model of politics. If politics can be considered a game, then no level of politics is more game-like than international politics.[2] Here, we see the most easily identifiable and powerful of political players, nation states competing for power, prestige, and economic resources on a global gameboard. Presidents, prime ministers, secretaries of state, and ministers of defense identify their goals, measure their resources, and implement their strategies before the eyes of the entire world. The game of international politics is not hidden: its results are felt by everyone.

Are there rules of international politics? If so, where do they come from and can they be enforced? And, is international politics more often a zero-sum or a nonzero-sum game? In other words, does the typical international game end with a clear winner and a clear loser, or with one of many possible combinations of winners and/or losers? Finally, if the game model is appropriate for the analysis of international politics, is it more appropriate than the systems model?

To answer these questions, we must return to the distinction between two images of international politics. Is it a game or system governed almost exclusively by the struggle for power among sovereign nation states, with few recognized rules, or a game or system governed by a set of rules recognized and accepted as binding by most of the players? The first model clearly emphasizes the concept of *power;* the second, the concept of *law.* We can go no further without a more detailed examination of these central concepts, first *international power,* then **international law**.

INTERNATIONAL POWER

Most students of international politics have made *power* their central concept. Consider the words of the best-known exponent of what is called the **realist school** of international politics: "International politics, like all politics, is a struggle for power. Whatever the ultimate aim of international politics, power is always the immediate aim."[3] Each nation state enters the international arena with its national interest and various military, economic, and political sources of power. Its foreign policies use the latter to achieve the former. The structure of the international political system is determined then by the degree to which nations can accommodate their national interests, and the distribution of power in the world.

National interest is just about as difficult to define as "public interest," but actually, they are closely related. Each describes interests that entire nations are supposed to have. The realist assumes that each nation does have objective interests—interests that go beyond the special interests of the population at a particular time. The most obvious (and sometimes the only one discussed) is **national security**. In the Hobbesian world of the realist, every nation's main concern is protecting itself from the ambitions of other nations. Power, then, is usually defined as the ability to control the actions of other nations or resist the attempts of other nations to control you. It is not surprising that according to this theory of international politics, the most important source of international power is *military might*. In fact, realists sometimes suggest that there is no clear distinction between the political and military in international politics. An influential nineteenth-century theorist once wrote that "War is nothing else than the continuation of political transactions intermingled with different means."[4]

This is not to say that realists glorify war, nor do they equate international power with the continual use of military force. The point is, rather, that in a system of competitive sovereign nation states, with no authoritative body at the center to decide who gets what, the essential element of control and order is the capacity of nation states to *threaten* military force. Thus, international politics emphasizes coercive power above other forms. In this light it is also easier to understand a concept that has become so important in theories of nuclear strategy, the concept of **deterrence**.

The idea is that, once one nation possesses the ultimate weapon, other nations must acquire similar weapons, not to use them, but to deter the first nation from using its weapons. However, this leads to a situation of escalating weapons acquisition, as each nation attempts to keep abreast of the others. Each nation emphasizes the "defensive" nature of its weapons, yet "defensive" here usually means developing a more efficient way to deliver even more devastating nuclear warheads. Given the realist's assumption, the notion of deterrence seems to make sense. Since each nation is trying to further its national interests, and only power (primarily coercive) can achieve them, then each must use its ultimate threat, that of a nuclear attack, to protect itself. No nation wants to start a nuclear war, but all must attempt to gain and then retain the ability to do so.

To critics of deterrence theory, the problem is that nuclear weapons are themselves a source of instability. Thus, building more nuclear weapons to increase a nation's ability to deter other nations only increases the chance that if conflict occurs, it will be the final conflict.

Now, those who emphasize the centrality of power in the conduct of international politics are not describing an anarchic world. Disorder is not necessarily the consequence of sovereign nation states using power to pursue their national interest. There can be order if there is a **balance of power**. This concept plays a role similar to that of the laws of supply and demand in capitalist economic theory. Both explain how order results from the interaction of individual actors without the need for a strong central authority. Each notion is based on the ideas of balance and equilibrium.

The balance of power concept suggests that order will result from the way that power is distributed among the nations of the world. The most popular variation emphasizes the desirability of a fairly equal distribution among a number of nations—that way, if one nation attempts to increase its power, the other nation will be able to bring it back in line. This implies a shifting balance of power as various nations adjust their power to maintain the equilibrium. Historians suggest that this was the basis of international politics during much of the nineteenth century. With the defeat of Napoleon and France, the nations of Europe attempted to play the game of balance of power. The foreign policymakers of these nations did seem conscious of the importance of preventing any of their number from getting too powerful and thus upsetting the balance.

As we move from the nineteenth century through the first half of the twentieth century, we find the original balance of power theory less applicable to international politics. As the nations of the world emerged from World War II, it became obvious that there were to be two dominant nations, the United States and the Soviet Union. The power of each was so much greater than that of other nations, that the multi-nation balance of power theory no longer worked. The international political system had become **bipolar**, with two very powerful blocks of nations, each led by a dominant nation, struggling for supremacy. We are, of course, referring to NATO led by the United States, and the Warsaw Pact led by the Soviet Union. It seems to follow from the bipolar model that international politics will be conducted at higher levels of tension because the stakes are higher and the moderating influence of other nations will be less evident than in the classic balance of power model. And, the tension-producing role of nuclear weapons must be added to the equation. It is no accident that the two dominant nations are the first great nuclear powers.

The bipolar model is still useful in describing international politics, but there are several qualifying factors. The most important is the increasing significance of the developing nations, called collectively, the **Third World**. The economic and political rise of nations throughout Asia, Africa, and Latin America means that international politics is more than a game between the First World (the United States and allies) and Second World (the Soviet Union and allies). Few observers would argue that the Third World nations are as powerful, or that they are even a unified bloc. The point is rather that as they develop, they make more demands on the international system; in addition, because of their economic and strategic significance, the big powers must take them seriously. Add to all of this the rise of somewhat independent major powers such as Communist China, and the bipolar model, while still valid, must be modified again.

INTERNATIONAL LAW

So far, our discussion of international politics has revolved around the concept of power. This is because of the centrality of sovereign nation states in the international system. As we have just seen, any order that results is attributed to the creation of a balance of power among the nation states. But, what about another possible source of international order: law? Are there binding rules that apply to the interaction of nations, similar to those that regulate the internal affairs of nations? And, if there are, where do they come from, and how are they enforced?[5]

Given all that we have said about the role of power in international politics, it might seem somewhat incredible that anyone could seriously believe that international law is a significant factor in the relations of nations. Depending on one's starting point, there are several ways to react, each representing a tradition in the analysis of international law. At one extreme are those who suggest that the belief in a viable international legal system is incredible—in a world of sovereign nation states, any discussion of binding international rules is primarily academic, since no nation is willing to accept as legitimate rules that supersede its own.

At the other extreme are those who believe that international law can develop into a body of universal rules that will replace conflict and force as the primary way to resolve disputes throughout the world. A third position falls somewhere in between, but closer to the first than the second. It accepts the centrality of the sovereign nation state and defines international law as the body of rules of international behavior that nation states are willing to accept because they facilitate their interaction and help maintain some order. According to this view, which has been the most widely held by students of international law, the nation state is a given. The main topics of international law—treaties, national boundaries, neutrality, the use of the seas, the standards of diplomacy—all take for granted a system of sovereign nation states. International law, then, is designed to regulate the behavior of nation states.

Two obvious and related questions arise at this point. If there is such a thing as international law, where does it come from, and who is responsible for applying and enforcing it? In 1945, the agreement that established the most important international court, the International Court of Justice (ICJ), identified several sources of international law. It is as complete a list as one is likely to find. The first source is **international custom**—general principles that are accepted throughout the international community. Examples include the rules of diplomacy, such as the need to protect foreign embassies and to grant foreign diplomats immunity. Most of these customary rules are based on common sense; they describe some of the practices that facilitate the orderly interaction of nations. A second source of international law (which overlaps to some extent with the first) consists of **general principles** derived from national legal systems. Examples include the right of a nation to protect itself, and respect for the rights of other nations.

Treaties, that is, agreements among nations, are another source of international law. Treaties can range from agreements between two nations—a peace treaty that ends a war, for instance—to an agreement among many nations, such as the agreement that established the United Nations. A fourth source of international law consists of the **decisions of international courts**, most importantly the ICJ. Finally, the **writing of respected legal scholars** can serve as a source of international law.

This is an impressive list. But, its most interesting feature is probably what is not included, the statutes of a legislature or the orders of an executive. This is because in the international political system, there are no authoritative policymakers, no legislature or executive. Thus, none of the sources listed above are binding on nation states. This is the problem of international law.

Customs, traditions, and scholarly opinions can operate, and some, like the rights of diplomats, are taken seriously by most nation states, but only if nations accept them. The same is true of legal decisions. The **International Court of Justice** has made about fifty decisions since its creation in 1945 (less than two per year). It should be noted, also, that no nation can be forced to accept the Court's authority; in effect, a nation decides if it wishes the Court to take jurisdiction of a case involving it. If we applied this principle to the national legal system, an individual charged with a crime could declare that the courts had no jurisdiction over him, and could get away with the crime. This leads to a related problem of international courts: they have no enforcement power. Even if nations submit themselves to an international court, they reserve the right to accept or not accept its decisions. Since it has no enforcement powers of its own and no executive to carry out its decisions, there is little the Court can do about a nation that refuses to go along with one of its decisions. Actually, enforcement is often left up to the individual nation states. It is commonly agreed, for instance, that an act of piracy on the high seas can be prosecuted by any nation state.

A more dramatic example is provided by the International Military Tribunal created in 1945 by the victorious allies, to try World War II war criminals. Meeting in Nuremberg, Germany, this court operated from the assumption that individual participants can be held responsible for their actions during a war. Thus, the Court could prosecute Nazi leaders for crimes against peace and humanity, and reject the defense that such prosecutions are unjustified when a military or political leader is simply carrying out the orders of a superior. But, behind the moral and legal principles was the power of victorious nations.

This leads to a few more words about treaties as a source of international law. It could be argued that treaties are the most important source of international law, since they are actually negotiated and signed by nation states and are thus more binding. There is something to this; treaties are, in a sense, contracts and thus are supposed to be honored by all parties to them. This is, in fact, one of the general principles of law that is supposed to guide the actions of nations. The problem is that since a treaty is negotiated by a nation with its national interest in mind, it can unilaterally renounce it, if it decides that its interests are no longer being served. If a nation takes this course, it usually cites a violation committed by the other parties or claims that the state of affairs under which the treaty was negotiated has so changed as to make the agreement meaningless.

But, the impression should not be left that international law is of no significance. If there is no real system of binding international law, there is still evidence that nation states value the order that can result from the existence of at least some international legal principles. As long as their sovereignty is not threatened, nation states are likely to accept such rules. Consider the fact that international diplomacy is still possible, even in a world of high tension and uncertainty. **Diplomacy** refers to the discussion that takes place between the official representatives of nation states. To facilitate such a process, nations grant the diplomats of other nations diplomatic privileges and immunities, such as immunity from criminal prosecution.

INTERNATIONAL ORGANIZATION

Some students of international relations see the development of international organizations as the only real hope for international order. On one hand, there are those who view an organization such as the United Nations as the basis for world government—a set of institutions that can make authoritative decisions and legislate rules that are binding on the peoples of the world. This implies the evolution of a global system in which sovereign nation states are no longer dominant. On the other side are those who view international organizations as debating societies with rhetoric and propaganda as their only products.

The real nature of international organization probably lies somewhere in between. Let us see why, by briefly examining the structure and function of the most important international organization, the United Nations.[6]

On October 24, 1945, fifty nations signed the Charter of the United Nations. Since then, more than one hundred have been admitted. The Charter was the result of decisions made by the United States, Great Britain, and the Soviet Union about two years earlier that they establish "at the earliest practical date a general international organization, based upon the sovereign equality of all peace-loving states, and open to membership of all such states, large and small, for the maintenance of peace and security."

This statement tells us several important things about the United Nations. First, its goal is to help maintain peace and security. The latter word suggests that there may be continuing reasons for insecurity. Second, the United Nations assumes as given an international system of sovereign nation states. Surrendering one's sovereignty has never been a condition for membership.

The original goal and strategy of the United Nations was **collective security**. It assumes that nations will be secure if they pledge themselves collectively to resist the aggressive actions of one or more of their number. The signers of the United Nations charter also pledged themselves to the reduction of hunger, disease, and illiteracy throughout the world. This was viewed not only as a humanitarian objective, but as a way to remove some of the major causes of political instability and thus international insecurity.

The United Nations charter established several institutions to achieve these goals. They are the General Assembly, the Security Council, the Economic and Social Council, the Secretariat, and the already mentioned International Court of Justice.

The **General Assembly** is composed of all members of the United Nations. Each nation has one vote. The General Assembly is primarily a forum for discussion (some might say propaganda), rather than decision making, but its significance can be lost amidst the emotional speeches that are so often a part of its meetings. The General Assembly offers nations the opportunity to speak instead of fight, and it can, with an overwhelming vote, influence the thinking of the international community.

Still, the **Security Council**, as its name indicates, was viewed from the very inception of the United Nations as the main peacekeeper. This is clearly demonstrated by its size—only fifteen members—and its rules. Five members were given permanent seats: the victorious "big" powers of World War II, the United States, the Soviet Union, the United Kingdom, France, and the People's Republic of China. The other ten seats are filled, on a rotating two-year basis, by elections in the General Assembly.

The single most important fact about the Security Council is the requirement that all important decisions (those involving questions of security and peace) be agreed to by all five permanent members. This clearly gives each of them the right to veto any proposed resolution, a right that has been exercised quite often, most frequently by the Soviet Union. Some students of the United Nations bemoan the veto, suggesting that it prevents any meaningful collective action against aggressive nations. But, this puts the emphasis in the wrong place. If collective action is difficult, it is not because of the veto power. The rules of the Security Council reflect the basic conditions of the international political system: no nation is willing to allow other nations to cross its borders in the name of collective security. This is, of course, especially true of the most powerful nations. Thus, the United Nations could function as an international peacekeeper only if the big powers were confident that they could prevent any collective action that was not in their own interests. But, this is the very thing that prevents the UN from taking action in major conflicts.

Many major international conflicts have occurred since the founding of the United Nations, but few have been resolved by an act of collective security by the Security Council. The United States was able to begin UN action against the North Korean invasion of South Korea only because the Soviet Union was boycotting the organization. It also helped that in 1950, the General Assembly had passed a resolution (the Uniting for Peace resolution) that allows it to recommend collective action when the Security Council is deadlocked.

But, this does not address the basic reasons for the limited ability of both the General Assembly and the Security Council to take collective action to maintain or restore peace. They are both composed of sovereign nation states who, thinking primarily of their own interests, find it difficult to support action against a friend or ally, much less themselves.

The **Secretariat** is the administrative branch of the United Nations. Headed by a secretary-general who is nominated by the Security Council and elected by the General Assembly, the Secretariat has become a kind of international civil service. Its 20,000 employees, drawn from many nation states, have in many cases developed a real sense of international loyalty. Thus, if movement toward a higher level of international cooperation is to take place, it might have to come from this global bureaucracy. As a matter of fact, the secretary-general has frequently assumed the roles of international troubleshooter and diplomat. Notable examples include Dag Hammerskjöld and U Thant.

Some advocates of international cooperation see the greatest hope in the **UN's Economic and Social Council**. Its primary function is to use a variety of agencies to promote human welfare. This mandate includes supporting worldwide human rights, improving the health of the world's population, and working for international economic stability. Some of the best-known international programs such as UNICEF (United Nations Children's Emergency Fund) work under the Economic and Social Council's direction.

An examination of these and the other institutions of the United Nations leads to this conclusion. The UN is neither as important as some think, nor as potentially significant as others believe. It is not about to become a world government. This is because the absence of a

truly authoritative decision maker remains the primary characteristic of the international political system. The United Nations is a confederation, and a weak one at that. However, despite its reputation as a forum for talk rather than a vehicle for action, the United Nations is at least a step beyond the anarchy of totally unregulated nation states.

INTERNATIONAL ECONOMICS

The main objective of the United Nations and regional international organizations such as NATO, SEATO, and the Warsaw Pact is collective security. But another reason for international cooperation is just as compelling: the desire for economic stability. Actually, since politics and economics are so closely linked, the goals of political and economic stability are not easy to separate. But, since up to this point we have focused on the political and military dimensions of international relations, let us turn our attention to the international economic system.[7]

There are several perceptions of international economics, each emphasizing a different facet of reality. The first recognizes that economic systems are interdependent. There is an international economic system, in which what goes on in one national economy will probably affect other national economies, and the resulting interaction can become very complicated. For instance, consider what happened when the oil-producing nations drastically increased the price of crude oil in the early 1970s. Not only did this send a shock wave through the oil-importing nations, but it led to huge revenues for many of the oil exporters. It is estimated that by 1977, Saudi Arabia had accumulated $150 billion in financial reserves. Much of this money was invested in the West, especially in the United States. American banks now have on deposit billions in oil dollars.

But the story does not stop here, because the banks have sent much of this money to Third-World nations in the form of loans to finance their development (which includes buying oil). Many economists believe that the accumulated debt of the developing nations, now more than $200 billion, represents the greatest threat to international economic stability. The reason is simple—developing nations like Mexico and Brazil are finding it difficult (if not impossible) to repay the loans. Thus, the banking systems of the West are threatened, the economies of the developing nations are threatened, and the ability of the oil producers to continue selling their oil is threatened.

Because national economic systems are intertwined and the resulting interaction can have negative consequences if left unregulated, international economic organizations have developed in an attempt to bring more order to the world economy. Among the more important are the **International Monetary Fund (IMF)** and the **World Bank** (the International Bank for Reconstruction and Development), both agencies of the United Nations.

The IMF, with a present membership of over 130 nations, was established to encourage monetary cooperation by controlling exchange rates and by setting up a fund of foreign currency that can be used by members during times of financial difficulty. The World Bank was created to provide loans to needy nations. Funds come from the contributions of member nations. From immediately after World War II until the late 1940s, the World Bank helped finance the rebuilding of areas destroyed during the war. Since that time, the emphasis has shifted to loans to developing nations. It is clear that the IMF and the World Bank exist because economic and political leaders throughout the world see them as being instrumental for a more stable international economy. All nations can suffer if exchange rates are unstable; and all nations, including the more developed ones, are threatened if less developed nations cannot finance their continued development. Thus, the very existence of international organizations designed to loan money indicates that nation states recognize how dependent they are on each other.

Just as there are regional political organizations so also are there regional economic organizations such as the European Economic Community, better known as the **Common Market**. The significance of this organization of ten European nations is its attempt to create an economic community that has no national tariff barriers, and which allows the free movement of workers and capital across national boundaries. The creation and successful operation of this kind of international economic organization is a major step toward a more stable global economic system. But its significance goes beyond the economic. There is evidence that as nations cooperate through necessity at the economic level, they begin to think more seriously about cooperating at the political level. Thus, as a consequence of the Common Market, the nations of Western Europe have begun building a regional political system, called the European Community.

Many students of international affairs argue that the most important development in international economics, and perhaps international politics, is the growing significance of a type of nongovernmental institution, the **multinational corporation**.[8] A national corporation becomes multinational when its activities can no longer be contained within the boundaries of a single nation state. Although most of us still tend to think in terms of American corporations, British corporations and German corporations, for examples, economic realities indicate that many if not most large corporations consider the world their market. This makes many traditional economic and political concepts obsolete. The basic problem is that individual nation states can no longer control the activities of the mighty international corporations. In the words of one student of international economics, "In a period when the world is still divided along national lines that reflect different ideologies and states of development—business has become, quite without design, the most powerful supranational force in the world."[9]

Examples can be found in almost every industry. Some of the most interesting are found in the automobile industry. While automobile companies are associated with particular nations, the fact of the matter is that most of them have in one way or another become multinational corporations. Many have large foreign subsidiaries—General Motors makes Opels in Europe, and Volkswagen and Honda build some of their models in the United States.

Many automobile corporations have working relationships with automakers in other countries. Chrysler of the United States imports several models made by Mitsubishi of Japan, and sells them in the United States as Dodges and Plymouths. But, the most significant kind of multinational development is the merger between corporations from different nations. The best-known recent merger took place between the largest French automaker, Renault (partially owned by the French government), and the American Motors Corporation. Their first joint effort, the Alliance, was designed in France and is being built in Kenosha, Wisconsin.

The point is, then, that while nations accuse each other of unfair economic tactics and threaten to impose new tariffs on foreign automobiles, automobile companies are developing new organizations that go beyond national boundaries. This is seen most visibly if we turn from automobile manufacturing to automobile racing. Several decades ago Grand Prix racing cars represented nations and were painted in national colors. Today, they wear the colors of their sponsoring companies, many of which are multinational corporations.

The political consequences for multinational corporations are either positive or negative, depending on one's philosophy of international politics. To those who value the stability of the nation state system, multinational corporations are seen as a new source of instability, since none can be effectively regulated by a single nation state (the largest multinationals have assets greater than the GNP's of all but a handful of nations). On the other side are those who suggest that it is the further development of the multinational corporation that gives the world the best chance of moving beyond the competitive and self-destructive nation state system into a global society based on economic cooperation and cross-national synthesis.

In an earlier section, we noted that there are several perceptions of the international economic system. So far, we have focused on aspects of international cooperation. But, there is another perception of international economics, also based on reality. It recognizes that economic strengths and resources—such as natural resources, technological developments, and strategic location—can be used as sources of power in the struggle for power among nation states. Thus, Saudi Arabia can threaten to cut oil production if the United States does not change its Mideast policy, and the United States can threaten to reduce its grain shipment if the Soviet Union continues its occupation of Afghanistan. It is clear, then, that we are back to power politics, except now, instead of using military might as a source of coercive power, nations use economic might as a source of both coercive and utilitarian power.

In an interesting way, military and economic power become joined, since one of the most desirable and thus marketable commodities in the international economy is arms. Tanks, guns, and missiles have both military and economic significance. They are sold for profit to those who will use them for military purposes, but they always end up having a political impact. This is why governments are almost always involved in the sale of arms.

THE FOREIGN POLICY PROCESS

International politics can be analyzed from several perspectives. So far, we have taken a broad approach by emphasizing such concepts as national power, international law, and international organization. But another perspective looks at the way that foreign policy is made within nations. At this level, we concentrate less on the grand global struggle for power and security among nation states, and more on the factors within political systems that guide decision makers in their selection of policies.

According to some observers, it is obvious that the foreign policy process of any nation reflects its national interest and the distribution of power within the international system. This perspective is similar to the rational model of budget making—budget makers sort out their nation's priorities and then allocate available government revenue accordingly. As we saw in our discussion of budget making, this model is not false so much as incomplete. Decision makers who deal with international politics do attempt to identify societal needs, and their foreign policies are usually grounded in some notion of the national interest; but note, it is *their* perception of the national interest. The point is simple: policies, both domestic and foreign, are made by decision makers who are not blank slates—they come to the policymaking arena with personalities, political styles, attitudes, ideologies, and interests.

Can anyone, for instance, believe that it made no difference that Richard Nixon and Henry Kissinger were the main architects of American foreign policy during the late 1960s and early 1970s? The fact that Kissinger was a close student and admirer of the nineteenth-century balance-of-power approach to international politics, surely did affect American policy in Southeast Asia, the Middle East, and Europe.[10]

Some students of foreign policymaking have even suggested that the relative power of decision makers within their own political systems can be as important an influence on foreign policymaking as their perception of the national interest. In other words, international politics is not only a struggle for power among nation states, but is affected by the struggle for power within national governments. Thus, political and military leaders might formulate and support certain policies because of their possible impact on their political career.

It has been argued, for instance, that when President Kennedy decided to support the invasion of Cuba at the Bay of Pigs by Cuban exiles in 1961, and then ordered a blockade of Cuba to remove Soviet missiles one year later, he was paying attention not only to the international balance of power but to his own standing in American politics. A successful invasion of Cuba, leading to the downfall of Fidel Castro, surely would have enhanced his political reputation, but the plan backfired. When the Bay of Pigs invasion failed, Kennedy had to find a way to refurbish his tarnished image. The discovery that the Soviet Union had placed intermediate-range ballistic missiles in Cuba presented Kennedy with the opportunity. His strong response, culminating in the decision to set up a naval blockade of Cuba, served several purposes. Most analyses of the missile crisis agree that Kennedy's response was appropriate, given the situation. It made clear to the Soviets that the United States was serious, but left Soviet leader Nikita Khrushchev a way out.

However, the blockade was also the best way—short of armed attack—for Kennedy to prove that he was a tough political leader.[11]

Let us consider the Cuban missile crisis from the standpoint of Kennedy's counterpart, Nikita Khrushchev. We can interpret the Russian's bold decision to place Soviet missiles in Cuba as an attempt to do something spectacular to regain the support of powerful military and political groups who were beginning to question his leadership. The fact that Khrushchev was forced out of power just two years later suggests that his political strategy did not pay off.

Some might argue that too much can be made of such considerations of personal power; they would suggest that foreign policymakers do think primarily of the national interest. But, the reply says, it is easy for them to define national interest in terms of their own political interests, especially in a crisis situation. It is also true that in a game that emphasizes power, one's chances of implementing what one considers good policies in the future, depends on one's ability to maintain and increase power in the present.

It would appear that foreign policymaking is less public and more specialized than its domestic counterpart. But one should not conclude that foreign policymakers operate in a political vacuum. This is obvious when we take the broad view—contemporary international politics is, by its very nature, a struggle among nation states. But it is just as true of the domestic environment of foreign policy. Policymakers are subject to the demands of various interest groups, each with a stake in the policies that are—or are not—adopted by the government.

The American Israel Public Affairs Committee (AIPAC) is a good example of such a group. Supported by contributions, primarily from the American Jewish community, AIPAC maintains a full-time operation which, by all accounts, is one of the most effective in Washington. Its main objective is to work for a continuation of a pro-Israel policy in the Middle East. In this effort, its main sources of power are a high degree of organization and a highly politicized American Jewish community, constituting only 2.8 percent of the population but, because of higher-than-average voting turnout, about 4 percent of the voting public. It should be noted that AIPAC is an American group working for the interests of a foreign government, not an official agent of a foreign government. There are, at the same time, many lobbyists who register as agents of foreign governments and whose job it is to influence American policy in favor of their client governments.

Given the success of AIPAC, it is not surprising that the much smaller Arab-American community has in recent years become a more active and effective interest group. Its most important organization, the National Association of Arab Americans, has been attempting to move the American government toward what it considers is a more "balanced" (less pro-Israel) Middle East policy.

As we have already seen, international politics is closely intertwined with international economics. Many foreign policy decisions have economic consequences. It is understandable, then, that various economic interests (corporations, labor unions, banks, farmers) pay close attention to and even influence the making of foreign policy. For instance, the oil industry is very concerned about Middle East policy, and American grain producers have come to realize that the status of Soviet-American relations can have an economic impact on their industry.

It seems safe to conclude that except for the most basic issues of war and peace (Vietnam was, and the nuclear freeze may become, such an issue), most questions of foreign policy attract the attention only of those groups who have a direct stake in them. In liberal democracies this means that interest groups will attempt to influence policymakers through the lobbying process. But it would be a mistake to assume that foreign policymakers in nondemocratic systems are immune from domestic political pressures. In authoritarian, even totalitarian, systems foreign policy will reflect, at least to some extent, the political effectiveness of the most powerful groups in society. In the Soviet Union, for instance, the Communist Party is clearly the main policymaker, but the various branches of the military, industrial, and agricultural interests can make their presence felt. The major difference is that such nondemocratic political systems are less open than liberal democracies.

SUMMARY

In order to understand politics in all of its dimensions, we must examine how nation states interact with each other. Although there is an international political system, it is different in certain important ways from national political systems. The main difference seems to be the absence of an authoritative decision-making mechanism to decide, on an international level, who gets what. The main reason for this lack of world government is the existence of sovereign nation states. However, it can be argued that because of increasing political and economic interdependence and the threat of nuclear war, nation states must cooperate.

Most students of international politics have identified power as the central element in the international political system. According to this view, international politics is the process by which sovereign nation states use power to achieve their national interests. International order results from a balance of power among the nation states.

This emphasis on power seems to deemphasize the role of law. However, many students of international politics recognize a limited role for international legal rules—basically, those that nation states are willing to abide by.

Similarly, international organizations such as the United Nations would seem to be of limited significance. Clearly, the United Nations is not a world government. However, if one has lower expectations, international organizations can be seen as useful in providing a forum for discussion among sovereign nation states.

It could be argued that if a greater degree of order is to occur in the international political system, it will result from the continued development of an international economic system of ever more interdependent national economies and multinational corporations.

NOTES

1. The most influential advocate of this approach is Hans J. Morgenthau, *Politics among Nations* (New York: Knopf, 1972).
2. For an interesting game analysis of international politics, see Steven J. Brams, *Game Theory and Politics* (New York: The Free Press, 1975), chap. 1.
3. Morgenthau, *Politics among Nations,* p. 27.
4. Carl Von Clausewitz, *On War,* ed. and trans. by Michael Howard (Princeton, N.J.: Princeton University Press, 1976).
5. See Werner Levi, *Contemporary International Law* (Boulder, Colo.: Westview Press, 1979).
6. See A. LeRoy Bennett, *International Organization: Principles and Issues* (Englewood Cliffs, N.J.: Prentice-Hall, 1984).
7. See Joan E. Spero, *The Politics of International Economic Relations* (New York: St. Martins, 1981).
8. For an examination of several issues involving multinationals, see David Apter and Louis Goodman, eds. *The Multinational Corporation and Social Change* (New York: Praeger, 1976).
9. Lester R. Brown, "The Multinationals and the Nation-State," *VISTA: The Magazine of the United Nations Association,* vol. 8, 1973, p. 15.
10. It is interesting in this regard to read Kissinger's memoirs: *For the Record* (Boston: Little, Brown, 1981) and *Years of Upheaval* (Boston: Little, Brown, 1982).
11. These and other explanations are explored in Graham Allison, *Essence of Decision: Explaining the Cuban Missile Crisis* (Boston: Little, Brown, 1971).

16

A CONCLUSION

We have now completed our survey of the basic elements of politics. The main purpose of this brief chapter is to put the first fifteen chapters into perspective and to show how the various factors that were discussed in these chapters are related. We will pull together the main points by stating several conclusions about politics.

Every society needs a process to decide who gets what, to maintain order, and to help people achieve their goals—this process is politics. Politics is necessary because most of the things that people want (benefits) are scarce and/or costly. It is clear that benefits and costs are handed out in varying amounts to different individuals, groups, and nations. One of the main objectives of this book is to examine the factors that lead to this result, and to raise questions about their impact on other things, such as political stability.

Because politics involves interacting players (individuals, groups, parties, governments, nation states) who devise strategies to achieve their goals, it helps to view the political process as a strategic game involving both conflict and cooperation. The game model also tells us that politics cannot be understood apart from the rules that govern it. It also helps to realize that the political process operates as a system, receiving inputs (demands and supports) from the society and making decisions (outputs) that affect the society. The systems model makes it clear that politics does not exist in a vacuum. It is also obvious that in the contemporary world, the most important political systems are the one hundred and sixty or so nation states.

One of the most important factors that affects the political process is power. Governments need power to back up their decisions and citizens need power to obtain a greater share of the benefits. Power comes in many forms and draws upon many resources. The most effective political actors are probably those who know how to use a variety of types of power. A relationship that stands out is one between authority and political stability: the more legitimacy a government has, the more stable it will probably be.

Wherever one looks, political power is distributed unequally, but the degree of inequality varies from system to system. The most equal distribution is found in liberal democracies; the most unequal, in authoritarian and totalitarian systems. Still, it is reasonable to assume that in all systems there are groups called elites that have more power than others. Some students of politics argue that the main questions to ask of any political system including a democracy are, How many elites are there? How much power do they have? What proportion of the population has a hand in their selection?

As we have seen, the systems approach tells us that politics does not exist in a vacuum; instead, it is part of a larger environment. The broadest part of this environment is culture, the concept we use to describe the basic values and orientations of the society. The political culture is made up of those values and orientations that are related directly to the political process. Some political systems exist within an integrated political culture, some within a fragmented political culture. This distinction describes the degree to which people share political orientations and allegiances. The basic conclusion seems to be that political stability is more likely in an integrated culture. People acquire their political values and orientations through the socialization process. They learn from various agents of socialization such as the family, school, and the government itself.

Two other very important parts of the environment of any political system are the economic and ideological systems. Politics and economics are so closely intertwined that it is difficult to separate them—most political policies have economic consequences and most economic decisions are affected by the decisions of government. In addition, most economic and political systems have evolved out of ideologies. Thus, an examination of the major ideologies—capitalism, liberalism, communism, socialism—involves a consideration of not only basic values, but politics and economics. Another linkage exists, this time between culture and ideology. We should not be surprised to find that in a society that has a dominant ideology, the culture will reflect the ideology. Ideologies vary along several important dimensions, including the role that government is supposed to play in the society and economy.

At the heart of every political system is a government, a set of institutions that makes, interprets, and administers political policies. Governments take on these functions because in most societies, they have more authority than other institutions. The stability of any political system is largely dependent on the degree to which its governmental institutions are able to establish authority.

Every governmental system has several levels, but the relationship among the levels varies greatly, with the unitary system and its powerful central government as the most typical kind of arrangement. A handful of systems can be considered federal; they are designed to balance power between a central and regional (state) governments. There are very few if any confederations since these decentralized systems are inherently unstable. In terms of the distribution and scope of power, authoritarian systems are the most common. Since the highly centralized unitary arrangement is also the most prevalent, it follows that most political systems are unitary and authoritarian. However, it should not be concluded that unitary systems have to be authoritarian. The liberal democratic and unitary government of Great Britain is a case in point.

Every government performs legislative, executive, and judicial functions. In some systems, these functions—especially the first two—are combined or fused in a single institution. In others, they are divided among several institutions. Since some liberal democracies use the fusion of powers system and some the separation of powers system, there appears to be no relationship between the structure of government and whether the system is democratic. This is because of the special characteristics of each type of institutional structure. The separation of powers system is designed to reinforce democratic competition by dividing power and government functions among several institutions. The fusion of powers system emphasizes the importance of making political leaders responsible to the people by concentrating power in the hands of one institution and group of leaders.

The most pervasive type of political institution is probably the bureaucracy. Bureaucracies are a part of all governmental systems for two main reasons. First, they perform an absolutely essential function: implementing governmental policies. In addition, because of their hierarchical organization, bureaucracies develop greater stability and continuity than other political institutions and thus are more likely to last. As a result, bureaucracies have become more and more important and have come to play an increasingly significant role in policymaking, not just policy implementation. This has blurred even further the already fuzzy distinction between politics and administration.

Contrary to a widely held opinion, courts are a significant part of many political systems. We do not have to question the impartiality of judges to realize that their decisions often determine who gets what. The most common function of courts, performed in all civilized societies, is to resolve disputes among members of the society, within a system of law. In some nations, most notably the United States and a few other liberal democracies, courts have assumed an even greater role in the political process. Through the power of judicial review, they have taken on the job of interpreting constitutions and deciding when other actors in the political system have violated the constitution. Most nations have not seen fit to extend this power to their court systems.

Despite their centrality to all political systems, there is more to politics than the institutions of government; just as important are the ways that people participate in the political process. There are many forms of participation. The variety is most extensive and the opportunities are greatest in liberal democracies. But participation takes place even in nondemocratic systems. People in all systems have opinions that are heeded by prudent government leaders, but public opinion is taken more seriously and has more impact in democratic systems. Voting is the most visible and significant type of participation in liberal democracies, for it is the primary way that government leaders are selected and kept responsible. Voting turnout varies significantly from system to system. There are many social, economic, and psychological factors that are related to turnout. In general, upper-income, higher status, more highly educated people who feel that their vote really counts, vote more often than those with the opposite characteristics. We also know that when it comes to deciding how to vote, a number of factors are important. The most significant are party identification, the candidate's image, and the issues.

More and more political participation is organizational; that is, coordinated by and channeled through political organizations such as parties and interest groups. This is, no doubt, a manifestation of the general institutionalization of politics. The general function of these organizations is to provide links between the society and the political system. In most political systems, there are clear differences between political parties and interest groups. The most important one seems to be that the main objective of parties is to get their leaders into government office, while interest groups spend most of their time trying to influence those who already hold office. There are, however, exceptions—systems where the two types of organizations and their functions overlap to a large extent. Then, there are political systems where neither political parties nor interest groups are important. Although no two parties are exactly alike, they can be compared along several dimensions. These include the number of viable parties in the system, party membership, the degree of discipline in the party, and the level of ideology in the party. While there are many possible combinations of these characteristics, in general, parties tend to reflect the characteristics of the larger political system of which they are a part.

Some political observers see interest groups in a negative light, as organizations representing special interests and destructive of the public good. Others see them as an essential part of any pluralistic society. Interest groups are the main vehicles for making the society's various demands on government. Through this debate one fact seems to emerge: no society is totally monolithic and thus every society has various interests. The question is not whether or not they exist, but how well organized they are and to what extent the government allows them to compete for power within the political system.

Some forms of political participation must be considered unconventional: outside of, even in opposition to, the regular political process. Even though these radical and revolutionary activities are understandably viewed as dangerous by defenders of the existing system, they must be considered political activities, since their objective is to change the basic process of deciding who gets what, albeit perhaps through the use of violence. Every society undergoes change; the key political questions that distinguish different groups from each other are how much change is viewed as necessary, and what methods of change are viewed as acceptable. Answers to these questions range from the conservative "as little as possible, and then only through accepted channels," to the revolutionary "as much as possible through the use of violence." Many theories have been formulated to explain why revolutions occur. The most important factors cited are a disequilibriated society, a widespread sense of relative deprivation, and social, economic, and political expectations that are rising faster than the government's capacity to satisfy them.

Politics takes place not only within nation states but among them. An analysis of international politics begins with the question, Do the concepts and theories that explain politics within nations also apply to politics among them? The basic elements are similar: a set of players (nation states) interacting as they attempt to achieve their goals. However, there is one significant difference; the international political system lacks a central authority, a government that makes authoritative decisions. Thus, it is often argued that the only determinant of who gets what among nation states is the distribution of international power. An alternate theory reserves an important role for international rules; this suggests the existence of international law. But a question arises: Who enforces these rules?

It is easy to view the world of contemporary politics with bewilderment and dismay. Given the fast-developing agents of change and the sources of conflict, one can begin to wonder about the survival rate of stable and just political systems. The record of the last century is not impressive, yet there is hope. (Witness the movement of the Philippines back into the category of liberal democracy.) But hope depends on an understanding of the political process, the importance of power, the role of ideologies, the way that institutions make decisions, and the ways that citizens can participate in the political process. The final realization must be that, like it or not, politics will continue to have a profound impact on all of our lives.

POLITICS

AN INTRODUCTION TO

GLOSSARY

Ability-to-pay principle—A principle of taxation which assumes that as the income of a person increases, so should his or her tax rate. Progressive taxes are based on the ability-to-pay principle. (p. 59)

Absolute monarch—A monarch (king or queen) who claims unlimited power. (p. 187)

Access points—The individuals and institutions of government that make decisions and are open to the demands of interest groups. (p. 279)

Achievement culture—A culture in which people are evaluated in terms of what they have achieved. (p. 112)

Administrative elite—Groups of administrators or bureaucrats, drawn from the same social and educational background who have gained significant power in some political systems. (p. 212)

Agents of socialization—Those individuals, groups, or institutions from whom people learn their political values and orientations. (p. 125)

Alienation—The feeling that one is not part of the political system; a factor in voting turnout. (p. 255)

Anarchist—Someone who views politics and government as unnecessary, or even harmful. (p. 5)

Anti-trust—Policies pursued by modern governments in capitalist systems to prevent the concentration of economic power and thus to maintain economic competition. (p. 139)

Ascriptive culture—A culture in which people are evaluated in terms of their inherited social status. (p. 112)

Authoritarian system—An elitist political system in which the elite controls the political system, but does not attempt to control all aspects (economic, social, cultural) of society. (p. 88)

Authority—Another name for legitimate power; usually vested in an office or process. (p. 78)

Autonomous socialization—The type of socialization that is unintentional, that is, the result of ongoing processes that continue from generation to generation without direct conscious control. (p. 124)

Balance of power—The idea that international order results from a fairly equal distribution of power among nation states. (p. 306)

Benefits—Things that people want from their society. Includes economic benefits such as income and property; social benefits such as freedom, equality, and security; and political benefits such as power. (p. 40)

Benefits-received principle—A principle of taxation which assumes that the amount of tax one pays to the government should be proportionate to the benefits one receives from government. It is the basis for users fees such as highway tolls. (p. 59)

Bicameral legislature—A legislature which has two houses or chambers. (p. 182)

Bipolar—A concept used to describe the present international system which is dominated by two great powers, the United States and the Soviet Union. (p. 307)

Blank-slate theory—A theory of human nature which assumes that humans have no inherent nature but are instead the product of their environment. (p. 9)

Brainwashing—A type of manipulative power in which people are controlled by breaking down their psychological resistance and instilling in them a new set of values. (p. 76)

Broker party—A non-ideological party which attempts to put together a broad coalition of groups in order to win elections. (p. 270)

Brown v. Board of Education—A case decided in 1954 by the United States Supreme Court which declared unconstitutional the "separate but equal" doctrine. (p. 24)

Bureaucracy—An administrative agency established to carry out specialized functions. (p. 202)

Cabinet department—An executive agency in charge of a particular function of government; in some systems it is called a ministry. (p. 211)

Cadre party—A political party headed by a small group of leaders who run the party but have very little control over who does or does not become a member. (p. 267)

Capitalism—An economic system based on the principles of supply and demand, the market, private property, and the profit motive. (p. 136)

Capitalist imperialism—An important concept in Lenin's theory which explains the continued survival of capitalism; capitalist nations extend their lives by colonizing the peoples of Asia, Africa, and Latin America. (p. 151)

Charisma—A kind of personal charm or magnetism possessed by some, which leads to personal power. (p. 79)

Chief of state—The ceremonial or symbolic head of a political system. (p. 187)

Civil law—Legal rules designed to handle disputes among individuals; similar to private law. (p. 221)

Coercive power—Controlling the behavior of others through the use of threats. (p. 72)

Collective Security—One of the founding principles of the United Nations; the idea that nation states will be secure if they promise to collectively resist the aggressive actions of one or more of their number. (p. 311)

Common law—A type of law which results from the interpretation and legitimizing of customs and tradition by judges. (p. 220)

Common Market—An organization of ten European nations designed to create a European economic community. (p. 314)

Communism—The last stage of history in Marxist theory; a classless and stateless society. (p. 149)

Confederation—A political system in which the regional governments, such as states or provinces, have the final authority. (p. 172)

Conquest Theory—A theory about the origins of politics which assumes that politics begins when someone gains control of others in a society, usually through an act of force. (p. 12)

Conservative—Anyone who wishes to maintain things as they are—a supporter of the status quo. (p. 288)

Conservative ideology—Any ideology which justifies the existing social, economic, and/or political system. (p. 135)

Constituents—The citizens of a political district who the representitive represents. (p. 248)

Constitution—The basic framework of a political system; the fundamental rules which give the system its basic character. (p. 23)

Constitutional law—Legal rules which deal with the basic framework of the political system, with relationships among the parts of government, and with the government and the citizens of the political system. (p. 221)

Constitutional Monarch—A monarch (king or queen) whose power is not recognized as unlimited or absolute. (p. 188)

Contract law—The type of civil law that deals with agreements. (p. 221)

Contract theory—A theory about the origins of politics which assumes that politics begins when the people of a society agree to be governed by political leaders in order to achieve greater order, freedom, or other political objectives. (p. 12)

Council of Ministers—The most important administrative body in the government of the Soviet Union. (pp. 193, 199)

Coup d'etat—The seizing of power by one political elite from another elite through the use of force. (p. 189)

Credibility—The degree to which others believe that a political actor will actually carry out a threat; an important factor in the successful use of coercive power. (p. 74)

Criminal law—Legal rules designed to handle situations in which an act considered harmful to society has been committed. (p. 221)

Cross pressures—Factors which pull a potential voter in opposite directions; often lead to non-voting. (p. 255)

Cultural pluralism—A society which is divided into distinct cultural groups. (p. 101)

Culture—The basic values of a society. (p. 111)

Cynicism—A lack of faith in government. (p. 255)

Delegate theory—A theory of representation which assumes that representatives should do whatever their constituents want them to do. (p. 97)

Demands—In the systems model, a type of input that includes the requests of government made by individuals and groups, to satisfy various needs and wants. (p. 32)

Democracy—A political system in which power is placed in the hands of the people. (p. 89)

Democratic consensus—Widespread agreement within a society that the political system should operate according to the democratic rules of the game. (p. 101)

Democratic socialism—A type of socialism which is critical of capitalism but rejects the need for revolution and instead works for socialist change through the democratic electoral process. (p. 155)

Destalinization—In the Soviet Union, the policy of discrediting Joseph Stalin; it began in 1956, three years after his death. (p. 190)

Deterrence—The act of preventing a nation from taking action against another country through the possession of powerful weapons—in the modern age, nuclear weapons. (p. 306)

Dialectical process—An important part of Marxist theory; argues that history develops through a series of class conflicts. (p. 148)

Dictatorship of the proletariat—According to Karl Marx, the period after the Communist revolution during which the working class will take over the political and economic system. (p. 151)

Diplomacy—Discussions that take place among the official representatives of nation states. (p. 310)

Directed socialization—A type of socialization which is consciously directed by government or some other agent of socialization. (p. 124)

Direct democracy—A liberal democracy in which people themselves make the policy decisions. (p. 91)

Disequilibrium—A situation in which the basic parts of a society do not correspond to each other; can lead to revolution. (p. 294)

Dissonant situation—Situation in which an individual's opinions conflict with each other. (p. 243)

Divine right—The claim, made by some kings throughout history, that their authority comes directly from God. (pp. 141, 188)

Dominant party system—A political party system which has several parties, but is dominated by one party. (p. 272)

Economic and social council—An agency of the United Nations that coordinates a number of international programs to promote human welfare. (p. 312)

Economic benefits. *See* **Benefits.**

Economic systems—The ways that material values are produced and distributed in different societies. (p. 133)

Efficacy—The degree to which one feels that his or her vote is important; an important factor in voting turnout. (pp. 115, 253)

Elite party—One of the central concepts of Lenin; an organization of knowledgeable and dedicated Marxists who lead the revolution and then reshape the society that comes after the revolution. (p. 151)

Elitism—A theory of politics which argues that all political systems are controlled by a small minority (elite). (p. 102)

Elitist democracy—A type of political system in which the people select the elites that will govern them. (p. 108)

Equality principle—A principle of taxation based on the belief that using the same tax rate for every income level leads to the fairest tax. (p. 59)

Executive department—The highest level of government bureaucracies—also called cabinet department or ministry. (p. 211)

Exploitation—A concept central to Marxist theory; refers to the ways that the capitalist class takes the product of the working class and sells it for profit. (p. 150)

Extraordinary majority—Any majority greater than a simple majority; 2/3 or 3/4, for instance. (p. 98)

Federal system—A political system in which authority is divided between the central and regional governments. (p. 173)

Feedback—Information distributed to a society about the outputs of the political system. (p. 32)

Fragmented political culture—A political culture in which people are divided into two or more distinct cultural groups, each with its own political values and orientations. (p. 119)

Fusion of powers—A governmental system in which political power and functions are combined into a single governmental institution. (p. 177)

Game model—A model of politics which views the political process as a game, similar to football, baseball, chess, and other strategic games. (p. 31)

Game of chance—A game (such as roulette) in which the outcome is determined by luck (the roll of the dice) and thus is beyond the control of the players. Politics involves some chance but is not considered a game of chance. (p. 18)

Game of skill—A game (such as golf) in which the outcome is primarily the result of the skill of the players. Politics involves skill but is not considered a game of skill. (p. 18)

Game of strategy—A game (such as football) in which the players are interdependent—they must consider the goals and objectives of their opponents. Politics is considered a game of strategy. (p. 18)

General Assembly—The largest institution of the United Nations; all member nations are represented. (p. 311)

General culture—The basic values, orientations, and behavioral norms of any society. (p. 111)

General principles—One of the sources of international law. Legal rules derived from national legal systems. (p. 308)

General Secretary of the Communist Party—The head of the Communist Party in the Soviet Union—the most powerful office in the Soviet political system. (p. 193)

Government—The institution found at the center of a political system which makes authoritative political decisions for the society. (p. 164)

Government corporation. *See* **Public corporation.**

Gross national product—The total value of goods and services produced in a nation during a year. (p. 44)

Guerrilla tactics—Revolutionary tactics, usually attributed to the Chinese leader Mao Tse-tung, which emphasize hit and run military tactics and the winning of the hearts and minds of the people. (p. 153)

Guns and butter—The choice that most national governments must make, between more spending on national security (guns) or more spending on social programs (butter). (p. 53)

Hierarchy—A basic principle of bureaucratic organization; a clean-cut chain of command within an organization. (p. 208)

House of Commons—The elected and most powerful branch of the British Parliament. (p. 180)

House of Lords—The non-elected and less powerful branch of the British Parliament. (p. 180)

Human rights—Anything, life, liberty, property for instance, that a society believes every citizen is entitled to. (p. 94)

Hypothesis—An educated guess about relationships in the world; tested by making systematic observations of the world. (p. 17)

Ideology—Any coherent set of values and beliefs about society, economics, and politics. (p. 133)

Independent Regulatory Commissions—Administrative agencies which are established to regulate a particular industry or segment of society and are given some independence from other government institutions. (p. 212)

Indirect liberal democracy—A liberal democracy in which the people's main function is to elect representatives, who then make decisions for them. (p. 92)

Influence—Another name for *personal power;* based on the respect that others have for a political actor. (p. 79)

Inputs—According to the systems model, the elements that are received by the political system from society; include demands and supports. (p. 32)

Integrated political culture—A political culture in which most people have the same political values and orientation. (p. 119)

Interest group. *See* **Political interest group.**

International Court of Justice—An international court created in 1945 which has no binding authority over the nation states of the world. (p. 308)

International custom—A source of international law; general principles of conduct that are accepted throughout the world. (p. 308)

International law—A set of legal rules that is considered binding by the nations of the world. (p. 305)

International Monetary Fund—An agency of the United Nations which was established to encourage monetary cooperation among the nations of the world. (p. 314)

Iron Law of Oligarchy—A principle formulated by the sociologist Robert Michels, which says that all human organizations end up being controlled by a small elite. (p. 103)

Judicial review—The power, possessed by a few courts around the world, to declare the actions of other branches of government illegal or unconstitutional. (p. 224)

Justice—A basic principle of politics; usually refers to the goal of the members of a society to receive what they consider a fair share from their economic and political systems. (p. 38)

Laissez-faire—The theory that the political system should allow the economic system to operate without government regulation; a basic principle of original capitalism. (p. 38)

Law of torts—A type of civil law which deals with those situations where the actions of one individual may harm another individual. (p. 221)

Legislation—The laws and policies produced by legislatures. (p. 180)

Legitimate political violence—Acts of political violence carried out by the established government. (p. 291)

Legitimate power—The right to control or make decisions for others; another name for authority. (p. 78)

Liberal democracy—A political system in which the people, not an elite, have ultimate control of the system. (p. 90)

Liberalism—An ideology based on the principles of individual freedom; historically, closely associated with capitalism. (p. 140)

Lobbying—Any attempt by an agent of an interest group to influence the decisions of a government official. (p. 281)

Loyal opposition—In a parliamentary governmental system, the party that has not won a majority and is expected to criticize and oppose the party in power. (p. 181)

Majority rule—One of the two major requirements of a liberal democracy; the decision-making rule which specifies that whenever a vote is taken, the alternative which receives at least 50 percent + 1 must be selected. (p. 97)

Manipulative power—A type of power in which someone is controlled without being aware of it; examples are brainwashing, propaganda, and socialization. (p. 76)

Marbury* v. *Madison—A case decided in 1801 by the United States Supreme Court which established the Court's power of judicial review. (p. 225)

Market—The economic process, central to the capitalist system, which through the interplay of supply and demand, determines what is produced and what it will cost. (p. 137)

Marxism—The social, economic, and political theories of Karl Marx, which criticized capitalism and predicted that the final stage of human history would be a univeral classless and stateless society. (p. 147)

Marxism-communism—The variety of socialism which is associated with the theories of Karl Marx. (p. 146)

Marxism-Leninism—The ideology which resulted from the additions Lenin made to original Marxism; they include the ideas of an elite party and capitalist imperialism. (p. 151)

Mass public—According to some theorists such as C. Wright Mills, a powerless mass of people who have almost no influence on the political process. (p. 105)

Mercantilism—A type of economic system prevalent in Europe during the 17th and 18th centuries, which assumed that the economy should be regulated by government in order to increase the wealth and power of the nation. (p. 138)

Middle level of power—One of the levels of power in C. W. Mills' power elite theory. It is made up of the visable political actors. (p. 105)

Military dictatorship—A type of authoritarian political system in which the elite is made up of military leaders. (p. 189)

Military-industrial complex—The combination of military and corporate leaders which some theorists believe control the American political system. (p. 105)

Ministry—An executive agency in charge of a particular function of government; in some systems it is called a cabinet department. (p. 211)

Minority rights—Protection for those who are not in the majority; examples are freedom of speech and religion. (p. 98)

Modal political culture—A way to describe the dominant cultural values of a society; it refers to those values and orientations that are most common in the society. (p. 116)

Model—A simplified way to think about something complex (such as politics) through the use of analogies which compare it with something more familiar (such as games). (p. 17)

Mode of production—Karl Marx's term for the economic system. (p. 148)

Monopolistic one-party system—A political party system in which only one party is allowed to function; closely associated with totalitarian systems. (p. 272)

Multinational corporation—A corporation which operates in several nation states. (p. 314)

Multi-party system—A political party system in which more than two parties compete fairly equally for power. (p. 275)

Multiple elites—A situation in which several groups compete for power and the support of the masses. (p. 107)

Multiple-member district—A legislative district which has two or more representatives. (p. 248)

National interest—Those interests which the nation as a whole supposedly has; the most important is national security. (p. 305)

National security—Making a nation safe from the aggression of other nation states. (p. 305)

Nation state—The most important political entity in the international political system. A nation state has three elements: a people, a territory, and a sovereign government. (p. 302)

Natural development theory—A theory about the origins of politics which assumes that political systems are not consciously created, but simply develop because of the inherent social nature of humans. (p. 12)

Natural law—A type of law which is based on certain self-evident principles or derived from a higher source such as God. (p. 219)

Natural rights—Certain human activities (such as speech and religious observance) and possessions (such as property) which some philosophers believe cannot be justifiably taken away by society or government. (p. 141)

Nineteenth-century liberal—A contemporary thinker who accepts the principles of early liberalism. (p. 145)

Non-decision making—The practice, used by many political elites, of exercising control of preventing issues from getting into the decision-making process. (p. 106)

Nonlegitimate political violence—Any violent acts designed to change a legitimate government. (p. 291)

Nonzero-sum game—A game in which the winnings and losses of the players do not equal zero. Some games of this sort are positive (more winnings) and some are negative (more losses). (p. 29)

One-party system—A political system in which only one political party functions. (p. 272)

Opinion vacuum—A situation in which few citizens have expressed their views about a particular issue or policy. (p. 242)

Outputs—According to the systems model, the elements that are sent into society by the political system; they include the decisions of government. (p. 32)

Parliamentary system—A governmental system such as that found in England, in which the dominant political system is the legislature, usually called Parliament. (p. 178)

Parochial political culture—A political culture in which the people identify more with their local regional, tribal, or ethnic groups than with the central government. (p. 116)

Participant political culture—A political culture in which the people identify with and accept the authority of the central government and also believe that they should take an active role in the political process. (p. 118)

Partisan identification—Another name for party identification; the degree to which one feels part of a political party. (p. 255)

Party discipline—The degree to which the leaders of a political party can control the behavior of the rank-and-file members. (p. 268)

Party identification—The degree to which one feels part of a political party; related to voting behavior. (p. 257)

People's democracy—A political system in which an elite has control but claims that it rules in the best interests of the people. (p. 90)

Per capita income—An economic statistic which measures the average income of the population of a society; obtained by dividing the nation's total income by its population. (p. 44)

Permanent revolution—Mao Tse-tung's belief that the Chinese revolution must continue until Chinese society is radically changed. (p. 153)

Personal power—Control that results from the respect that others have for the personal qualities of political actors. (p. 79)

Personification of the public—The mistaken belief that the public speaks as one voice on all issues. (p. 240)

Plessy v. Ferguson—A case decided in 1896 by the United States Supreme Court, which established the "separate but equal" doctrine. (p. 24)

Pluralism—A society in which there are many social, economic, and political groups competing for power. (p. 277)

Plurality election—An election in which the winner is the candidate who receives the most, but not a majority of, votes; always possible when there are more than two candidates. (p. 248)

Policy—A governmental decision which indicates how a particular goal is to be achieved. (p. 166)

Politburo—The most powerful institution in the Communist Party of the Soviet Union. (p. 198)

Political benefits. *See* **Benefits.**

Political culture—The basic feelings that the people of a society have about the political process. (p. 111)

Political interest group—A group of people with shared interests who organize and make demands on government. (p. 275)

Political party—A group of individuals that seeks to direct the policies of the political system. (p. 265)

Politics—The process in any society which decides who receives the benefits and who pays the costs of society. (p. 4)

Popular control—One of the two main requirements of a liberal democracy; the power that the people have to ultimately control the political system. (p. 93)

Positional conservatism—Defending the status quo. (p. 146)

Positional sense of ideology—Defining ideologies in terms of whether they support or oppose the existing system. (p. 135)

Positive law—Law which is created by humans. (p. 219)

Power—The ability to control someone else's behavior, to get them to do something they would not otherwise have done. (p. 70)

Power elite—According to C. Wright Mills, a group made up of economic, military, and political leaders, which supposedly controls American society. (p. 105)

Prefect—In the French political system, an agent of the central government who monitors the activities of a local government. (p. 171)

President—One type of chief executive, usually found in the separation of powers political system. (p. 191)

Presidential system—A governmental system, such as that found in the United States, which has a strong chief executive called a President. (p. 178)

Pressure group—Another name for an interest group. (p. 277)

Prime Minister—The political leader of a parliamentary system. (p. 191)

Private law—Rules designed to handle disputes among nongovernmental individuals and institutions. (p. 221)

Procedural rule—One type of government decision; describes how decisions are to be made and enforced. (p. 166)

Progressive tax system—A tax based on the ability to pay principle in which the tax rate increases as one's income increases. (p. 60)

Propaganda—A type of manipulative power in which a political candidate, idea, or policy is sold through the use of certain motivational techniques. (p. 76)

Property law—A type of civil law that deals with property rights and obligations. (p. 221)

Proportional representation—A system of representation in which the proportion of seats a party wins in the legislature is equivalent to its percentage of the popular vote. (pp. 249, 274)

Public corporation—An economic organization, created and owned by a government, which has been established to perform a particular economic function. (p. 213)

Public interest group—An interest group which claims to represent broader interests than the typical special interest group. (p. 278)

Public law—Rules designed to handle disputes in which the government is involved. (p. 221)

Public opinion—An expressed feeling that people have about an issue or policy. (p. 239)

Pure public goods—Benefits (such as clean air) which are good for everyone in a society, and thus, good for the society as a whole. (p. 39)

Radical—Someone who believes that a major part of the political system needs basic change. (p. 289)

Radical ideology—Any ideology which criticizes or rejects the existing social, economic, and/or political system. (p. 135)

Reactionary—An ideology which advocates going back to a system which it is believed was better than the present: also, one who accepts such an ideology. (p. 145)

Realigning election—An election in which large numbers of people change their party identification. (p. 261)

Realist school—A theory of international politics which emphasizes the struggle for power among sovereign nation states. (p. 305)

Referendum—A method of direct democracy in which people vote on a specific policy issue. (pp. 92, 247)

Reformer—Someone who believes that a particular part of the political system needs change. (p. 289)

Regressive tax system—A tax which is the opposite of a progressive tax in that the tax rate increases as income decreases. (p. 60)

Relative deprivation—The belief that an individual or group is receiving less than other individuals or groups; considered a source of revolution. (pp. 295–96)

Revisionists—Those socialists who were viewed by Marxists as traitors to Marxism because they revised some of Marx's basic ideas; one of the sources of contemporary democratic socialism. (p. 155)

Revolutionary—One who believes that the political system is in need of violent, radical change. (p. 291)

Revolutionary political culture—A political culture in which many people feel that the central government should be drastically changed, even overthrown. (p. 118)

Rights—Actions that people are entitled to do. (p. 141)

Rising expectations—The state of continually expecting more from one's society and government. If the government finds it impossible to satisfy the increasing demands, a revolution could occur. (p. 296)

Scope of power—The range of societal activities that a political elite controls. Thus, the scope of power of a totalitarian elite is greater than that of an authoritarian elite. (p. 89)

Secretariat—The administrative branch of the United Nations. (p. 312)

Security Council—The institution of the United Nations which is given the primary responsibility of maintaining international security; it has five permanent and ten nonpermanent members. (p. 311)

Separation of powers—A governmental system which divides power and political functions among several branches of government. (p. 177)

Simple majority—Fifty percent plus one. (p. 98)

Single-member district—A legislative district which has only one representative. (p. 248)

Socialism—Any of several related ideologies which are critical of the capitalist market system and the class system which supposedly is always part of the capitalist economy. (p. 146)

Socialization—The process through which the people of a society learn values. (p. 123)

Special interest group—An interest group which supposedly represents a narrow, specialized interest and has no concern for the common good. (p. 277)

Status quo—The existing state of affairs. (p. 143)

Subject political culture—A political culture in which the people identify with and accept the authority of the central government, but do not see themselves as participants in the decision-making process. (p. 117)

Substantive decision—Governmental decisions which decide who gets what. (p. 166)

Supply and demand—The basic components of the market in a capitalist economic system. (p. 137)

Support—In the systems model, input that refers to the degree to which individuals and groups accept and back the policies, institutions, and decision makers of a political system, or the political system itself. Support can be positive or negative. (p. 33)

Supreme Soviet—The most important legislative institution in the government of the Soviet Union. (pp. 193, 198)

Systems model—A model which views politics as a system, analogous to other systems such as automobiles or human bodies. This model assumes that politics is an ongoing process in which the political system interacts with a larger environment through a series of inputs and outputs. (p. 32)

Technocrat—A government official whose authority is based on special knowledge or skills. (p. 207)

Third World—The less developed nations of the world. (p. 307)

Totalitarian democracy—A political system in which the power of the majority is unlimited. (p. 98)

Totalitarian dictator—The leader of a totalitarian political system, who leads his party in attempting to gain total control of the society. (p. 190)

Totalitarian system—An elitist political system in which the elite not only controls the political system, but also seeks to control all aspects (economic, social, and cultural) of the society. (p. 88)

Transfer payments—The process in any social system which provides benefits to some by increasing the costs to others. (p. 39)

Treaty—An agreement among nation states. (p. 308)

Trust—An important component of political culture. It refers to the degree to which individuals and groups are willing to trust others with political power. (p. 115)

Trustee theory—A theory of representation which assumes that representatives should do what they think is best, not whatever their constituents want them to do. (p. 97)

Two-party system—A political party system in which two parties compete fairly equally for power. (p. 273)

Unconventional political participation—Types of political participation which operate outside the normal political process. (p. 287)

Unicameral legislature—A legislature which has one house or chamber. (p. 182)

Unitary political system—A political system in which the central government has final authority. (p. 171)

Unlimited majority rule—A political system in which the majority can do anything it wants. (p. 98)

Utilitarian power—Controlling the behavior of others through the use of promises. (p. 75)

Veto group theory—An elitist political theory which argues that in modern political systems it is easier for elite groups to block policies they do not like, than to achieve the policies they do like. (p. 108)

Vote of confidence—A vote taken in a parliamentary system to discover if the parliament still has confidence in the prime minister. (p. 197)

Voter preference—The decision made by a voter to select one candidate or party over others. (p. 250)

Voter turnout—The percentage of eligible voters who actually vote. (p. 250)

Welfare capitalism—A characteristic of modern capitalistic systems in which the government, through various social programs such as unemployment compensation, helps individuals who have been dislocated by the economic system. (p. 140)

Winner-take-all election—An election, usually associated with single-member districts, in which the candidate who receives the most votes becomes the sole representative of the district. (p. 248)

Who gets what—A definition of politics which views it as the process which allocates the benefits and costs for society. (p. 5)

World Bank—An agency of the United Nations which was created to provide loans to needy nations. (p. 314)

Zero-sum game—A type of game in which the winnings of one player equal the losses of the other, resulting in the sum of zero; describes a situation of total conflict. (p. 28)

ACKNOWLEDGMENTS

Cover photo: © Steve Gottlieb
Part I, p. 1; George Bellerose/Stock, Boston
Chapter 1, p. 11; Paul Conklin
Chapter 2, p. 22; Ebony/Johnson Publishing
Chapter 3, p. 52; Paul Conklin
Part II, p. 67; J. P. Atlan/Sygma
Chapter 4, p. 82; J. P. Atlan/Sygma
Chapter 5, p. 94; Brown Brothers
Chapter 6, p. 126; Drawing by Milligan, © 1982 The New Yorker Magazine, Inc.
Chapter 7, p. 136; Sara Krulwich/NYT Pictures
Part III, p. 161; Everett Johnson
Chapter 8, p. 167; Lionel J. M. Delevinge/Stock, Boston
Chapter 9, p. 184; Brad Markel
Chapter 10, p. 207; Drawing by Victor © 1981 The New Yorker Magazine, Inc.
Chapter 11, p. 225; Bill Fitz-Patrick/The White House
Part IV, p. 233; Wide World
Chapter 12, p. 259; Photoworld/FPG
Chapter 13, p. 276; Wide World
Chapter 14, p. 290; Zimberoff/Sygma
Part V, p. 299; Wide World
Chapter 15, p. 313; Reprinted with special permission of King Features Syndicate, Inc.

Tables

pp. 43, 55, 57: From *The New Book of World Rankings* by George Thomas Kurian. Copyright © 1985. Reprinted with permission of Facts on File, Inc., New York.

pp. 44, 45: From *The World Almanac & Book of Facts,* 1986 edition, copyright © Newspaper Enterprise Association, Inc. 1985, New York, NY 10166. Reprinted by permission.

p. 50: From 1986 *Information Please® Almanac.* Copyright © 1985 by Houghton Mifflin Company. Reprinted by permission of Houghton Mifflin Company.

INDEX

A

Ability-to-pay principle, 59
Absolute monarch, 187–89
Access points, 279
Achievment culture, 112, 113
Administrative elite, 212
Afghanistan, 43, 44, 45, 48, 90
AFL-CIO, 280
Age, and voter turnout, 252–53, 254
Agents of socialization, 125–29
Alienation, 255
Amendment (constitutional), 98, 99
American-Israeli Public Affairs Committee (AIPAC), 318
American Medical Association, 107, 282
American Petroleum Institute, 83
American Revolution, 142, 144
Anarchists, 5–6
Anderson, John, 30, 31
Antitrust suits, 139
Apathy
  in public opinion, 242–43
  voter, 237
Aristocracy, 87
Aristotle, 8, 10, 13, 87–88, 91, 98, 121, 164, 293, 294
Armed forces, 56–57
Ascriptive culture, 112–13
Athens (ancient), 91–92
Australia, 90, 178, 246, 273
Authoritarian system
  access to information in, 96
  definition, 88–89
  elitism in, 102, 105–6
  executive in, 185, 193
  legislature in, 177
  unitary government in, 171
Authority, in decision making, 78, 80–81
Autonomous socialization, 124–25

B

Babylon, 203
Balance of power, 306–7
Bangladesh, 43, 44–45, 48, 111
Bargaining, 29–30
Bay of Pigs invasion, 317
Begin, Menachem, 71
Belgium, 48, 90, 189
Benefits, 37–54
  and government budget, 48-54
  hierarchy, of, 41–48
  inequality of, 62–64
Benefits-received principle, 59
Bernstein, Edward, 155–56
Bicameral legislature, 182–83
Bill of Rights (U.S.), 99
Bipolar system, 307
Blackmun, Harry, 225
Blacks
  and voter turnout, 252, 254
  voting rights of, 245
Blank-slate theory, 9
Bradley, Bill, 79
Brainwashing, 76
Brazil, 43, 44, 45, 48, 114, 313
Brennan, William, 225
Brezhnev, Leonid, 193
British Broadcasting Corporation, 213
Broker party, 270, 272
Brown v. *Board of Education*, 24, 25, 226
Budget
  and distribution of benefits, 48–54
  and distribution of costs, 54–62
  in the United States, 37, 38, 49–54
Bundesrat, 180, 183
Bundestag, 177, 180, 181, 182, 183
Bureaucracy, 202–14
  as anarchy, 207
  definition, 202
  functions of, 210–211
  history of, 203–4

  in Marxist-Leninist system, 213–14
  model, 204–10
  types of, 211–13
Burger, Warren, 225
Burke, Edmund, 143–45

C

Cabinet (Great Britain), 25
Cabinet department (U.S.), 211–12
Cadre party, 267
Campaign, 260–61, 280
Canada
  armed forces in, 57
  culture, 26
  as liberal democracy, 90, 178
  political parties in, 273, 274
  spending in, 55
  taxes per capita, 63
Capitalism, 136–40
  abuses in, 156
  definition, 136
  versus democratic socialism, 158
  versus Marxism, 147–50
Capitalist imperialism, 151–52
Carter, James E. "Jimmy," 26–27, 115
Castro, Fidel, 80, 193, 317
Charisma, 79–80, 81, 82, 89, 258
Chief of state, 193
China. *See* People's Republic of China
China (ancient), 203
Chon Too Hwan, 114
Chung Hee Park, 114
Churchill, Winston, 79, 185, 258
Civil law, 221
Coercive power, 72–75, 78, 80, 89, 106
Collective security, 311
Common Cause, 278
Common law, 220
Common Market, 314